The Florida Land Boom of the 1920s

# The Florida Land
# Boom of the 1920s

GREGG M. TURNER

McFarland & Company, Inc., Publishers
*Jefferson, North Carolina*

Unless otherwise indicated, photographs are from the author's collection.

LIBRARY OF CONGRESS CATALOGUING-IN-PUBLICATION DATA

Turner, Gregg M.
The Florida land boom of the 1920s / Gregg M. Turner.
p.    cm.
Includes bibliographical references and index.

**ISBN 978-0-7864-9919-9 (softcover : acid free paper)** ∞
**ISBN 978-1-4766-2062-6 (ebook)**

1. Real estate development—Florida—History—20th century.    2. Real estate investment—
Florida—History—20th century.    3. Land speculation—Florida—History—20th century.
4. Florida—Economic conditions—20th century.    5. Florida—History, Local.
6. Migration, Internal—United States—History—20th century.    7. Florida—
Emigration and immigration—History—20th century.    I. Title.

HD266.F6T87  2015          333.3309759'09042—dc23          2015010797

BRITISH LIBRARY CATALOGUING DATA ARE AVAILABLE

On the cover: *Judge Real Estate Number* by Ruth Eastman,
January 16, 1926 (Florida Ephemera Collection,
Special Collections & University Archives Department,
University of Central Florida Libraries, Orlando, Florida)

Printed in the United States of America

*McFarland & Company, Inc., Publishers
Box 611, Jefferson, North Carolina 28640
www.mcfarlandpub.com*

For Anne, Mike, Dolly, Moe and Beefer

# Table of Contents

After eighteen months the spectacular migration of men and money to Florida from all over the United States is still unchecked. Contrary to universal prediction, the great land boom has grown bigger and bigger. It has reached the proportions, one may say, of an historical event. Men have made thousands of dollars in Florida by the mere flourish of a pen; land that they have never seen has brought them millions. How has all this come about? Where is it to end?

—The *Times* of London, 6 November 1925

# Preface

This book explores the epic land boom that unfolded in Florida during the 1920s. What happened here that decade became one of the greatest building and migration episodes in our nation's history.

I first came across the phenomenon several years ago while writing another book. It intrigued me to no end, so much so that I began to search for more information, even collecting memorabilia. Before long a casual interest began to snowball into a serious passion. I then thought about writing a book on the topic, especially since no serious introduction or overview of the canvas existed. Before doing so, though, I penned two smaller works about this fascinating period: *Venice, Florida in the 1920s* and *Florida Railroads in the 1920s*. Both have sold well.

Convinced that there was readership interest in this remarkable era, I began the big project in 2011. Soon, I was searching for important source documents, verifying dates and events, journeying to countless libraries, museums and historical sites, and jotting down endless notes. After culling and organizing the research material, the task of writing the book began. Afterward, hours of editing and polishing followed.

In the pages ahead I trace how the Twenties land boom in Florida evolved, describe the key players, consider the critical role that the media and advertising played, look at how the railway and highway renaissance took root, something about the crooks who stepped across the stage, and why the phenomenon eventually collapsed. But the majority of the book focuses on some of the many communities that were either created by the speculative fever or were forever transformed by the real estate craze. Period images and ephemera fill out the narrative. Overall, I've tried to recount the events with both the devotee of history in mind along with an interested reader. Hopefully neither will be disappointed.

Researching and writing the book involved many individuals and organizations. Without exception, everyone I encountered offered professional and courteous assistance. I am especially indebted to Dr. James Cusick, curator of the P. K. Yonge Library of Florida History, University of Florida; Dr. Gary Mormino, professor at the University of South Florida; Dr. Mitchell Zuckoff professor at Boston University; and to author and academic Seth Bramson of Miami Shores. I am also grateful to staffers at the Florida Historical Society in Cocoa, the Florida State Library in Tallahassee, and to Dawn Hugh and Rebecca Smith of the History Miami Archives and Research Center (formerly the Historical Museum of Southern Florida). Special thanks are certainly owed to Colleen Superak of the Lee County

Library System; Diana Peguese, senior LTA librarian, Florida Gulf Coast University; Dorothy Korwek, Venice Area Historical Society; Carole Goad, Sebring Public Library; and to Dana Thimons of Nova Southeastern University. I would also like to extend my appreciation to Mary Jane and Herb Oberman, as well as to Gary Laird. Lastly, helpful suggestions regarding content and editing were cheerfully rendered by my academic colleagues Catherine Weller, Lori Bufka, Gary Lewis, and Charles Hammond, Jr.

To one and all my sincerest thanks!

# Introduction

The United States paid Spain $5,000,000 for Florida on February 22, 1821—62 cents an acre. The King of Spain, Floridians say, spends much of his time now wishing his country had held on a little longer.

—*Nation's Business*, May 1925

Daniel Boorstin, the Pulitzer Prize–winning author and former Librarian of Congress, once asked his readership, "If Southern California boomers [of the 1880s] could sell city lots in a barren desert where water was nowhere to be seen, could not the Florida boomers [of the 1920s] sell city lots that were three feet under water?" The renowned scholar, humanitarian and world authority on all things Americana proceeded to answer his own question: "American salesmanship and advertising proved more than equal to the challenge."[1]

This book explores the subject about which Boorstin speaks; that is, the epic land boom that gripped Florida during the fabulous 1920s. Devotees of the state's storied past generally agree that Florida truly became Florida in that decade, that not only was its image as a pioneer state forever erased but that the Florida dream—that of a better life in a tropical clime—was reinvented for all time.

That our subject became one of the greatest building and migration episodes in American history cannot be argued. In fact, it "outstripped in numbers and speed" the human stampedes to the Klondike, Oklahoma and the Indian Territory and the Mormon pilgrimage to Utah, as well as the land grabs in Oregon, Kansas, and Pike's Peak.[2] "At its core," writes the eminent Florida historian Gary Mormino, "the 1920s boom involved furious speculation and investment in property, especially in south and central Florida. Miami and Fort Lauderdale, St. Petersburg and Sarasota, all came of age in the 1920s. Across the state abandoned subdivisions also became graveyards of dreams."[3]

Despite its epic dimensions, the Twenties land boom was not the first to have manifested in Florida. In reality the state's real estate potentialities had attracted home seekers, immigrants, farmers, and investors long before the Florida Territory had been established in 1822. There was, for example, an impressive migration of peoples and building in British-owned "East Florida" between 1782 and 1784—at St. Augustine and along the upper reaches of the St. Johns River—which precipitated a population uptick there from 6,000 to over 17,000 persons. Of greater import was the famed Forbes Land Purchase of 1806, when an English investment firm acquired a stupendous land claim of over one million acres near the

3

Apalachicola River, a transaction it negotiated with the Creek Indians with the consent of the Spanish government. Equally instructive was the founding and up-building of St. Joseph—the "wickedest City in the Southeast"—that blossomed during the territorial era. And of even greater significance was the land boom that erupted on the peninsula during the 1880s that involved several spectacular developers such as Henry Flagler, Henry Plant and Henry Sanford.

Whereas the real estate extravaganza of the Twenties was in a class of its own, one hastens to acknowledge that an even greater one unfolded thirty years later. Fueling the 1950s boom was the first wave of Social Security retirees, the pesky mosquito being controlled, the introduction of window air conditioning, and the arrival of countless ex-military personnel who, having trained here during the Second World War, returned for the state's inviting climate and low cost of living. Oddly enough, another land boom would take root thirty years afterwards in the 1980s, when owning a Florida condominium or second home became *de rigueur* for many middle and upper-class Americans. And, in recent memory, there was the incredible real estate mania and run-up in property values that commenced around 2002, a real estate boom that eventually spiraled out of control and crashed horribly, the pain from which is still being felt in many Florida quarters.

**Untold numbers of Spanish-styled homes arose in Florida in the 1920s. This beauty at the Davis Islands development was designed by Tampa architect Franklin Adams. Typical period elements included a red-tiled roof, colorful canvas window awnings and a stucco exterior.**

Although each of the foregoing episodes embraces unique and colorful details, the land boom of the 1920s was, for many, the most kaleidoscopic. Beyond the perfunctory activities of buying, selling, and building, this saga teems with brilliant marketing, community boosters, the creation of ready-made cities (like Coral Gables, Hialeah, Boca Raton and Venice), and the opening of thousands of residential subdivisions, many of which having ornate entrances. Lavish hotels also arose that decade (such as the Vinoy and Don Ce'Sar in St. Pete, the rebuilt Breakers in Palm Beach, the Hollywood Beach Hotel, and the Miami Biltmore), as well as countless Spanish-inspired apartment buildings, hundreds of opulent mansions, and countless smaller homes. Further, impressive commercial complexes were constructed along with stunning municipal buildings, causeways, and graceful bridges—such as the one linking St. Augustine with Anastasia Island, "The Most Beautiful Bridge in Dixie." Many country club and fraternal facilities were built too, as were imposing churches, elegant theatres (Tampa Theatre was regarded as the finest in the South), and noteworthy school buildings. A railway renaissance also took place that decade as did a bevy of important road-building projects. Even a unique architectural theme emerged, today called Mediterranean Revival (a blend of Spanish, Italian, Mediterranean and Moorish details), which developers and builders embrace to this day.

That the Twenties event had a seamy side was also true. Criminally speculative schemes evolved, many investors were defrauded and a host of crooks stepped across the stage, like Charles Ponzi of Ponzi scheme fame. (His forte was selling building lots through the mail that were under swamp water.) The abuses and indiscretions prompted a smear campaign against Florida by out-of-state critics. To combat the negative press, Governor John Martin hosted a New York news conference entitled "The Truth About Florida," where he and prominent businessmen defended the land boom along with the state's honor and financial stability. But the erstwhile efforts did not eradicate the bad actors, or the banking irregularities and failures. Two destructive hurricanes would impact the real estate mania, while the invasion of the Mediterranean fruit fly brought further misery to the Florida economy. Then, the 1929 stock market crash occurred.

Although a good literature has surfaced over the years about certain aspects of the Twenties boom, no formal introduction or overview of the subject exists, a deficiency that this work hopes to remedy. Many questions, of course, still persist. For example, when the phenomenon precisely commenced—or ended—has never been definitively established, though many sources are quick to cite 1922 and 1926, respectively. (Your author contends it began in 1919 when Carl Fisher launched a nationwide advertising campaign for Miami Beach real estate. There is also evidence that building lots and homes were still selling briskly as late as 1927 at such places as Howey-in-the-Hills and at the ready-made City of Venice.) Another conundrum is how many bona fide fortunes were actually made during that zany era, by whom, and in what amounts. Equally vexing is why the state tardily prosecuted unscrupulous developers and speculators, or why no statistics survive confirming just how many persons came to Florida that decade in search of the American *El Dorado*.

Our story begins in the "Magic City" of Miami shortly after the Armistice was signed. Gradually, the construction and speculative fever intensified and began resonating up the

**The Miami Biltmore Hotel was the crowning achievement of the ready-made city of Coral Gables. Today elegantly restored, it continues to beckon guests from the world over. When opened in 1925 it was the tallest structure in Florida.**

so-called Gold Coast, "that millionaire-jeweled strip seventy-two miles long and two to seven miles wide from Miami northwards to Palm Beach, between the Everglades and the Atlantic Ocean."[4] Then, in what seemed the twinkling of an eye, the land booming began erupting all over the peninsula, at Orlando, Winter Park, Lake Wales, Sebring, around Tampa Bay, and southward to Sarasota, Venice and Fort Myers. Nearly every peninsula town and city was sucked into the land boom's vortex. Hardly affected was the Panhandle, though Pensacola, together with the St. Andrews Bay area and Apalachicola, eventually experienced "boomlets" in the phenomenon's waning hours. Further, several old gracious Florida cities— like Tallahassee and Gainesville—which were usually avoided by northern visitors in winter witnessed little of the speculative fever and thus suffered only fractional losses when the frenzy subsided. Oddly enough, one of the last communities to embrace the insanity was the "Gateway City" of Jacksonville, the largest municipality in the state, whose citizenry at the boom's onset merely watched the flood of humanity pass through its gates en route to the supposed "gold" downstate.

Without question the post–World War I economy helped drive the Twenties boom along with the ready availability of capital and credit, this despite a sharp eighteen-month recession that began in January 1920 as the nation adjusted to peacetime. Also fueling the pandemonium was an army of community boosters, developers, builders, and realty magicians, all of whom did their earnest best to get Americans to come to the Sunshine State and investigate the so-called "effortless riches."

**Dwight James Baum conceived the magnificent Municipal Court House complex in Sarasota, one of many that opened in Florida during the Roaring Twenties. In the same city, the renowned architect also designed an estate for circus-king John Ringling (courtesy Florida Memory, State Archives of Florida).**

And, my, did they come! Tourists, families, widows, promoters, investors, salesmen, speculators, job seekers, business owners and farmers as well as sham artists. Many crossed the state border in their newfangled motorcars that often brimmed with household supplies, suitcases, farming tools, food, pets, children, and family possessions. Others journeyed southward in fancy touring cars, coupes, pick-up trucks, flashy limousines, overcrowded buses, even motorcycles. Still others arrived by ship at such ports as Jacksonville, Miami and Tampa. How many came by train will never be known; Florida was then but a thirty-six-hour train trip for two-thirds of the nation's population. As more people came, the buying, selling, and ballyhoo rose to a fever pitch. If one fact summarized the madness of the decade it was this: "Enough land was subdivided in Florida in the 1920s as to re-house the entire population of the United States at that time."[5]

Another critical ingredient driving the Florida boom was the media. As one chronicler summarized, "Systematic propaganda stressed the undeniable fact that Florida was an unappreciated playground."[6] Almost from the get-go, local and national newspapers and magazines became awash with stories about the quick real estate fortunes being made, the glories of the Sunshine State, its salubrious climate, or the agricultural possibilities. National magazines frequently sported colorful covers of a Florida scene or went so far as to devote entire issues to the real estate euphoria of the Twenties. A spate of promotional books about Florida appeared. Songs were composed about countless Florida cities or a specific attraction. So captivating did Florida and its growth become that it eventually became fodder for such novels as Elizabeth Kennedy's *Daughter of the Sun* (1939), Theodore Pratt's *The Big Bubble* (1958), Wyatt Blassingame's *The Golden Geyser* (1960), and John Maccabee's *Miami Millions* (1980).

Among the many sidebars of our story was Prohibition, created by the Eighteenth Amendment. Most Floridians blatantly ignored the Volstead Act which enforced the legislation, including public figures, politicians, police chiefs, and city mayors. Small wonder, therefore, that boom-era visitors and investors relished the footloose atmosphere which only added to their perception of the tropical paradise. Ultimately the state legislature abandoned any serious attempt to halt the production, importation, and distribution of intoxicating liquors. Cargoes of wine and spirits from Bimini, Cuba and the Bahamas continued to be landed on both Florida coasts during the Twenties, using all manner of vessels. A bottle of beer then retailed for a dollar; bottles of whiskey sold for three dollars and up; moonshine was priced less. Liquor consumption skyrocketed, especially in South Florida where it reached astounding levels. (Fort Lauderdale became known as Fort Liquordale.) Floridians, along with real estate prospects and investors, became convinced that liquor traffic was so elaborately organized that it was virtually impossible to eradicate.[7]

Florida had a population of 968,470 persons when the Twenties land boom began. By 1925—as a direct result of the land boom—that figure would rise to 1.26 million. In fact, between 1920 and 1930, the growth rate of the state soared to fourteen times the national average. Except for Tallahassee, every major Florida city became a Standard Metropolitan

New railway stations by the dozens arose across Florida during the Roaring Twenties. The developer of Venice—the Brotherhood of Locomotive Engineers—paid for this 1927 complex, to the delight of the Seaboard Air Line Railway. Today it is beautifully restored.

Area that decade. Further, thirteen new counties were established between 1921 and 1925—three in the northern sector of the state while ten were fashioned out of the peninsula's southern tier. As the boom reached its zenith hour in 1925, the permanent population of Miami stood at 71,419, up 165 percent over the year 1920; Lakeland at 17,064, up 142 percent; Orlando at 22,272, up 140 percent; West Palm Beach at 19,132, up 121 percent; and Tampa at 94,808, up 84 percent. Even the ancient Spanish enclave of St. Augustine, which experienced only a modest economic uptick in the boom years, could boast some ten thousand inhabitants.[8]

Readers may recall that it was during the 1920s that the United States became the richest nation in the history of the world. Business, industry, and consumerism flourished as never before. Social and class implications also intensified, just as Thorstein Veblen—the Norwegian-American sociologist and economist—said it would in his seminal work, *The Theory of the Leisure Class*. In it, Veblen coined the phrase "conspicuous consumption" for the practice of individuals acquiring wealth and toys so as to create a pecking order. In writing about the decade John Kenneth Galbraith, the renowned Harvard economist, proclaimed that "the Florida land boom was the first indication of the mood of the Twenties, the conviction that God intended the American middle class to be rich."[9]

It was during the 1920s that the progressive reforms of prior governments gave way to a series of Republican presidents who espoused national optimism, prosperity and a "new era" in the country's history. But this new era also triggered numerous cultural upheavals. The moral compass of the nation shifted. Consumer credit came of age, and before long Americans desired everything from motorcars to cigarettes, from refrigerators to cosmetics, nylon stockings, radios, vacuum cleaners, and phonographs. Movies with sound were released; jazz and flapper girls appeared. It was also a time when many middle class Americans became infatuated with something that heretofore had been reserved for the manor born: taking an extended winter vacation or owning a second home. And for many there was no better place to pursue such dreams than Florida—the so-called "Empire in the Sun," the "American Riviera," and "The Nation's Winter Playground." As economist Galbraith further elaborates: "Men and women proceeded to build [in Florida] a world of speculative make believe, a world inhabited not by people who have to be persuaded to believe, but by people who want an excuse to believe. In the case of Florida, they wanted to believe that the whole peninsula would soon be populated by the holiday makers and the sun-worshippers of a new and remarkably indolent era."[10]

Our story ends, as all real estate boom-and-bust cycles must, in collapse. What occurred was not pretty. Among those that would record the eventual return of sanity was then-author Henry Villard, who observed at decade's close, "The further one gets into Florida, the more one is impressed with the absence of ballyhoo. All the extravaganza of picture-pretty cities, all the fantastic hokum of lot-selling and lot-buying, all the hypnotism of get-rich-quick, which used to transform the most unsuspecting tourist into a frenzied financier, has vanished like a soap bubble. Dead subdivisions line the highways, their pompous names half-obliterated on crumbling stucco gates. Lonely street lights stand guard over miles of cement sidewalks, where grass and palmetto take the place of homes that were to be."[11]

There is already one generation in existence, perhaps more than one, to whom our story will come as something of a surprise. Nevertheless, conspicuous reminders of the Twenties land boom proliferate in the Florida landscape, heady reminders of a zany, bygone era. But by no means was this the last boom that the Sunshine State would witness. As author Villard goes on to say, "The very persons getting out of Florida today are going to return tomorrow for ... *they all have sand in their shoes.*"[12]

# 1

# Those Effortless Riches

A new world arose in Florida, a world of fronds and palms and palaces, of
Moorish shops, Italian streets, Castilian clubs, and Neapolitan ice cream.
— *The Great American Bandwagon*, 1928

No pilgrimage into Florida's land boom of the 1920s can commence without first acknowledging that which occurred forty years earlier in Southern California, another garden spot of America "whose soft climate of winter and the dry cool sea-breezes of summer, in the long line of sunny days with nights made for the soundest sleep, made people stay."[1]

Even the most casual of comparisons quickly reveals that the Florida extravaganza was strikingly similar to what had unfolded in the six southern counties of the Golden State in the 1880s. In fact according to one historian it is only from a financial perspective that these two boom-and-bust real estate episodes materially differ. Whereas just $200 million were spent on all real estate transactions in Southern California that decade, "three-fourths of that amount was spent just on the promotional improvements of a single Florida development, Coral Gables. Where California prices ran into the thousands, Florida prices were counted by the tens of thousands."[2]

The Southern California land boom was characterized by the "feverish platting of subdivisions, towns, and witnessed untold land sales and a building-construction flurry."[3] The very same activities occurred in Florida four decades later. Prior to the California mania, visitors mostly went there in the winter months and, "like birds of passage, the whole flock took wing as soon as the almanac announced that spring had come, leaving only a few who concluded to settle."[4] The touristic patterns that unfolded in Florida prior to the Twenties were identical. But in the summer of 1885—like Florida in the summer of 1925—the spring exodus of visitors never manifested. Instead, a tidal wave of humanity poured into Southern California that began investing and speculating in real estate opportunities. "New settlements, like the Redlands, were springing up here and there; Los Angeles, Pasadena, and San Bernardino were growing rapidly; on the north, Santa Barbara and San Buenaventura were beginning to feel the effects; and, even San Diego began to rub its eyes after the long sleep that followed the collapse of the Texas Pacific Railroad some twelve years back."[5]

Persons from every station in life—rich and poor, high and low—would succumb to the California fever, including the "the rich merchant who heretofore had gone to Florida and, hearing that wealthy people were now going to Southern California, concluded that he would try it."[6] There also came, just as they did in Florida, men and women of cultivation

PROFESSIONAL JEALOUSY

*Top:* Ever since the 1880s, Florida and California have battled one another for tourists, homeseekers, farmers and immigrants. The dueling sometimes became comical, as this 1925 cartoon attests. *Above:* Real estate auctions in Florida were sometimes conducted under tents. Many attendees dressed up for the occasion. Sometimes gifts were freely given away for attending—a box of chocolates, perhaps a meal, and on occasion even a new Ford motorcar.

along with the moneyed class, the *hoi-polloi*, immigrants, invalids, climate and health seekers, and farmers by the hundreds "who were tired of vibrating for seven months in the year between the fireplace and the wood-pile, dodging cyclones, or taking quinine."[7] Both land booms also attracted "schemers and promoters of all kinds with a little money which they were anxious to increase at the expense of someone else and without risking any of their own, together with capitalists who had heard that the country was prosperous."[8]

Whereas one might think that it was Florida's boosters, developers, and marketing magicians who originated the art of real estate ballyhoo, or it was they alone who knew all about "shearing the lambs," the truth of the matter was that these parties more often than not took a page from the Californians, whose bravado of four decades prior they imitated or improved upon. Case in point was the subject of public relations and promotion. As the land boom in Southern California intensified, the region's promotional machinery began issuing more and more publicity to every corner of the United States. Seductive articles, written by professional writers, ad men, and residents quickly found their way into newspapers, magazines, pamphlets, and guide books. The public relations machinery of Florida pursued the same strategy in order to create favorable impressions.

Period literature extolled Southern California's glorious climate, the cheap living costs, the "healthfulness and picturesqueness" of the land, the fertility of her soil, not to mention the cornucopia of money-making opportunities. The very same themes would be trumpeted by the Florida media. Enticing marketing pieces were also issued by the railroad companies of Southern California, which aided newcomers and immigrants with travel or relocation plans. Literature issued by Florida's companies, especially those of the Florida East Coast Railway, were even more sumptuous, thanks to advances in four-color printing technology.

Glenn Dumke, the able chronicler of the Southern California boom, notes that "men often stood excitedly in line for days at a time so as to get first choice of lots in a new subdivision."[9] The same hysteria often prevailed in Florida, like at the Davis Islands in Tampa where man-made islands were laced with bridges, lagoons and canals. In October 1924, prospects stood in line for forty hours hoping to buy lots in the not-yet-built Hyde Park Section. First day sales amounted to $1,683,000 (today's money: $20,935,233). Dumke further relates that "exuberant auction sales were often accompanied by brass bands and free lunches."[10] Band music also proved popular at Florida land auctions, as well as chicken barbecues and fish-fries. To handle the incoming tide of humanity the railroads of Southern California "traced out for themselves, with lizard-like speed, a complex network of trackage."[11] The Twenties boom in Florida spawned a railway renaissance that ultimately established the state record for total miles of track and frequency and level of train service.

Los Angeles, the City of Angels, became the epicenter of the Southern California land boom, its population soaring by 500 percent in the 1880s. Some 2,000 real estate agents dashed about the city "seizing lapels and filling the balmy air with windy verbiage."[12] The epicenter of the Florida land boom in the Twenties became Miami, the Magic City, where in the greater metropolitan area some two thousand real estate offices existed. Some 25,000 agents went about hawking lots, houses, and acreage midst considerable "hand-shaking, back-slapping, and general boosting."[13] In conclusion, the land boom in Southern California of the 1880s teemed with "uproarious enthusiasm, reckless waste and wild extravagance," appellations that fittingly describe what took place in Florida during the Roaring Twenties.[14]

* * *

About the time the Southern California land boom emerged, the Florida peninsula was undergoing an economic and demographic transformation. Many towns and businesses began to flourish in the 1880s. Immigrants, tourists and newcomers began pouring in, farmers were beginning to prosper as never before and considerable railway construction was under-way. Much of the renaissance was attributable to the work of several spectacular developers, among them Henry Flagler, Henry Plant and Henry Sanford.

What attracted these and other moguls—aside from the state's inviting climate and fertility of soil—was the resumption of a lucrative land grant scheme that the Florida Leg-islature had unveiled in 1855, but that had laid dormant since the Civil War and Recon-struction. Under this largesse a railroad company could freely receive nearly 4,000 acres of state-owned land for every mile of new track a rail firm would construct, provided the work met certain specifications.[15] The bait worked! Not only did railway promoters go on to make fortunes in the conveyance of passengers and freight, but they also easily entered the lucrative world of real estate.

It fell to Governor William D. Bloxham (1835–1911) to extricate the land-granting Internal Improvement Fund (IIF) from its malaise. This Bloxham did by selling, in 1881, four million acres of "swamp and overflowed land" in Florida to Philadelphia industrialist Hamilton Disston, at the amazingly low sum of twenty-five cents an acre. Nevertheless, pro-ceeds from the sale restored the IIF to solvency, whereupon the land grants to railway com-panies and other entities resumed with zest, so much so that legislators began giving away more land that had been originally conveyed to the state from the Federal government. Regardless, the railway network became substantially enlarged, and the respective companies began to aggressively market their newly-acquired real estate to homesteaders, immigrants, health seekers, businessmen, tourists, farmers, and all manner of potential shippers.[16]

During the next two decades most of Florida's independent railroads (excluding Flagler's Florida East Coast Railway) were acquired by large out-of-state entities, such as the Louisville and Nashville Railroad, the Southern Railway, the Seaboard Air Line Railway, and the Atlantic Coast Line Railroad. They, too, had aggressive traffic and public relations depart-ments, and in time they issued fanciful brochures and guidebooks about Florida that described its myriad attractions and real estate potentialities. Overall, these promotional pieces went far in arousing and educating Americans about the state. Much of the real estate that had been acquired by the underlying rail firms (through the IIF) was sold to these prospects at attractive prices with low-interest or no-interest loans. In some cases land was freely given away if settlers would occupy and improve their new holdings. In all the endeav-ors helped transform the perception of Florida from being a remote wilderness for invalids, rheumatics, and those suffering from lung and pulmonary disorders, to that of a worthy touristic destination, a place of desirable residency or, as one brochure proclaimed, "a Paradise on Earth."

An important beneficiary of railway promotional efforts became Miami which, within a few short decades of its founding, became the poster child for the 1920s land boom. Pre-viously, in 1896, the first train of Flagler's Florida East Coast Railway steamed into the prim-itive setting. By 1915, area business leaders had organized a Board of Trade, a forerunner of the Miami Chamber of Commerce. Propaganda about the setting was distributed far and wide, and before long tourists and newcomers began arriving in record numbers while busi-nesses began to spring up like toadstools.

Flagler, who at first was skeptical about advancing his railway south of West Palm Beach, ultimately erected in Miami the plush Royal Palm Hotel (at the juncture of the Miami River

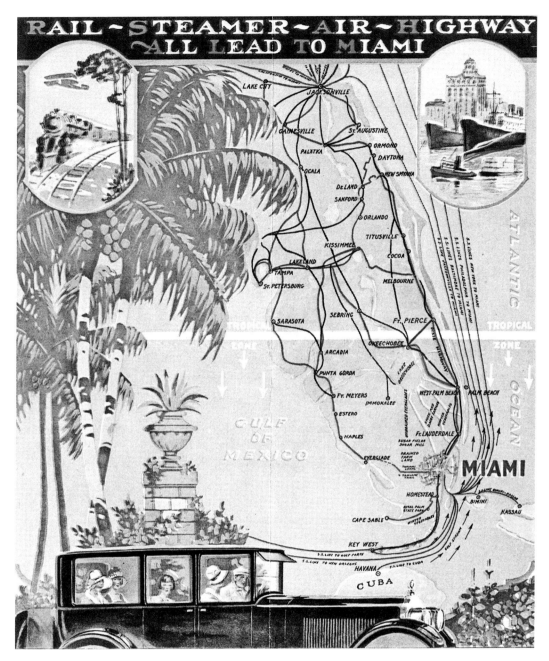

**The Twenties land boom began in greater Miami. Before long, all manner of advertisements and maps began pointing the way to the Magic City, whether the traveler was arriving by motorcar, train or ship.**

and Biscayne Bay) that became a watering hole for bluebloods, politicos and captains of industry. Other Flagler benefactions included sidewalks; paved streets; water, sewage and utility lines; land for churches and municipal buildings; a substantial terminal dock; and a country club. Before long the Florida East Coast Railway began promoting a popular $350 package tour for Americans who desired a five-week stay in Florida, replete with meals, accommodations in Flagler-owned hotels, and railroad transportation.[17] In 1912, the elderly tycoon officially opened his "ribbons of steel" south of Miami to Key West, a stupendous engineering feat across the keys and open waters that, according to historian Seth Bramson, was "unequalled, unparalleled in U.S. and possibly world history."[18]

In addition to having railway transportation, other attractions that helped secure Miami's place in the sun were the Dade County Agricultural Fair and the opening of the famed Collins Bridge (1913) to Ocean Beach, later called Miami Beach. Not long afterwards a car caravan arrived in Miami over the newly-completed Dixie Highway, which linked Chicago with the Miami suburb of Buena Vista.[19] Heading the colorful cavalcade was the highway's promotional genius Carl Fisher, owner of the Indianapolis Motor Speedway, whose name would be inextricably linked in the Twenties to the development of Miami Beach.

Convinced that the motor car would play a significant role in American life, the Miami City Council began to install, in 1918, over six hundred billboard signs along popular roadways leading to Miami that reminded the passersby about the wonders of the Magic City—a marketing technique borrowed from those clever Californians! (The slogan "Magic City" had been coined by promoter E. V. Blackman, a former Methodist preacher turned publicist, long before he had ever seen the setting.) Another noteworthy Miami attraction was Elser Pier on the downtown waterfront, then the largest amusement and arcade structure in the southeast. Small wonder, therefore, that Miami became the epicenter of the 1920s land boom. In fact, so great would the speculative fever here become that city fathers eventually passed an ordinance that forbade the sale of real estate in city streets or even showing thereon of a real estate map!

Beyond the aggressive efforts of communities like Miami, several state agencies were also busily oiling their publicity machinery. As far back as 1868 the Florida Department of Immigration had been issuing collateral pieces about the state. In subsequent decades this agency, along with Florida's Department of Agriculture and the Florida Development Board (forerunner of the Florida Chamber of Commerce), began to seriously promote tourism. According to the noted historian and author Paul George, these collective efforts produced "a spate of guidebooks, travel accounts, and articles in national periodicals which marveled at Florida's assets and its unlimited potential for tourism, real estate development and agriculture." George also notes that "the image of Florida as a new Eden blossomed."[20] Whereas just 33,000 visitors came to Florida during the winter season of 1874–75 and collectively spent some three million dollars, fifty years later—at the height of the 1920s land boom—it was estimated that some 2.5 million visitors were within the state's borders who collectively spent some $445 million.[21]

* * *

Another factor having implications for the Twenties land boom was the First World War (1914–1918). Readers may recall that the United States had tardily entered the hostilities and only after the sinking of the unarmed passenger liner *Lusitania*, the famed "Zimmerman telegram" being made public, and the resumption of unrestricted submarine warfare along the Atlantic seaboard. These events prompted President Woodrow Wilson to seek a Declaration of War against the Imperial German Government less than a month after his second term in office had begun. Congress obliged on 6 April 1917. The financial cost to America of fighting the encounter would prove immense—about $33 billion, not counting the billions loaned to Allied governments. But more disturbing was the human toll of Americans: 113,000 soldiers—51,000 in battle; 62,000 from disease.[22]

Harnessing the American economy for wartime purposes proved a complex task. Essential to the process was the cooperation of industry including the nation's railroads which, at that moment, were playing a vital role in the Florida economy. Just after Christmas Day, President Wilson took possession of the nation's railroads and placed them under control of the United States Railroad Administration, which oversaw their operation until they were returned to stockholders on 1 March 1920—just as Florida's land boom was getting legs.[23]

Ever since the war had commenced in Europe in 1914, Florida's railways had experienced an uptick in freight traffic owing to the extra shipments of citrus, vegetables, beef, lumber, and phosphate, much of that traffic bound for America's European allies. Another revenue stream came from the movement of soldiers and, to a lesser extent, the carriage of munitions and wartime supplies. In all, some 42,000 Floridians would come to serve in the war, and most all were transported, domestically, by trains.

In addition to moving record amounts of freight, wartime supplies, soldiers, and normal passenger traffic, Florida's railways also experienced an unexpected revenue stream· the carriage of "rich and pleasure-loving Americans who found they had to seek some other winter paradise than Italy or France or the Mediterranean; and although it was at first towards the better-known State of California that their eyes turned, it soon became evident that in Florida there were potentialities that were greater still."[24] Exactly how many such persons became acquainted with Florida in this way is not precisely known; however, we do know that shortly after America entered the hostilities Miami was completely overwhelmed with tourists, so much so that it had to turn away an estimated 10,000 persons for lack of proper accommodations.[25] No doubt many would have otherwise gone to European destinations.

These combined revenues furnished a handsome return for Florida's railways during the war years. But the extra business also extracted a huge toll on track, locomotives, rolling stock and equipment. Further, the wartime prosperity was not enjoyed throughout all quarters of the Florida economy. As one business publication remarked, "Outside of lumber, turpentine, foodstuffs, and a few wooden ships, Florida profited little from the general scheme of things. It had, for instance, no great industrial cities furnishing munitions of war. In fact when the war was over and the transformed munitions plants elsewhere speeded up production of corsets, typewriters, and automobile parts, Florida folks sat tight."[26] Fortunately, they did not have to wait too long for something good to happen.

America approached the Twenties with an enormous industrial capability that had not been damaged in any way by the war. Although many persons had sacrificed luxuries, workers had managed to save money during the war years. Farmers, too, were flush with funds from fulfilling American and European agricultural orders. In fact, on 6 May 1917, Florida governor Sidney Catts proclaimed a "National Crisis Day" and urged Florida farmers to produce even more food and encouraged food conservation throughout the state.[27]

In retrospect, American factory employees were able to accumulate savings as a result of overtime and double shifts at facilities that produced war-related material and munitions. As financier Bernard Baruch notes in his monumental tome about the wartime era, "laborers throughout the land turned with favor towards war work, both because it was the patriotic thing to do and they liked the prestige and satisfaction of it, and because it paid unusually high wages."[28]

Not only did farmers and workers prosper, but so did factory owners and investors, it being remembered that the United States was supplying the Allies with all manner of supplies long before the first American soldiers had been dispatched abroad. Confirming this was the fact that, in 1915, the Dow Jones Industrial Average had enjoyed its biggest annual percentage gain in its entire history—a staggering 86 percent.[29]

This overall postwar prosperity put America's bankers and financiers in a rather expansive mood. Capital and credit became readily available both during and after the war, except for the sharp brief recession cited in the Introduction. When the Armistice was signed on 11 November 1918, American industry was operating at peak efficiency. The production of automobiles, furniture and domestics soared owing to pent-up purchasing demands of Americans as well as European consumers, whose manufacturing plants had often been decimated. Another trend emerging in the postwar era, one that very much would have significance for Florida, was this: "City and country real estate began to appreciate *fantastically* in value."[30]

If any one person captured the mood of postwar America it was history professor and author Dr. Alfred Hanna of Rollins College in Winter Park. Hanna claimed that "at the close of World War I, Americans had pockets bulging with war profits with little opportunity of spending them. Expensive as the war had been in materials and tragic in its loss of life.... Americans were pleasantly excited at the thought of their new international importance and their increased wealth. They wanted to go places; they had money to pay their way; the family jalopy in which to travel; and the long Dixie Highway beckoning towards Florida sunshine which the advertisers said was the answer to chilblains [overexposure to cold] as soon as the first blizzard struck the old homestead."[31] Hanna also observed that Florida real estate projects were beginning to rapidly unfold after the war, endeavors that not only offered a "quick gain, but large gains; eight percent on any investment was common; and there was no lack of tempting opportunities to make ten or fifteen percent or more."[32]

\* \* \*

From the land boom's infancy to its ultimate collapse, three governors would come to preside over Florida. The aforementioned Sidney Catts became the state's chief magistrate in 1917 and remained in office until 1921. West Florida was the political stronghold of Catts, where he became a devoted friend of rural voters. Frequently he would remind farmers and provincials that they had only three real friends in the world: "Jesus Christ, Sears, Roebuck & Company, and Sidney J. Catts."[33] A native of Alabama who eventually became a Baptist minister and an insurance salesman, Catts is largely remembered for attempting to enforce prohibition laws, championing racism, and fanning the flames of anti–Catholicism. Little did he do for land boom promoters and developers, though he did support the construction of new roads.

Succeeding Catts was lawyer-banker Cary Hardee of Live Oak, a former state's attorney and Speaker of the House of Representatives. During the Hardee administration (1921–1925) the Legislature amended the Florida state constitution so that "no tax upon the inheritance or upon the income of residents or citizens of this State shall be levied by the State of Florida or under its authority." This 1923 initiative, which delighted land boom promoters and developers, was swiftly approved by the legislative members primarily because it would induce wealthy persons to make Florida their legal residence. In the following year, Hardee would open the famed Gandy Bridge, then the longest automobile toll bridge in the world, between St. Petersburg and Tampa, this in the presence of sixteen state governors and thousands of celebrants. Beyond these events, the somewhat reticent politico did little else for the Twenties land boom.

In contrast to the gubernatorial records of Catts and Hardee was the one fashioned by John Martin, who presided over Florida from 1925 to 1929. Running for office as the "businessman's politician," the youthful and handsome attorney had thrice been mayor of Jacksonville. In short order Martin became the political "face" of the land boom, declaring that a Florida governor should be "daring and imaginative, a living advertisement for the splendors of the sub-tropic paradise of oranges, palm trees and white sand."[34] Martin vigorously supported real estate development and railroad expansion, along with the construction of new roads "from one end of the state to the other, before the people now living were in the cemetery." He also vigorously defended the state's reputation, especially when out-of-state gadflies took aim at the land boom's excesses and indiscretions.

\* \* \*

Our chapter concludes with the topic with which we began: California. Ever since 1905 the Florida Department of Agriculture had issued a fact-filled booklet to the public entitled "Florida's Resources and Inducements" which painted an inviting and convincing picture of the Sunshine State. In the 1923–24 issue, Governor Hardee took aim at Florida's old western nemesis. "Among the States," he said, "Florida has only one competitor in climate. But there both the heat in summer and the cold in winter are more intense than they are in Florida, often rising above one hundred degrees in summer and falling below twenty-five degrees in winter. In that State the rainfall is so scant that irrigation is necessary to the production of all crops. In Florida, though, the rainfall is reliable and abundant during practically all the seasons."[35]

The dueling between the two states never ceased during the Twenties. Promotional pieces produced here naturally proclaimed the superiority of Florida's climate, its attractions and the fabulous opportunities over anything available in California. Those emanating from the Golden State touted their advantages over Florida.

Among those who poked fun at the ongoing feud was the American comedian Will Rogers, who wrote an entertaining article about the subject for the *Saturday Evening Post* (29 May 1926). In it, the witty celebrity noted that Florida literature always bragged about having the longest seacoast of any state in the Union. "We have 1,145 miles," said one promotional brochure, "and that is 100 miles more than California has." Notice they emphasize the word California! Why didn't they say how much more they had than New York or West Virginia? No, they must outdo California! "Now, I ask, what does a large seacoast have to do with the quality of a state? According to the latest returns from Rand McNally, Siberia has quite a mess of seacoast, but I have never heard of any emigration going on there; that is, voluntarily, on account of their seacoast. Clam diggers and lighthouse keepers are the only two professions that I know of that thrive off long coast lines."

Rivalries aside, the curtain was about to go up on what became one of America's greatest building and migration episodes. Although the Golden State also experienced a land boom in the Twenties, what manifested in the Sunshine State forever erased the perception that Florida was a pioneer state. In fact it would soon become known as one of the true garden spots in all of America.

# 2

# Communities of Note

The rush is on, the fever is raging and the boom cities in Florida are filled to overflowing. People crowd the sidewalks day and night and spill over into the streets. Construction gangs are working three shifts. Food and shelter are at a premium. In every town and city, real estate offices flourish like green bay trees. In downtown Miami there are twenty offices to the block. They are jammed with salesmen—nickered, coatless, hatless, sleeveless, young men scouring the town for buyers.

—*The New Republic,* 14 October 1925

This chapter, along with chapters 4 and 6, explores several Florida communities that played a unique role in the Twenties land boom. The list—admittedly somewhat arbitrary—includes developments that either had been established before that phenomenon began and as a result of it came of age, or were actually conceived as a direct result of that building and migration frenzy. Books about each could easily be written and in many cases superb ones have. Space limitations here preclude anything more than a brief summary of each, though in no way should this marginalize or diminish their fascinating story or importance.

## Miami

According to author and satirist Kenneth Roberts, the infant setting of Miami first consisted of "two small buildings and a storehouse. Sometimes as many as ten Seminole Indians would be seen in the vicinity of these buildings at one time, and the occupants of the dwellings would scarcely be able to sleep that night because of their excitement at seeing such a throng of people."[1]

That was hardly the case during the Roaring Twenties. As one chronicler waxed: "In less than a quarter of a century, miles of rainbow-hued dwellings, bizarre estates, ornate hotels, and office buildings grew from mangrove swamp, jungle, coral rock, and sand dunes. Islands dredged from Biscayne Bay are now glorified by exotic plantings and houses of many types and styles. Great wealth, lavishly spent on these synthetic isles and shores, has gone into the building of a winter playground designed to attract those, pleasure-bent, who follow the sun. To the first-time visitor its shining spires, its tropical foliage, the incredible blue of its waters, the cloud formations that tower in the background—all sharply etched under an intense, white sunlight—appear as ephemeral as a motion-picture set."[2]

What became known as the "Magic City" was less than thirty years old when the Twenties land boom commenced. Its population in 1920 stood at a mere 30,000 persons. Three years later, according to historian Paul George, that number rose to 47,000 inhabitants—an increase of fifty-five percent.[3] By summer's end in 1924, just as the land boom began roaring out of control, the City of Miami would issue nearly $3.6 million in new building permits (today's money: $44,781,249), the second highest total of any city in the South.[4] In fact a study released that year by the United States Department of Labor confirmed that Miami outranked every other American city in terms of per capita housing construction. Not only did construction soar, but so did Miami's physical size. By 1925 the greater metropolitan area swelled to forty-three square miles owing to the annexation of such burgs as Coconut Grove, Silver Bluff, Allapattah, Lemon City, Buena Vista, and Little River. That year alone no fewer than 970 subdivisions were platted in greater Miami, 174,530 deeds were filed with the Dade County clerk, and 481 hotels and apartment houses were erected.

Regardless where one gazed in the Magic City during the mid–Twenties, the building craze seemed never ending. One writer proclaimed that "the song of the hammer and the saw sounds throughout the land. New building is at every turn. New subdivisions surround

Downtown Miami became choked with traffic in the land boom years. Pedestrians often took their life in their hands when crossing East Flagler Street. Even trolleys had to be contended with (courtesy Florida Memory, State Archives of Florida).

*Crank up the Lizzy, an' all git aboard,*
    *We're goin' down south, so hurry up an' load!*
*I know she rattles, an' the radiator leaks!*
    *But she'll git us thar safe, even if she squeaks!*
*Git the axe an' saw, an' the big fryin' pan;*
    *An' the tent an' pegs.  An' oh, my lan'!*
*Don't forgit the matches, an' the ole tire pump!*
    *Hustle around now, an' keep on the jump!*
*The weather-man says, that's a blizzard comin';*
    *So crank up the Lizzy an' keep 'er a-hummin'!*
*Head 'er fer Floridy, as fast as we can go;*
    *An' we'll beat that blizzard, first thing we know!*
*We'll pitch our tent, by a runnin' stream,*
    *An' the rest of the winter, 'll be one long dream!*
                          —S.S.R.

**Motorists by the tens of thousands came to Florida in the 1920s. Many arrived in "tin Lizzies" built by Ford. As this postcard reveals, many brimmed with clothes and household goods. Many would begin a new life in the Sunshine State.**

the towns and cities, reaching far into the countryside. The sharp staccato of the air hammer tells of structures of steel, and they seem to be rising skyward in half the city blocks. Miami has a new sky line of skeleton steel. As seen from across Biscayne Bay, the towering steel frames dominate the sky line. Carpenters and masons are just beginning to fill in with brick and tile. Contractors and builders are said to be booked to capacity for months ahead. On this account, and for the added difficulty of getting material shipped in, it is becoming quite a problem to initiate more building of any kind."[5]

So great did the demand for construction materials and supplies become in Florida that, in late summer 1925, embargoes were issued by the state's railways to alleviate the traffic

**Most every real estate firm in Miami did an amazing business in the land boom. Sales of lots and homes took place every day. In 1926, Buchanan & Burton even represented properties in distant locales. The Everjune Gardens subdivision on the chalkboard was situated near Sarasota.**

congestion. Particularly hard hit was Miami, which was served by the Florida East Coast Railway. Whereas sailing vessels and steamships also helped land the much-needed cargoes, that December the harbor of Miami became blocked by the grounding of one vessel and, in the following January, by the overturning of another at the mouth of the harbor's turning basin. Dozens of arriving ships thus had no choice but to anchor off Miami Beach and wait, sometimes weeks on end, before they could enter the port.

It was difficult to estimate just how many firms and individuals were directly and indirectly involved in Miami real estate during the Twenties. "The butcher, the baker, the candlestick maker, and their wives will buy a lot for you or sell you one. Those in Miami who

A stunning landmark of the Twenties was the Miami News Tower, which opened in 1925 to house the famed paper. Schultze and Weaver conceived the structure, modeling its spire after the Giralda bell tower atop the Cathedral in Seville, Spain (courtesy Florida Memory, State Archives of Florida).

haven't got their best ear and eye ready to spot a real estate deal are so few they don't count. But what I speak of are the hordes of men and women, mostly young—many of them very young—who have flocked here from the four corners and are engaged in what is practically a curb market in real estate covering the whole of the Miami business section and operating over the whole state of Florida."[6]

By one estimate some 2,000 real estate offices were located in the greater Miami area at the land boom's height in 1925 together with some 25,000 agents. On Flagler Street, the city's commercial nerve center, sales pitches were conducted in offices, on sidewalks, at curbside, in broad daylight and at night, often to music and roving bands. Expensive cars and buses stood at the ready to convey prospects to a particular listing, subdivision, or new com-

*Liberty* **magazine was one of many American publications that reported on Florida's land boom of the Twenties. Covers were often creatively conceived, and the two characters seen here seem to be relishing their southbound odyssey.**

munity. "At times," notes Paul George, "the sidewalks along Flagler Street were impassable due to the great number of realtors transacting their business."[7] So acute did the congestion become at times that pedestrians had to literally walk out into streets in order to get anywhere in the downtown district, the Magic City then possessing the highest per capita ownership of motorcars in all of America.[8]

The aforementioned author Kenneth Roberts, who witnessed the Miami real estate orgy first hand, was amazed at the intense pressure placed upon unsuspecting sales prospects. "Some of the firms keep impressive-looking salesmen standing just outside the building in which the firms do business. These salesmen are large handsome men for the most part, strikingly dressed in white trousers, pearl gray coats, white shoes, white belts, white neckties, and straw hats tilted knowingly toward the right ear. If one stops for a moment to admire a window display, one of these salesmen is very apt to come up behind him and tempt him with honeyed words. It is almost futile to struggle against these salesmen! Unless one possesses an iron will, he will weakly permit himself to be coaxed within the portals of the office where he will spend the better part of an hour looking at real estate maps and hearing large sums of money bandied about with the utmost carelessness and disrespect."[9]

Another locus of hysteria unfolded at the Miami passenger station of the Florida East Coast Railway, where trainloads of newcomers, tourists, vacationers and sales prospects arrived several times each day. "Like vultures, the real estate fraternity swarmed round the carriages like a hive of angry bees, most of them shouting all purple in the face with heat and excitement."[10] Major subdivisions in the region, together with the more aggressive real estate firms, had their best salesmen upon the platform whose job it was to cajole and browbeat the arrivals into at least viewing a real estate product. And lucky was the agent who had only to flash a prepared sales contract and get an innocent to sign on the dotted line without ever seeing the listing!

Building lots in downtown Miami sold for approximately $1,000 in the early 1900s. By 1925 they were priced between $400,000 and $1,000,000. Lots in premium locations, such as on busy Flagler Street, ran as high as $70,000 a running foot. Lots that were situated two miles from the city center that in previous years sold for $250 eventually commanded $50,000 or more. Stories of fabulous profits were never ending, as Kenneth Ballinger's superb book, *Miami Millions*, documents. In the peak year of 1925 perhaps $100 million was spent on real estate purchases.

Ballinger relates that the big developers were always on the hunt for acreage to subdivide. Among the manifold Miami settings they created were Paradise Park, Riverside, Flagler Terrace, West Gate and Normandy Beach. Bay Vista Park on Buena Vista Drive, west of the Dixie Highway and 2.5 miles from Miami's City Hall, auctioned five hundred building lots in February, 1925; terms were 15 percent down, 15 percent in thirty days and the balance in thirty-six equal payments. Sunny Isles ("The Tropical Venice of America") also drew auction crowds, as did Musa Isles on the Miami River, where sixty-five lots ranged in price from $1,000 to $1,500. Biscayne Park Estates, seven hundred acres of choice lots that boasted dark sandy loam, got platted on the Dixie Highway. Literature proudly proclaimed that the setting was a twelve minute drive from downtown Miami and "a safe distance from the City tax collector as well as the noise and confusion." Other popular Miami area subdivisions included Flagler Lawn, Flagler Manor, Coral Way Park, Brook Lawn, and the Buena Vista projects of Biltmore and Shadowlawn being developed by David P. Davis.[11]

In order to sell these vast inventories of lots, developers frequently hired highly skilled and expensive real estate auctioneers from California and New York. Kenneth Roberts confirms that prospects were frequently lured to the auctions with "free lunches, by the distribution of souvenirs, even by the giving away of automobiles. 'We give away,' advertised one subdivision owner, 'a new Ford car each Monday or its equivalent in cash, and other valuable gifts daily for the duration of the sale. And, we will entertain those who attend the sales with ANY AMUSEMENT WE ARE ABLE TO PROVIDE.' The exact meaning of the last phrase, however, is shrouded in mystery, but it makes its appeal to those who read between the lines."[12]

While dozens and dozens of new subdivisions surfaced in the Miami area during the Twenties, some never saw the light of day. One of the more intriguing speculations was Isola di Lolando, an artificial island community conceived directly in Biscayne Bay by the Shoreland Company (developers of Miami Shores) and the Venetian Island Company. Interestingly, several concrete pilings still remain aligned in water near the northern tip of Di Lido Island and the Julia Tuttle Causeway. Had its seawalls been completed and the man-made island filled in, no doubt a splendid Venetian-inspired enclave would have arisen. Alas, financial problems set in, hurricanes struck and the stock market crashed in 1929. And the island dream, like many subdivisions that decade, remained just that.

## Miami Beach

Hailed today in worldwide tourist literature as the "American Riviera," this appellation for Miami Beach is actually a throwback to the 1920s when the Florida East Coast Railway advertised its territory the very same way. Prior to 1913, this narrow tongue of land was a worthless jungle, a wilderness of mangroves, sea grapes, and scrub palmetto that was infested

George Wharff and son of Portland, Maine, journeyed to Florida in 1922. To prove it, they arrived home with palm fronds and coconuts. Their third passenger quietly rests on the front wheel fender.

with snakes and mosquitoes. The only way of reaching the beachfront was by ferry or excursion boat. But by the mid–1920s, "The island, ten miles long and from one to three miles wide, became a world of moneyed industrialists, boulevardiers, and stars of stage and screen; its atmosphere gay, carefree, and expensive."[13]

Miami Beach did not really flourish until after the Collins Bridge opened across Biscayne Bay to the Miami mainland in 1913. Though pioneer developers like John Collins, the Lummus brothers (Smiley, Bethel and Johnson) and Thomas Pancoast (former Miami Beach mayor) helped transform the setting by selling real estate and spearheading various business ventures, the mogul who became most closely identified with the setting during the Twenties was the indefatigable and hard-drinking Carl Graham Fisher (1874–1939). As comedian Will Rogers was fond of saying to audiences, "Had there been no Carl Fisher, Florida would be known today as the Turpentine State."[14]

From his days as a "news butcher"

Carl Fisher really put Miami Beach on the map in the Roaring Twenties. Here, the indefatigable entrepreneur pauses for a haircut—the ever-present cigar in hand. After the Florida land boom he rolled the dice on a development in Montauk, Long Island.

aboard railway trains in Indiana, Fisher had developed a special gift of seeing possibilities in things which everyone else regarded as impossible. Builder of the Indianapolis Motor Speedway and chief promoter of the Lincoln and Dixie highways, Fisher parlayed his fortune from the automobile head-light business into developing what became Miami Beach. After financially aiding bridge-building aspirant John Collins (a Quaker and horticulturist from New Jersey), Fisher proceeded to purchase and sell building lots on the beach. He also cleared Lincoln Road (where he envisioned an upscale shopping district); helped incorporate the town of Miami Beach; opened the Lincoln and Flamingo hotels among others; connected south Miami Beach and the Miami mainland with a trolley line (via the County Causeway, renamed the MacArthur Causeway in 1942); and conceived his celebrated Roman Pools and Casino at 22nd Street.

Fisher began to really introduce Miami Beach to Americans in 1919 through a series of highly-successful national advertisements that were conceived by the publicist and promotional artist Stephen Hannagan. Hannagan created ads that depicted attractive young women clad in bathing suits frolicking about Miami Beach, images that the creative genius

*Top:* Miami Beach was once known as Ocean Beach, and to reach it one took a ferry (owned by the Lummus brothers) from the Miami mainland at the foot of Flagler Street. Carl Fisher helped with the beach name change (courtesy Florida Memory, State Archives of Florida). *Above:* Carl Fisher's famed Roman Pools on Miami Beach drew the crowds; a windmill marked the locale. The salt air, sun, camaraderie, and grub-n-grog did wonders for the soul. Eventually Fisher sold the complex to another mogul, the amazing N. B. T. Roney.

called "cheesecake." In short order, tourists, investors, the hoi-polloi, along with the rich and famous, began to descend on the island to investigate what Fisher (and others) had for sale.

Many regard the advertising program that Fisher orchestrated as the starting point of the Twenties land boom. "Of all Florida resorts," notes author Polly Redford, "Miami Beach was the best publicized and, most important, it best reflected the spirit of the decade that later came to be known as the Roaring Twenties."[15] In her fascinating tome about the fabled setting, Redford claims that Fisher eventually discovered that sports-related activities drew more attention and attracted more sales prospects than did seductive female pictures on palm-fringed beaches. Accordingly, Fisher constructed a state-of-the-art facility for polo and hired polo instructors from England and staged at Miami Beach the first-ever polo game in Florida. (Even teams from England were imported). He also arranged dare-devil boat races, regattas, golf tournaments, tennis matches, along with swimming and diving exhibitions, events that he would personally spend nearly $350,000 a year upon.

Among Fisher's other triumphs was his posh Flamingo Hotel, the Beach's most imposing and fashionable resort that opened on New Year's Eve in 1920. Located at 15th Street and overlooking both Biscayne Bay and the Atlantic Ocean, the state-of-the-art facility boasted one-hundred-fifty rooms along with boat docks, boathouse, laundry facilities, a men's club, and

**Miami Beach developer Newton B. T. Roney made a fortune in Miami and Miami Beach real estate during the Twenties land boom. His name appeared on billboards everywhere in Dade County. Someday, his story will be fully told.**

retail shops. In the following year President Warren Harding stayed in one of the hotel's luxury cottages. The nation's Chief Executive also swam at the Roman Pools and played a game of golf, his caddy being a baby Asian elephant named Rosie—another publicity stunt staged by the famed developer.

By no means were Fisher's achievements the only ones that occurred in the Twenties. There was, for instance, the opening of the splendid Miami Beach Congregational Church (1921), the superb Pancoast Hotel (1923), the Fleetwood Hotel (1924), the Floridian Hotel (1925), and the spectacular $2 million Roney Plaza Hotel which opened in 1926. A number of lavish estates—built just before and during the boom itself—also began dotting the landscape, including those of store merchants J. C. Penney and S. S. Kresge; tire manufacturer Harvey Firestone, spark plug king A. C. Champion, car maker Harry Stutz, tobacco giant R. J. Reynolds, and whiskey kingpin Hiram Walker. A spate of homes for the less-wealthy arose too, many in the new Mediterranean style. A network of paved roads eventually made motoring pleasant on the island, and before long businesses began springing up like mushrooms. What was once an impenetrable jungle in 1913—the year Fisher first arrived here for his health—had become a jewel in Florida's crown thanks to the migration and building phenomenon of the 1920s.

No snapshot of Miami Beach in the Twenties can close without mentioning another real estate titan of the day—Newton Baker Taylor Roney, who, according to author Kenneth Ballinger, "made money spout out of ventures like rabbits out of a silk hat."[16] Roney hailed from New Jersey where he had been a lawyer, real estate operator and a political force. He built the posh Roney Plaza Hotel at Miami Beach along with thirty other buildings. Throughout the Twenties boom his name appeared on signboards across greater Miami, though the thrust of his endeavors took place on the Beach where, in 1918, he began an intense, seven year campaign of buying and selling. So great was Roney's business acumen that *National Magazine*, in its October 1925 issue, stated that he had made in the previous month "a profit of $1,000,000 an hour for eight consecutive hours in Miami Beach real estate."

According to Ballinger, Roney's investments had begun with five ocean-front lots for which he paid Johnson Lummus—another Beach mogul—$16,000. (He resold them all for $150,000.) Around 1923, the master became responsible for organizing the Miami Beach Bank and Trust Company and supplied the first funds for the original *Miami Tribune*. By 1925, Roney would own commercial real estate properties that housed some two hundred shopping units—from Collins Avenue and Third Street to Twenty-Third Street, all within two blocks of the ocean. Prior to the erection of the Roney Plaza Hotel, the real estate wizard had acquired eight smaller hotels. One of his most picturesque Beach ventures was a Spanish-styled village he christened Espanola Way, which consisted of eighteen commercial buildings designed by architect Robert Taylor. Interestingly, the site became area headquarters for Al Capone's gambling syndicate. Decades later, the Cuban-born American entertainer Desi Arnaz started here the rumba craze, while the location would later serve as a ready-made set for the 1980s television series *Miami Vice*.[18]

In March, 1925, Roney paid $2,500,000 for eight homes and virtu-

*Florida's Finest Hotel*

## The Roney Plaza

### On the Ocean at Miami Beach

*Luxurious, Romantic, Exclusive*

## The Roney Plaza

Is Florida's greatest ocean front hotel, situated less than 200 feet from the rolling surf of the South Atlantic at Miami Beach.

Luxury, refinement, service, location and management have been combined to provide in The Roney Plaza a palatial winter and summer palace for men and women of the most discriminating tastes.

The Roney Plaza will be operated on the European Plan, with à la carte dining room service.

*Booklet on request*

**W. G. McMEEKIN, Manager**

Collins Ave. and 23rd St.                    Miami Beach, Florida

*Golf          Tennis          Polo          Surf Bathing          Yachting*

**The Roney Plaza Hotel was nothing short of spectacular. The entrance was breathtaking, the rooms beautifully decorated. Every amenity and convenience was available to guests.**

ally all the seaside holdings of the Carl Fisher companies, from Fifteenth to Twentieth streets. (Included in the transaction was Fisher's first home—"The Shadows.") Just before this huge outlay, Roney had acquired Fisher's famed Roman Pools, his popular Casino, and all the adjoining stores.[17] Someday, Roney's remarkable story will be fully told. It is safe to say that his legacy—like all the real estate moguls of that remarkable decade—helps form the fairytale story of Miami Beach.

## Hialeah

Five and a half miles northwest of Miami proper lies today's bustling community of Hialeah, one of many ready-made cities built from scratch during the Twenties land boom. Abutting the Miami Canal (a continuation of the Miami River), Hialeah had once been a staging area for the Seminole Indians who called it Hi-a-le-ah, or "high prairie." From this

*Left:* Many Florida developers baited sales prospects with a free bus or car trip. This one for Hialeah, printed on card stock, was distributed throughout Dade County. After the sight-seeing the development sales pitches began in earnest. *Right:* A giant in the early airplane industry was Glenn Curtiss of Hammondsport, New York. After he cashed out of his airplane business, he took his fortune to Florida and, among other endeavors, created three ready-made cities (courtesy Florida Memory, State Archives of Florida).

locale, tribal members would camp and then bring their goods and wares into Miami for trading and provisions, whereupon they would return to their reservation in the Big Cypress Swamp.

What became the City of Hialeah was, in 1921, a huge grassy parcel owned by the Curtiss-Bright Ranch Company. The firm's founder, Missouri cattleman and rancher James H. Bright, dubbed the 17,000 acre spread "Brighton." That year only a small ranch office dotted the property together with two dairy barns and a few farm buildings.

Bright had begun his real estate empire back in 1909 with a single square mile of property. He organized a cattle and poultry business in 1911, and five years later gave property to the famed aviator Glenn Curtiss for an airstrip. Over time Bright's firm would purchase some fourteen thousand additional acres of land, largely for dairy farming. In 1919 he planted three hundred acres with a special grass from Cuba, and in doing so created exceptional grazing lands for his renowned herds of Brahman bulls.[19]

Hialeah, by 1922, would boast a business section, post office, a flourishing school (for one hundred and fifty children), a community church, an eighteen-hole golf course, more than two hundred residences, a motion picture studio, a model dairy farm, a fully-functioning water works, an electric light system, roads and "a future big with promise." That same year Bright, and his fellow developer Glenn Curtiss, amazed themselves by selling one million dollars of realty in a ten-day period.[20]

A New York native, aviation genius Glenn Curtiss (1878–1930) discovered at an early age that he was blessed with unusual mechanical skills. In the beginning of his career he repaired and sold bicycles for a living, manufactured and raced motorcycles, and eventually supplied gas engines for America's first airships. He also obtained the first pilot license ever issued in America (1911), actually built airplanes, conducted airplane experiments with inventor Alexander Graham Bell, and eventually developed and manufactured travel trailers. His sprawling Curtiss Aeroplane and Motor Company in New York underwent a financial reorganization in 1920, at which time its founder cashed out with reputedly thirty-two million dollars. Curtiss then moved to Florida where he founded eighteen corporations, served on various civic commissions and donated extensive land and water rights, indeed remarkable achievements for an individual who possessed only an eighth grade education.

Curtiss had met Bright in 1916. In order to become one of Bright's business partners, Curtiss bought out Bright's brother, whereupon the two embarked on plans to sell building lots and to create a ready-made city. Together they formed the Curtiss-Bright Company to create Hialeah, which would occupy twenty-six blocks of the Curtiss-Bright Ranch Company holdings. Though lots were sold as early as 1920, the actual plat for Hialeah was not finalized until the following year. According to author Seth Bramson, Bright himself paid for laying out the new city along with "the streetlights, sidewalks, and coral rock streets."[21] His aviator partner is thought to have funded the remainder of the project.

The two developers ultimately commissioned a municipal architect in New York to design their ready-made community. Among the drawings that party rendered was a "birds-eye view" of the future city, which included a gridiron of streets together with amenities and various subdivisions. So as to properly receive sales prospects, a combination welcome station and real estate office building was erected at the corner of County Road (today Okee-chobee Road, U.S. 27) and 1st Street in Hialeah. The complex sat directly across from the

**Towering above Hialeah was a wooden likeness of Jack Tigertail, a Seminole Indian. His outstretched hand points to the welcome center and real estate office at the made-from-scratch community. In the foreground is the Okeechobee Road, Route 27.**

Miami Canal, where a dock was installed permitting water-borne prospects and visitors to disembark and visit the community. Also on the canal side of County Road, in full view of approaching motorists and watercraft, the developers erected a towering, wooden welcome sign depicting Jack Tigertail, a Seminole Indian, in native dress, whose outstretched hand pointed visitors to the welcome center.

Hi-a-le-ah, as the setting was spelled in early promotional literature, formally opened to the public in 1923 as the "Gateway to the Everglades" and "The First Town West of Miami." By May of the following year, dozens of new homes had been completed with a pueblo architectural theme, including ones for both Bright and Curtiss. About this time the partners hired a noted New York industrial designer, Fay Leone Faurote, to create a stunning promotional brochure about Hialeah, replete with a pastel color cover, development photographs, and convincing copy—a marketing piece that is today greatly prized by collectors.

To facilitate the growing intake of visitors and prospects, Curtiss and Bright acquired a number of coach busses to carry prospects around their thirteen-square-mile fiefdom. On 10 September 1925, Hialeah officially became an incorporated municipality with over 1,500 inhabitants. By that time approximately twelve thousand lots and parcels had changed hands; sales had topped the $2,800,000 mark. By now the myriad career achievements of Curtiss were widely known in America, and his portrait eventually appeared on the cover of *Time* magazine.

As the land boom years progressed, Hialeah's reputation began to turn on amusement and sport. The famed Hialeah Park Race Track drew nearly 18,000 attendees on opening day in 1925. (The racing of dogs preceded horses). To encourage the construction of a state-of-the-art horse racing facility, Bright deeded one-hundred-sixty acres of land to Joseph Smoot and colleagues, who further developed the track as well as the Miami Jockey Club, the latter having 1,000 stables. Special trains, courtesy of the Florida East Coast Railway, ran directly to the world-class facility thanks to a spur track. A full-time "snake catcher" was hired to patrol the racing track innards! Though severely damaged by the 1926 hurricane, the rebuilt facility of 1930 eclipsed the previous structure; bougainvillea vines with coral and magenta blooms smothered the betting mansion.

Another period attraction drawing crowds to Hialeah became Seminole Lodge, which touted an eatery along with a dance floor and cabaret. The fast-paced Spanish game of Jai-alai was played to great acclaim at the Hialeah Fronton. The Hialeah Shooting Club also possessed a loyal clientele, while golf devotees rejoiced in the greens of the Hialeah-Miami Municipal Golf Course. Another flourishing enterprise became the Hialeah facility of Miami Motion Picture Studios. Among the many productions filmed there was D. W. Griffith's *The White Rose*.

Sadly, the 1926 hurricane destroyed or damaged nearly 70 percent of all homes built in Hialeah; twenty persons perished. Despite the setback and the demise of the land boom, Hialeah survived because it retained a good mixture of location, attractions, business, agriculture, and housing. Today its population stands at 225,000 persons, the sixth largest city in Florida. Hialeah also has the distinction of being home to the second largest population of Cubans and Cuban-Americans in all of America.

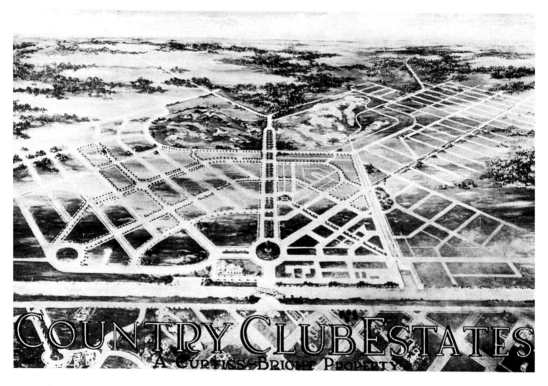

**Sales prospects for Country Club Estates, another Curtiss-Bright community, were given this artist's plat to help visualize the setting-to-be. Today we know the city by a different name: Miami Springs.**

# Country Club Estates

Across the Miami Canal from Hialeah's welcome center blossomed another Curtiss-Bright development called Country Club Estates. From the outset its developers envisioned here a ready-made community with strict land and building covenants, so as to not repeat the chaotic sprawl that Hialeah experienced. Their desire was to have all homes conceived with a Spanish pueblo architectural theme. Lot sales commenced in 1922 for approximately $1,200 apiece, a somewhat large amount when similar lots in neighboring Hialeah went for as a little as $75.[22]

According to the company's sales brochure, Country Club Estates would be a "high-class residential and business property, surrounding the best golf course in South Florida." It was also promised that the new community would be carefully zoned and restricted. Sales offices were situated at both the development site and on East Flagler Street in downtown Miami. Interestingly, Curtiss eventually learned that deep below Country Club Estates there existed numerous fresh water wells, of such magnitude that they would one day furnish much of the drinking water for greater Miami.

The "Country Club" appellation meant, of course, golfing. In 1923, Glenn Curtiss sold 183 acres of land within the new development to the City of Miami for $90,000. The latter developed the tract, naming it the Miami Springs Golf Course. Nearly eight decades later, in a twist of events, the City of Miami sold the golf course back to (what became) the municipality of Miami Springs for $5 million.[23]

To stimulate sales within their new development, Curtiss opted to give away selected home sites with the proviso that the recipient would promptly build a new home. The first four homes within Country Club Estates were clustered at a quadrangle in order to take advantage of a water pump operated by hand. Curtiss, himself, moved to Country Club Estates and had a suitable mansion erected in the Spanish pueblo style at 500 Deer Run, which he commissioned the noted Miami architect Martin Luther Hampton to design.

One of the more noteworthy projects completed within the ready-made community was the Hotel Country Club. Though work began on the imposing edifice in 1925, it did not open until four years later, well after the land boom crested. That same year a prominent American rented a home within Country Club Estates. Dr. John Harvey Kellogg of Battle Creek, Michigan, operated a world-famous sanitarium in the Wolverine State, one that heartily embraced holistic methods. (Kellogg himself invented the corn flakes breakfast cereal that still bears his name.) In short order Curtiss struck up a warm friendship with Kellogg. Learning that the renowned physician was seeking a southern branch for his sanitarium, Curtiss offered his newly-finished Hotel Country Club for consideration. In fact, the offer he tendered to Kellogg was hard to resist: keep the sanitarium open for just six months of the year and the annual rent on the hotel building would be just one dollar! Kellogg took the bait, and in 1930 the Miami–Battle Creek Sanitarium opened. Today the sprawling structure houses an adult living facility.[24]

In August, 1926, Country Club Estates was officially incorporated as a Florida city. Four years later, voters agreed to change the setting's name to Miami Springs, today a real gemstone among the myriad communities helping to form the greater Miami complex.

**City Hall was the grandest Moorish Revival structure in Opa-locka. The Arabian-themed community was the most exotic created in Florida during the land boom years. The structure, restored but modified, still stands and continues to amaze visitors and passing motorists.**

## Opa-locka

Another "ready-made city" carved from the vast Curtiss-Bright land holdings became Opa-locka, perhaps the most exotic community conceived in Florida during the Twenties land boom. Today it occupies about four square miles in northwestern Miami-Dade County. Native Americans originally called the setting Opa-tisha-wocka-locka which, in Seminole Indian parlance, roughly translates to "wood hammock in a swamp." Curtiss, who reduced the tongue-twister to just Opa-locka, engaged an architect who designed a city having a mixture of Arabic, Persian, and Moorish architecture—today called Moorish Revival. Launched amidst intense advertising, a number of original buildings and homes still stand. Some even sport domes along with minarets, crenellations, and crescent moons. Architecturally, it is thought to be the only city of its kind in America.

The architect whom Curtiss engaged for the project was Bernhardt Emil Muller (1878–1964), a Nebraska native who had attended the famed L'Ecole Des Beaux Arts in Paris. After travelling and studying throughout Italy, France, Austria, and Germany, Muller spent his formative career years in New York City where, in 1914, he opened an office. Around 1923 he was commissioned to design several Mediterranean and Spanish-styled homes in the Miami area.

Who actually conceived Opa-locka as a Moorish Revival fantasy remains something of a mystery. In a newspaper interview, Muller stated that after reading a new edition of *The Arabian Nights,* the idea of creating a city around a literary work began to manifest in his mind. Muller wired his ideas to Curtiss, who brought the architect to Florida to discuss

**When the Seaboard Air Line Railway was opened through Opa-locka in 1927, theatrics staged an Arabian skit for dignitaries aboard the Orange Blossom Special trains. Florida Governor John Martin (second from left) enjoyed the merrymaking as did Seaboard President S. Davies Warfield.**

his so-called "Dream of Araby." "I described to him [Curtiss] how we would lay the city out on the basis of the stories, using a story for each of the most important buildings and naming the streets accordingly. In each building we would tell the story by means of mural decorations and wrought iron work carrying out the various features of the story. The style of the architecture would be governed by the country in which the story was supposed to have taken place. Mr. Curtiss was fascinated with my ideas, and I made plans to actually create the phantom city of my mind."[25]

Curtiss, on the other hand, claimed that it was he who had submitted the fantasy scheme to Muller. Further still, a book about the ready-made city notes that it was the mother of Curtiss who suggested the Arabian Nights theme to her son based on another party suggesting it to her.[26] Regardless who conceived the theme, James Bright, business partner of Curtiss, was not especially enamored of the fantasy and subsequently encouraged his partner to move forward with the endeavor largely by himself.

According to architectural scholar Catherine Lynn, drawings and sketches from Muller's Fifth Avenue office in New York City began to arrive at the Curtiss home in 1925. Plans eventually included an impressive sales administration building for the Opa-locka Company, a bathing casino, an archery club facility, volleyball courts, a swimming pool with grandstand seating, an observation tower (where prospects could view the entire Arabian dream) and a variety of homes. Streets carried the names of those found in the Arabian Nights stories—Sultan, Ali Baba, Sharazad, Aladdin, and Sesame Street.[27]

Aggressive advertising played a big role in launching the ready-made city, which had been physically laid out by the noted city planner Clinton Mackenzie of New York. Numerous building lots were sold, and before long both homes and businesses appeared. One of the more interesting structures was a bank conceived as an Egyptian temple. But most of Muller's creative output remained as conceptual drawings or sketches, such as a gas station having Arabian details, a hot dog stand no less, a Christian Science church, and the impressive Hotel Aladdin.

The Seaboard Air Line Railway built through Opa-locka in 1926, en route to Miami from West Palm Beach. A splendid Moorish-inspired depot was subsequently erected on Ali Baba Avenue. On January 8 of the following year, the Seaboard line was officially opened using several sections of the company's famed Orange Blossom Special passenger train. Upon stopping in Opa-locka en route to Miami, the Honorable H. Sayer Wheeler, mayor of Opa-locka, and Carl Adams, president of the Opa-locka Company, together with 1,000 or so citizens, congregated that day whereupon Glenn Curtiss staged a remarkable demonstration.

An Arab scene unfolded for the attendees with a large cavalcade of steeds ridden by men dressed and colored as Arabs. Some participants were dressed in Asiatic costumes and many ladies and girls were attired as inmates of a Harem. In the skit, the Grand Vizier (Carl Adams) of the Opa-locka Arabs, accompanied by their personal bodyguards who were superbly mounted on desert steeds, dashed forth from the sacred mosque (City Hall) and calling their people to battle against the invasion of the snorting "Iron Horse" (steam locomotive). But the spirit of Mohammed spoke to the Grand Vizier and told him not to fear, but to actually welcome the Iron Horse and the Great Sheik (President S. Davies Warfield of the Seaboard Air Line Railway). The skit and reception dazzled Warfield's entourage—among them Florida governor John Martin—after which a reception was held whereupon the various sections of the Orange Blossom Special departed for Miami.[28]

Sadly, the land boom fizzled before Opa-locka could ever be completed. Building plans of the Opa-locka Company were put on hold in 1928, the stock market crashed in 1929, Glenn Curtiss died the following year, and the Great Depression of the 1930s set in. Soon, many of the Moorish-styled structures fell into disuse or decayed. Also, the ethnic demographics of the community changed. In 1959, Bernhardt Muller—at age 80—returned to the setting which he had not seen since the 1920s. "What Muller found upon returning was *not* the charming, beautifully-designed Moorish Revival town he had created. In addition to many altered or demolished buildings of his design, he found a collection of plain, unappealing structures, much like any other American town could exhibit, which he sought to avoid in his work."[29]

Muller died in 1964, but he would have been pleased to learn that the crowning achievement at his fantasy setting—the ornate City Hall building—was reopened in 1987 after a major restoration. Today, there is a growing civic and governmental movement to improve Opa Locka (notice the revised spelling) and reverse its economically depressed image, a setting that, in 2004, had the highest violent crime rate—for its size—in all of America.

# 3

# Marketing the Frenzy

In cities and towns men sold out their small shops on the western prairies and on New England hillsides; families disposed of their holdings; waiters, clerks, salesmen, writers, lawyers, mechanics and medicine men, all fevered by a dream of wealth, formed an astounding cavalcade to Florida in the 1920s. Sanity fled the scene; caution and common sense were out of hand and, out of mind.
—author Burton Roscoe, 1932

Among the ingredients essential to a successful land boom include real estate products, a ready supply of capital and credit, promotional machinery, a steady stream of able and willing buyers, and—most importantly—confidence. All were in evidence during the Florida boom of the 1920s, an event that ultimately captured the interest and involvement of countless Americans and many foreigners.

Among the cornucopia of real estate products available were building lots (sometimes on, near, or away from water); homes of every description (opulent, plain, small, large, new and old, most in subdivisions or ready-made cities); attractive apartment buildings; commercial properties and business blocks both small and large; hotels of every size and quality; farms, both gentlemen and experimental; ranchlands, timberlands, and pasturelands; raw and undeveloped acreage; citrus groves (which Northerners tended to call "orchards"); and a host of speculative opportunities, from oil drilling to banana plantations. Capital and credit was easily obtainable for most of the decade owing to a robust post-war economy and the demand abroad for American-made products and foodstuffs. Aggressive marketing and ballyhoo generated a seemingly endless stream of sales prospects, investors, newcomers, tourists, and speculators, especially after the Twenties boom started to receive national attention.

Then, as now, location greatly matters in real estate decisions. Many boom-era purchasers and investors came to Florida in search of an investment that was at or near an established community having infrastructure and services. Others relished seclusion and thus chose the countryside or farmlands. Purchasers desiring to be on or near the water—whether fresh or salt—invariably had to pay a premium for such. In fact so great did the demand for ocean-side property become that what was once loosely called seashore "soon became five, ten, or fifteen miles from the nearest brine."[1]

A very popular real estate product proved to be building lots, which could be bought one winter season and "flipped" the following year for a profit. As the boom wore on and demand intensified, lots started to be flipped the same winter season, perhaps the same month, and sometimes the very same day. Other purchasers retained ownership of a lot and erected thereon a home. As housing construction increased, contractors became greatly sought-after, even kowtowed to like potentates. Laborers, too, often became prima donnas, ready to quit at a moment's notice if it was suggested that they take a little less than an hour and a half for lunch. Monday mornings eventually became nightmares, and many of the best tradesmen didn't show up as there was pirating of labor all over the state.

Marketing the land boom required the expertise of many talented individuals and organizations, along with such state agencies as the Florida Development Board, the Florida Department of Agriculture and the Florida Bureau of Immigration. An army of community boosters also chased tourists and sales prospects together with zealous Chamber of Commerce members, Boards of Trade, countless realty firms, advertising wizards, public figures, politicos, developers, builders, experts in public relations, civic organizations (like the Kiwanis and Rotary clubs), not to mention banks, mortgage companies and investment firms. All wanted a direct or indirect slice of the action.

FLORIDA

"Land of Sunshine and Happiness"

Various Florida entities issued brochures and booklets during the zany 1920s. Many emphasized the tropical nature of Florida, as this winged nymph—holding oranges—symbolizes. The ad was prepared in soft pastel colors.

At first most of the foregoing parties conducted their own marketing initiatives, but as the boom fever heightened Governor John Martin called for an "All-Florida Development Conference" in West Palm Beach in March, 1925. "Two hundred representative men from every section of Florida then began planning and put into effect a program calculated to unify their respective efforts, to stabilize the economic foundations of the commonwealth, and to promote a wider knowledge of the sound realities underlying the speculative furor of the times."[2] The alliance proved enormously successful, and went far in bringing into Florida that summer and fall a tidal wave of humanity from every corner of the nation.

What, then, were some of the techniques and ploys that the marketing gurus of the day so cleverly employed? How did they reach their target markets? What did their collective efforts achieve?

Repetition is an old maxim in marketing, for repeating one's message over and over eventually yields positive results. Without question boom literature of the Twenties repeated certain themes to create a favorable image of Florida, or about a particular real estate setting, or to stir sales prospects into action. Perhaps the greatest theme trumpeted over and over was Florida's glorious climate. "Climate is Florida's stock in trade," noted one writer, "and it will bring visitors to Florida as long as transportation continues and human activity endures."[3] Another chronicler insisted that climate was "Florida's unanswerable argument."[4]

As to why the climate theme was so often repeated was that Florida lacked extremes of temperature, as most of the state is a peninsula extending into warm seas. But another contributory cause is astronomical: "It has longer days of sunshine in winter and shorter days of sunshine in the summer than the northern states, where extremes of heat and cold are so marked."[5] Frequently, boom-era literature claimed that Florida's climate could restore health, extend life and allow newcomers from northern climes to escape from frigid weather, frozen water pipes and blizzards.

Another theme hyped *ad nauseam* was the "Fountain of Youth" leg-

*Judge* magazine was another publication that reported on the land boom story in the Twenties. Covers often depicted intriguing scenes about the "effortless riches," such as this flapper number. Small wonder that, after thumbing the pages, many readers jumped in their cars and headed south.

end. Students of Florida history will recall that it was Juan Ponce de Leon—companion of Columbus on his second voyage to the New World—who, in March, 1513, "first sighted the shores of Florida from the deck of his flimsy caravel."[6] He named the land, which he thought was an island, *La Florida*. We are told that the robust Spanish conquistador, then age fifty, was familiar with the old Puerto Rican Indian story that the "island" he would one day claim for Spain was rich in gold and silver, and contained a magic fountain that, upon drinking its waters, would restore youth. That tribal members of that sect had sallied forth in search of it, long before Juan Ponce had arrived, could have been true, for "Andreas the Bearded, a West Indian, told the renowned Spanish historian Peter Martyr d'Anghiera that his father had found the spring in Florida and returned home restored with health and vigor."[7] Alas, Ponce's quests for the fountain, not to mention the gold and silver, proved in vain.

Nevertheless, the Fountain of Youth legend made good fodder for land boom literature principally because newcomers—then as now—were perpetually interested in recapturing their youth. One of the first boom-era articles that expounded the legend had been written by Edgar Arthur Howe for the *Saturday Evening Post* (26 February 1921). Even the famous financial sage Roger Ward Babson could not resist the story: "Juan Ponce de Leon had the right idea. He did not come to Florida to look for paper town sites, isolated acreage, subdivision auctions, or the other paraphernalia of exploitation. He went to Florida in search of a Fountain of Youth. And he found it; for Florida can add from five to ten years to the lives of people who will spend their winters there in quest of health and happiness."[8]

**Virtually every Florida community and county issued colorful literature during the 1920s, so as to attract newcomers and sales prospects. Orlando was no exception, and their publications were some of the very best, as collectors of today would confirm.**

Other themes frequently appearing in land boom literature were that Florida was the last pioneer state in America; that her soil was superior to that of California; that it was "blessed" with many natural resources; that it was home to innumerable historic and civic attractions; and that untapped business and manufacturing opportunities abounded. Further, Florida could (in the 1920s) be readily accessed by motorcar, train, ship, or bus.

Never overlooked in marketing pieces were the recreational and leisure-time themes enjoyed in Florida, such as golf, tennis, polo, croquet, horseshoes, horse racing, boating, sun bathing, swimming, fishing, and hunting. Even the merits of "loafing" were emphasized, as well as the cheap living costs, the abundance of cultural activities and the stability of Florida's banking system (despite it crashing after the land boom's glory years!). The state's numerous educational institutions were touted too, as was Florida's "grandiose future" and the fact that the legislature had constitutionally abolished state income and inheritance taxes.

Land boom brochures and pamphlets were usually handsomely conceived, whether they were issued by a state agency, a particular county, a development or community, or by a ready-made city or model farm. Most had covers printed in pastel colors that featured something of a tropical or fantasized setting. The interior pages usually contained black and white photographs of local attractions together with convincing growth statistics and a detailed map. Often times a particular setting, city, or county would issue more than one brochure as the decade advanced. The collateral pieces were free for the taking at visitor bureaus, Chamber of Commerce offices, railroad depots, bus stations, travel agencies, tourist attractions, municipal offices, libraries, etc., or they were freely mailed to the homes of sales prospects, investors, and would-be tourists.

Preparing a marketing brochure for a county or development often meant an opportunity to create a slogan. Some of the more memorable included West Palm Beach, "The Nation's Winter Home"; Clearwater, "The Golden Sunset City"; Winter Haven, "The City of 100 Lakes"; Sanford, "The Celery City"; Okeechobee, "The Chicago of the South"; Lake Wales, "The City of the Carillon"; Hardee County, "The Cucumber Capital of the World"; Kissimmee, "The Road to Contentment"; Fort Lauderdale, "The Tropical Wonderland"; Fort Myers, "The City of Palms"; Clewiston, "The City of Certain Income"; Deland, "The Athens of Florida"; Coral Gables, "Miami's Master Suburb"; Sarasota, "A City of Glorified Opportunity"; and, Cocoa-by-the-Sea: "The Friendly Land that Loves a Playmate."

The copy or text for pamphlets and booklets often contained a good dose of hyperbole. For example, one of several prepared for St. Petersburg informed readers that "here the sunshine, which floods the earth, finds its way into the hearts of men and women, bringing peace, health and happiness." West Palm Beach proclaimed in one of its brochures that "the rejuvenating influence of ocean breezes and balmy sunshine makes life worthwhile in the land where flowers grow." Hialeah, in turn, issued a promotional piece with nationalistic overtones: "Every American fortune had a small beginning. Think of the great American fortunes which have been made on town sites. Hialeah offers to the investor one of the great opportunities in America for town site investment with its attendant great profit-making possibilities."

Other developments that used hyperbole to good effect included Whitfield Estates on Sarasota Bay, "Where Chicago Spends the Winter." One of its brochure urged buyers to "act now because values are rising amazingly—yet prices are remarkably low, so that investors still have the opportunity that awaits the pioneer." Nearby at Longboat Shores (on Long Boat Key) one brochure read: "Now is the time! Buy now before the first price advance, ahead of the great rush of investors." The Haven-Villa Corporation in Winter Haven, whose development featured citrus groves, proclaimed that its offerings were "Your best opportunity to own one of the finest 10-acre groves in Florida's Scenic Highlands." Howey-in-the-Hills, in Lake County, whose sales were also keyed to citrus groves, noted in one of its brochures that "no bond had ever been issued that represents a safer investment than does an orange or grapefruit grove properly located and properly attended." Our prize, though, for the best boom-era hyperbole appeared in the January 1925 issue of the *Miamian*, a booster publication for Miami: "Go to Florida, where enterprise is enthroned—Where you sit and watch at twilight the fronds of the graceful palm, latticed against the fading gold of the sun-kissed sky—Where sun, moon and stars, at eventide, stage a welcome constituting the glorious galaxy of the firmament—Where the whispering breeze springs fresh from the lap of the Caribbean and woos with elusive cadence like unto a mother's lullaby—Where the silver cycle is heaven's lavaliere, and the full orbit is its glorious pendant."[9]

Another task cheerfully seized by marketing wizards was the naming of a new community or subdivision. A popular strategy was to use words, or combinations of words, that evoked a tropical image, perhaps a foreign destination, or something that suggested a magical, fantasized setting. At Ormond Beach, developer Walter Hardesty conceived Rio-Vista-on-the-Halifax, an upscale community he opened with sixteen model homes conceived in the "Mediterranean style." Further down the coast sat Daytona Highlands, whose homes featured "a rose-filled patio, a spraying fountain, bright-hued awnings, and swaying palms." (Note:

prior to 1926, Daytona occupied only the west shore of the Halifax River; on the opposite shore sat Seabreeze and Daytona Beach, separate municipalities. During the land boom, Daytona and the small hamlet of Port Orange began wrangling over the annexation of the peninsula south of Daytona Beach. Landowners in the disputed territory demanded they be included in Daytona. This was done in 1924. Two years later, Seabreeze and Daytona Beach voted for annexation and the three cities, with a single municipal government, were united under the name of Daytona Beach.)

And it was in Fort Lauderdale that farmer-turned-real estate investor Charles Rodes, a West Virginian native, conceived a Florida land boom first: the man-made "finger island" or artificial peninsula that created terra firma for lovely waterfront home sites. Rodes, who witnessed the building technique in Venice, Italy, dredged a series of parallel canals near the New River, lined them with concrete seawalls and filled them with reclaimed land. He called his development Venice, after the Italian city. The finger island technique was also used in other area subdivisions including those undertaken by builder W. F. Morang and Sons, whose creations included Rio Vista Isles, Lauderdale Isles, Lauderdale Shores, and Lauderdale Harbors. Idlewyld, on the north side of the New River, also used the ground-breaking technique. Small wonder, therefore, that the city began advertising itself nationwide as "The Venice of America." Before long developers on both Florida coasts began embracing the novel construction technique.

Because so many boom-era settings, homes and amenities were conceived in the Mediterranean architectural style, subdivisions were frequently christened with Spanish, Italian, Venetian or Moorish names. Some of the more memorable appellations included Rio Vista Isles, San Jose, Los Gatos, Las Olas, Alcazar, Alhambra, Andalusia, Cordoba, Granada Terrace, Venetia ("Northern Florida's Sub-Division Masterpiece on the St. Johns River") and Venetian Isles in Miami ("A Tribute to Man's Resourcefulness"). As we have seen, aviator-developer Glenn Curtiss turned to an Arabian Nights legend for his Moorish fantasy near Miami called Opa-locka. Even place names of rival Southern California settings were introduced, such as Santa Barbara, Santa Monica Highlands, Pasadena Heights, and Laguna.

Among those subdivisions touting a concocted name was "Floranada"—a word corruption of Florida and Canada—which was situated in Fort Lauderdale. Its developer, the American British Improvement Corporation, advertised the 8,000 acre setting as something of a second Biarritz on America's gold coast, perhaps a rival enclave to Palm Beach. Among its social and financial backers were Mrs. Edward T. Stotesbury of Philadelphia, Mrs. Horace Dodge Dillman of Gross Pointe, locomotive builder Samuel Vauclain, flour merchant John Pillsbury, and the Countess of Lauderdale, wife of Lord Thirlestane. Exclusivity was emphasized in sales literature; building lots began at $4,000. Even a residence for the King of Greece was spoken of. (Despite the hoopla, a *United Press* news release of 3 June 1926 noted that "Floranada" had failed, and that royalty and millionaires lost more than $9,500,000 in the speculation—roughly $115 million in today's money.)

Another east coast community advertised as a bastion of exclusivity was Indrio, in St. Lucie County, a word corruption of the Indian River and the Spanish word for river, Rio. Principal backer of this "Masterpiece of Civic Planning" was Pennsylvania investor Edwin Binney, the wealthy and inventive co-founder of Crayola Crayons in Easton, Pennsylvania.

## When You Build A Home —

OU often think of it—building a home! If you have already built, then you are planning another with perhaps "one more room"; with "this" changed or "that" added. Perhaps lack of proper restrictions has made really harmonious surroundings impossible for your present abode. Beside your carefully planned and properly designed Spanish bungalow there are houses which clash with yours. There may even be a noisy and unsightly repair shop across the street. But you cannot help it—*there are no restrictions!*

Look at the Daytona Highlands homes pictured on this page. They are varied and beautiful, yet they *harmonize.* There is no curtailment of individual taste at Daytona Highlands; you can build to suit your particular fancy. But everyone must build under protective regulations, thus making your home and your neighbor's home assured of harmonious environment for all time.

Homes in Daytona Highlands will bring splendid prices because they *are* protected. Those who own homes there are loth to part with them.

# DAYTONA HIGHLANDS
### Florida's Suburb of Hills and Lakes
Main Sales and Executive Offices
#### 162 S. BEACH STREET
DAYTONA                    FLORIDA

Are There Children in Your Home? Send for a copy of our Pictorial Alphabet. Address Educational Director, Daytona Highlands, Box 325 Daytona, Florida.

Sales prospects flocked to Daytona Highlands in Volusia County, though the elevation there above sea-level was minuscule. Nevertheless, an area attraction in the 1920s was Daytona's famed beach, where cars raced at high speeds on hard-packed sand.

# INDRIO

Home of
Your Dreams

*Left: A suggested Indrio home of Mediterranean architecture*

*Above: The Oval Basin, Indrio's proposed salt water bathing casino*

*Right: Suggested duplex apartment building for Indrio*

*One of the proposed plazas which will add charm to Indrio*

*Suggested treatment of a business thoroughfare in Indrio*

At Indrio is coming true your dream of a perfect life in a perfect setting. Here man is combining with nature to create an earthly paradise—an all-year home town where comfort and charm will predominate.

Indrio is on the far-famed Indian River, a stretch of emerald sea water separated from the Atlantic only by a narrow strip of tropical jungle land. Game fish abound in these nearby waters and wild fowl are plentiful. Sandy beaches and a rolling surf invite the bather.

When blizzards rage in northern cities, or heat prostrations are of daily occurrence, the climate here is delightful. In summer cool breezes sweep in from the sea, while winter days are made balmy by the Gulf Stream. 72 degrees is the average annual temperature.

## Fairest of Florida's Townsites

Nowhere else in Florida can be found a more beautiful, more healthful or more accessible spot in which to live. Indrio is but 60 miles north of Palm Beach on the Dixie Highway and Florida East Coast Railway.

Visioned by men of large affairs, with millions at their command, Indrio is already becoming a reality. Eminent architects and landscape gardeners have been engaged to make it America's most beautiful home town.

Parks, plazas, golf courses and boulevards are even now being laid out. These latter range from 100 to 200 feet in width, and will be generously planted with palms.

Architectural unity will be assured by the adoption of the appropriate Mediterranean type of architecture as standard. No residence lot will be less than 100 feet wide.

Indrio's projected improvements include a million-dollar hotel, salt water bathing casino, pleasure and boat piers, yacht harbor, tennis and roque courts, bridle paths and an 18-hole golf course. Electricity and pure drinking water will be available at low cost.

Visit Indrio when you come to Florida this winter. Compare it with all similar developments. The coupon below will bring you an illustrated brochure which further describes this miracle of city planning.

### PHELPS-HENDRICKSON COMPANY

*Exclusive Selling Agents for East Coast Development Company*

JOHN I. BEGGS, *President*    Box P22, INDRIO, *Florida*

*Indrio's waterfront as it will appear when completed, shewing the Indian River and beyond it the Atlantic Ocean*

*The proposed Indrio station of the Florida East Coast Railway, whose main line affords frequent service north and south*

PHELPS-HENDRICKSON COMPANY
Box P22, Indrio, Florida

Gentlemen: Please send me your illustrated brochure describing Indrio.

Name ..................................................

Address ..............................................

..............................................................

---

**Full-page magazine ads were often placed for burgeoning subdivisions. Those for Indrio, sixty miles north of Palm Beach, had an upper-class tone. Artist sketches depicted the future amenities, some of which were never built by developers because of financial reasons.**

Not at all a bastion of exclusivity was the Gulf coast vision of Boston real estate promoter Joel Bean who, in the early 1920s, platted "El-Jobe-An" (an anagram of his name) on the northern banks of the Myakka River in Charlotte County. Here, the developer erected a post office, general store, and hotel, and sold hundreds of building lots mostly by mail on convenient terms. But Bean's "City of Destiny" sputtered in the Great Depression, and today the setting is simply known as El Jobean.

Marketing wizards were also fond of attaching the word "city" to a ready-made town or new subdivision so as to indicate a future metropolis. (To incorporate a city in Florida in the Twenties one needed only $10,000 of agricultural produce output.) Helping to form the list were Cosmic City, Surfside City, Tropical City, Textile City, and Tamiami City. Picture City, near Hobe Sound, was conceived by the Olympia Improvement Corporation, which wished to create a Greek-inspired community where motion pictures could be produced. Two subdivisions—Olympia Beach and Bon Air Beach—were hatched, and for a brief time Hobe Sound was renamed Picture City. A Hollywood-like movie production facility was envisioned here; movie stars would be encouraged to live on Jupiter Island. Street names in Olympia came from Greek mythology—Zeus, Saturn, Mercury, Mars, Olympus, and Athena. In 1924, a Picture City building was acquired by Martin County and fashioned into the Olympia School. (Following the destructive 1928 hurricane, the Picture City founders abandoned their plans and all remaining assets were sold at a bankruptcy sale.)

Another fleeting fantasy was Interocean City, located in Osceola County, and so named because it was platted midway on the peninsula between the Gulf of Mexico and the Atlantic Ocean. Apartments, office buildings and Spanish homes arose, but most were never completed. When the land boom fizzled, only a silhouette of crumbling pink and tan stucco structures remained. Today the setting is known as Intercession City.

Another forgotten but well-advertised dream was Aladdin City, located some twenty miles southwest of Miami, "In the Heart of the Redlands." Aggressively promoted by the Aladdin Company of Bay City, Michigan, the firm specialized in "redi-cut" (prefab) homes for factory towns. Advertisements for the Dade County endeavor exhibited a strong Arabian theme. Houses would be delivered in kit form via railway cars—a land boom first. To confirm the developer's mettle, six chartered aircraft were flown to Florida with all necessary components for a new kit home. According to the *Homestead Leader* (15 January 1926), twenty-one workers—carpenters, electricians, plasters, plumbers and cement workers—commenced work at seven o'clock in the morning. By nightfall the first home was completed, replete with landscaping. Spectators were dumbfounded! Some eight hundred home sites were sold the first day. Two months later the developer laid the cornerstone for a bank building conceived in "Persian style." Only a small part of Ali Baba Circle and Aladdin Boulevard survive today, together with several renamed streets. Most of the Moorish-themed city has since reverted to agricultural use, the original plat having vanished.

Perhaps the most enduring city venture of the era proved to be Kelsey City. On his first visit to Florida in 1919, Boston entrepreneur Harry Kelsey bought 30,000 acres north of West Palm Beach. After selling his controlling interest in the Waldorf restaurant chain, Kelsey's East Coast Finance Corporation acquired more than 100,000 additional acres in Palm Beach County. The developer envisioned several agricultural industries including sugar cane farms, demonstration and stock raising farms, hog and poultry farms, citrus groves, along with truck and dairy farms.

Kelsey chose the scrub ridge near Lake Worth for his residential community, whereupon he hired Olmsted and Olmsted of Boston (sons of the illustrious Fredrick Law Olmsted) to handle design details. Conceived for working-class people, Kelsey City was one of Florida's first zoned communities that tastefully integrated residential, commercial and industrial components. Above a giant arch at the city's entrance, on the old Dixie Highway, a welcome sign read "Gateway to the World's Winter Playground." By 1922, property sales ranged from $250,000 to $500,000 per day. Unfortunately, the 1928 hurricane wreaked horrific damage upon Kelsey City, leaving it in economic shambles. Sir Harry Oakes and his Tesdem Company eventually bought about 80 percent of the setting. In 1939, residents voted to change the community's name to Lake Park.

Other boom settings in Florida that were advertised far and wide in the Twenties included Lennox, Fellsmere Estates, Okeechobee Highlands, Okeechobee Shores, Gardendale ("Lots Priced from $100-$500 with Only $53.33 Down!"); and, Poinciana, whose lots were largely underwater deep within the Ten Thousand Islands. Farming and citrus subdivisions were promoted too, such as Fort Pierce Farms ("20 Acres and Independence"); Penney Farms in Clay County (promulgated by department store kingpin J. C. Penney); Venice Farms (brainchild of the Brotherhood of Locomotive Engineers union); and Holly Hill Groves in Davenport.

A development of special note also tied to citrus production was Temple Terrace, located in the northeast section of Tampa, that was headed by developers Burt Hamner and partners D. Collins Gillette and Vance Helm. They formed Temple Terraces, which was comprised of some four to five thousand acres of groves devoted to Temple orange production (the variety then in its infancy), and Temple Terraces Estates, a residential setting of some seven hundred acres that would tout a professional golf course and fancy clubhouse together with Spanish and Italianate homes of various hues that sported red-tiled roofs. Promoters, who desired buyers to invest in both a home and the grove, hailed the setting in print as "a veritable fairyland surrounded by the Hillsborough River."

Practically every peninsula town and city in Florida was affected by the Twenties boom. Case in point was Fort Myers, winter home of Thomas Edison, which went head-over-heels that decade. As one writer exclaimed, "Subdivisions sprang up here like mushrooms in a sheep pasture after a warm spring rain."[10] Among the new subdivisions beckoning prospects were York Manor, Riverside, Valencia Terrace, Stadler Central Heights, Seminole Park, Edison Park, Carlton Grove, Allen Park, Kingston Grove, Mecca Gardens, Valencia Court and Twin Palm Groves. In 1922, the value of new construction permits issued amounted to $246,310; three years later they totaled $2.79 million. The *Fort Myers Press* also ran repeated advertisements for such subdivisions as Alabama Groves ("Will you wait until all this property is sold before you investigate?"); Palmwood ("It is without equal today and for the future"); Russell Park ("In September we sold more lots than all of last year!"); and San Carlos ("Oversubscribed $986,000 at the September 28th opening"). "The lush year for real estate sales people was 1925. Those who failed to make at least $10,000 were considered rank failures. Many made $50,000 or more."[11]

Innovations also occurred in how building lots were actually marketed. One writer notes that they were "often sold from blue-prints, for they look far better that way. Then the buyer gets the promoter's vision, can see the splendid curving boulevards, the yacht basin, the parks lined with leaning cocoanut trees and flaming hibiscus. The salesman can show the expected lines of heavy travel and help you select a double (two-lot) corner for a business, or a quiet water-front retreat suitable for a winter home. To go see the lot—well, it isn't done! In fact, often it isn't practicable, for most of the lots are sold predevelopment. The boulevards are yet to be built, the yacht basin must be pumped out, and the excavated dirt used to raise the proposed lots above water or bog level. Then they will be staked, the planting done, and the owner can find his lot."[12] When auctions were conducted with no blueprints for prospects to view, the auctioneer would vaguely wave toward a mangrove swamp and exclaim that the building lot was "off there somewhere."

Another marketing technique achieving prominence in the Twenties was the so-called "binder" system of sales. Under this scheme, a deposit or binder of just five or ten percent of the purchase price was legally sufficient to close a real estate deal. The first substantial installment—say twenty-five percent of the purchase price—could not be demanded by the seller until the title to the property cleared. And because of the extraordinary number of real estate transactions that were taking place during the boom in some cities, not to mention the accompanying paperwork congestion and chaos at both law and municipal offices, it often took anywhere from four to six weeks for a single title to be properly recorded and cleared.

It was during this interlude that a certain class of salesperson stepped into the picture: the "binder boy"

For ages, Fort Myers was a sleepy cattle town on the Caloosahatchee River. Although Thomas Edison established his winter home there, it was not until the 1920s that the population exploded. That decade city fathers adopted a catchy slogan: "The City of Palms."

(rhymes with "cinder"), who was usually a young, slick and somewhat dirty individual dressed in a white suit or soiled knickers who went about selling the very same property (for the new buyer) at a higher price before the first substantial down payment was due. In other words, re-sales were taking place far more rapidly than the law could follow them. As a result, the very same property might be sold six or ten times in as many days, all of which created an even greater paperwork nightmare. Naturally opportunities arose for all kinds of trickery. So long as prospects bought and real estate values soared, fortunes could be made in just a few weeks, even by the binder boys who, themselves, often sold their options for cash.

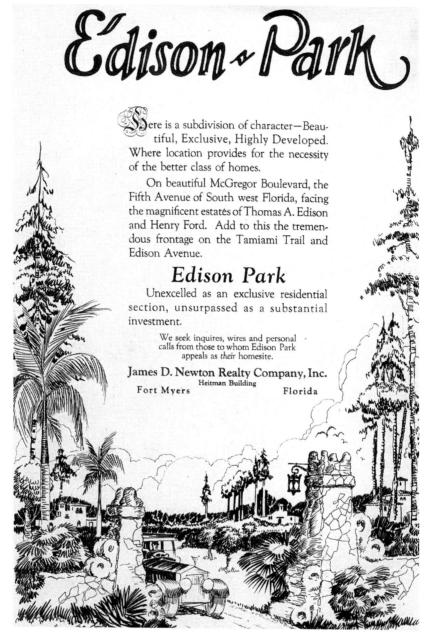

# Edison ~ Park

There is a subdivision of character—Beautiful, Exclusive, Highly Developed. Where location provides for the necessity of the better class of homes.

On beautiful McGregor Boulevard, the Fifth Avenue of South west Florida, facing the magnificent estates of Thomas A. Edison and Henry Ford. Add to this the tremendous frontage on the Tamiami Trail and Edison Avenue.

## Edison Park

Unexcelled as an exclusive residential section, unsurpassed as a substantial investment.

We seek inquires, wires and personal calls from those to whom Edison Park appeals as *their* homesite.

### James D. Newton Realty Company, Inc.
Heitman Building

Fort Myers                         Florida

**Edison Park was one of the more elegant subdivisions that sprouted wings in the land boom years. Its developer was youthful James Newton, a friend of Thomas Edison. Its superb entranceway on McGregor Boulevard still garners the attention of pedestrians and motorists.**

Without question, boom-era marketers used the power of newspapers with devastating efficiency. A mountain of favorable articles ran the gamut of interest—from covering how the speculative fever was gripping the state to unbelievable stories of overnight riches to the endless glories that Florida possessed. Others reported on the progress of a new community or subdivision. As one newspaper correspondent recalled, "Most of my work consisted in interviewing allegedly prominent visitors to the city or in drawing up great manifestos announcing fresh building schemes or in writing stirring accounts of local activities."[13] Demand for the articles became intense, especially from out-of-state newspapers. When truthful articles could not be supplied, Florida reporters and correspondents were known to fabricate propaganda, hype, bias, rumor, and gossip—sometimes outright lies.

On occasion a newspaper would hire a professional journalist, noted author, or public figure to write favorable copy. Clarence W. Barron, president of Dow, Jones and Company (publishers of the *Wall Street Journal*), frequently wrote articles about the Twenties land boom claiming, in a 1926 interview, that Florida was then holding "the eye of the world." Articles were dispatched over the national wire services by telegraph, whereupon they were "picked up" by daily and weekly newspapers throughout the United States and foreign countries. Whether containing fact or fiction, the articles went far in keeping the land boom story before the public. They also served to keep the advancing flood of humanity sweeping southwards down to Florida and believing the popular adage "One Good Investment Beats a Lifetime of Toil."

Newspapers also proved to be an ideal vehicle for advertising chiefly because they could reach a large audience at cheap cost. The format developers and marketers most often chose was the display ad, which had inviting copy and an appropriate image. Occasionally, a tear-off coupon might be incorporated which, when redeemed, brought further information or possibly free transportation and accommodation to view a development. Most ads were run in black and white; multiple exposures of an ad contributed to messages reaching a specific target market.

Often newspaper advertisements were cleverly conceived, such as the series prepared for the ready-made city of Venice that appeared in the *Chicago Tribune*. The community's developer, the Brotherhood of Locomotive Engineers of Cleveland, together with its Venice Company real estate division, entitled their successful series "One Hundred Things to Do at Venice." Each week a new ad focused on a specific attraction or activity of the development. One of the most popular was ad No. 21 entitled "Dancing in the Orange Grove." The pen and ink drawing depicted nattily dressed dancers gliding about the dance floor under orange trees that sported electrically-lighted oranges no less, this at the developer's Hotel Venice. Equally successful was ad No. 37, which carried the catchy headline "Loafing Actively."[14]

Like many made-from-scratch cities of the boom, Venice published its own newspaper to attract newcomers and sales prospects and to arouse investor interest. *This Week in Venice* was the local rag of the aforementioned Venice Company as was its slick successor publication, *The Venice News*. Articles in both papers covered every imaginable topic, from the latest construction activity to social gossip, from community events to interviews with anyone of the slightest importance. Display ads, which helped offset printing costs, were taken by commercial entities within the infant city. Among those specifically prepared by the Venice Company was this one: "VENICE—a tropical Sea—a wonderful beach—a city rich with the architectural beauty of the Italian Renaissance; Mystic palms—glorious nights—boats slipping noiselessly by; the wail of muted violins—the laughter of happy people—the crash and rumble of the surf. Truly a matchless setting! Venice, the new Resort Supreme of Florida's West Coast Riviera."[15]

Statistics confirm that Florida's printing industry profited handsomely during the Twenties land boom. The total spent on publications in 1921, of which newspapers and periodicals represented the largest share, amounted to $8 million. By 1925 that figure soared to $28 million thanks to land boom advertisements. Because the state became home to so many new residents during the 1920s, national manufacturers of goods—from cars to refrigerators—willingly placed more and more ads in Florida newspapers, from $3.6 million worth in 1921 to $18.4 million in 1925.[16] During the boom's palmy days, weekly Florida newspapers often became semi-weekly publications; tri-weeklies became dailies; and daily newspapers, which increased in numbers from thirty-three in 1921 to fifty-three in 1925, often chose to expand their facilities. Case in point was the *Miami Daily News* which, in early 1925, moved into a spectacular, twenty-six-story corporate tower (modeled after Spain's Giralda Tower) at Bayshore Drive and Northeast Sixth Street, then regarded as the finest newspaper plant in the South. (It's now called the Freedom Tower). That summer the same paper—one of four that covered the greater Miami beat—set a world record by publishing a single issue having no fewer than twenty-two sections—a whopping 504 pages!—most of which consisted of real estate advertisements.[17]

Although the *Miami Daily News* was the most popular newspaper in the Magic City, the *Miami Herald* refused to sit on its hands during the boom. In fact for thirteen months in 1925–26 it became the largest circulated newspaper, in terms of volume of business, in the entire world, surpassing the circulation numbers of the *San Francisco Chronicle*, the *Detroit News*, the *Chicago Tribune* and the *New York Times*. "Those were the days when customers with cash in their hands pleaded in vain for page advertisements that couldn't find space even in an 88-page daily. It was not unusual for the harried staff to turn down as many as fifteen pages of advertising in one day. This is recited as one of the almost unbelievable effects of Florida's land rush. From 48 to 56 pages daily was the low average up to July, 1925, and it went up to 88 pages daily quite frequently until the following February. The *Sunday Herald* usually ran from 112 pages to 168 pages. At one time there were twenty-five solid pages of classified ads alone in the *Sunday Herald* and it was not unusual in August and September to see twenty pages of classifieds."[18]

National magazines, too, did a land-office business during the land boom. Most all carried articles about Florida settings or about the state's wonders and attractions. A number of staff reporters and free-lance writers took credit for the publicity and propaganda. Occasionally such communications were viewed as educational, or non-biased accounts. Among the luminaries engaged for such was the business prognosticator Roger Babson, Standard Oil muckraker Ida Tarbell (her series appeared in *McCall's Magazine*), Gertrude Shelby (whose Florida odysseys were recounted in *Harper's Magazine*) and the aforementioned Clarence Barron, of Dow Jones publishing fame.

Though most magazine articles contained favorable copy, on occasion authors would blaspheme the land boom or perhaps prepare something satirical as the marvelous works of Kenneth L. Roberts attest. "Anyone who goes down to the land of alligators and citrus fruits expecting to pick gold coins off the streets or out of the air," he said, "is a candidate for solitary confinement."[19] Roberts, whose literary output included such serious works as *Northwest Passage* and *Rabble in Arms*, loved to squirt lemon juice into the eyes of the Florida real estate magicians and "seekers of Paradise" as well as crushing the hopes of get-rich-overnight speculators. He believed that most of the fabulous real estate profits made in Florida came about in one of two ways, "through the teeming imagination of press agents, or purely on paper."[20] His eleven articles for the *Saturday Evening Post*, which described the land boom and life in Florida, were melded into three classic books, one of which was hilariously titled *Florida Loafing: An Investigation Into the Peculiar State of Affairs Which Leads Residents of 47 States to Encourage Spanish Architecture in the 48th.*

Among the national magazines that took pleasure in covering the Florida land boom were *Collier's Weekly, Judge, Liberty, The American Review of Reviews, Literary Digest, Nation, Nation's Business, Country Life in America, Woman's Home Companion, Vogue, House Beautiful, Arts and Decoration, Outlook, New Republic, World's Work, Survey, Popular Mechanics, American Mercury, World's Week, Town and Country, Vanity Fair,* and *House and Garden. Life* magazine also ran stories about Florida and even dedicated an entire issue to the state on 26 November 1926. The November 1925 issue of *The American Review of Reviews* did likewise.

Like newspaper owners, magazine publishers were also keen to sell as much advertising space as possible to Florida marketers and developers. Advances in printing technology allowed many ads to be run in four colors and occupy full page or double page positions. Of exceptional beauty were those issued for the Davis Islands development in Tampa as well as those for the ready-made cities of Venice, Boca Raton, Hollywood-by-the-Sea, Indrio, and Miami Shores. But for sheer beauty none surpassed those rendered for Coral Gables by Denman Fink and Phineas Paist, of which several have been splendidly reproduced in a recent book by the noted Miami author Arva Moore Parks.[21]

Beyond issuing brochures, writing persuasive articles, or placing glamorous advertisements, boom-era promoters utilized other marketing strategies to attract sales prospects. One setting that broke ground in the relatively new field of "mass mailings" was Coral Gables—"That perfect city, the capital and metropolis of a visible and tangible heaven." Its advertising and promotion department dispatched thousands of customized letters to potential purchasers throughout the United States. As one employee recalled, "The main feature was a vast battery of electric duplicating machines, with double crews working in three, eight-hour shifts all through the twenty-four hours. These machines consisted of mechanically-driven typewriters worked somewhat on the Pianola principle; a slotted sheet representing a standard sales letter was placed on a roller, a switch was turned, and the letter was typed off at such a speed that it was actually impossible to see the keys moving with the naked eye. I believe I am correct in saying that an ordinary single-page letter could be typed in this way in fifteen seconds, and all the operator had to do was to fill in the name and address of the recipient at the top of the sheet. Each letter was thus an original copy, and was in so sense a circular."[22]

Other marketing tools proving useful were billboards and outdoor signs. A popular advertising message that Miami boosters displayed in the winter season atop buildings and along well-travelled roads simply read: "IT'S JUNE IN MIAMI." The slogan itself, coined by Everest Sewell of the Miami Chamber of Commerce, was even showcased in a lighted billboard in New York City's Times Square.

Underwriting a radio broadcast was another promotional technique used to good effect in the 1920s. The developer-controlled Chamber of Commerce at Venice actually sponsored a nationwide radio link-up in December, 1926 that featured the local Lopez Orchestra. Lis-

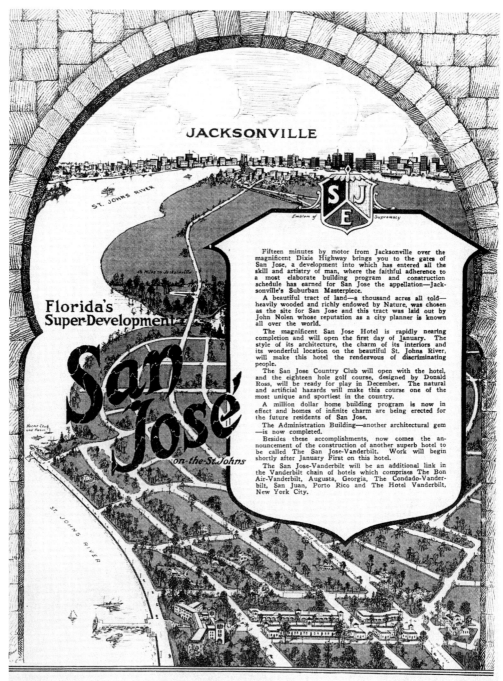

JACKSONVILLE

Florida's
Super-Development

San José
on-the-St Johns

*Emblem of*  S J E  *Supremacy*

Fifteen minutes by motor from Jacksonville over the magnificent Dixie Highway brings you to the gates of San Jose, a development into which has entered all the skill and artistry of man, where the faithful adherence to a most elaborate building program and construction schedule has earned for San Jose the appellation—Jacksonville's Suburban Masterpiece.

A beautiful tract of land—a thousand acres all told—heavily wooded and richly endowed by Nature, was chosen as the site for San Jose and this tract was laid out by John Nolen whose reputation as a city planner is known all over the world.

The magnificent San Jose Hotel is rapidly nearing completion and will open the first day of January. The style of its architecture, the charm of its interiors and its wonderful location on the beautiful St. Johns River, will make this hotel the rendezvous of discriminating people.

The San Jose Country Club will open with the hotel, and the eighteen hole golf course, designed by Donald Ross, will be ready for play in December. The natural and artificial hazards will make this course one of the most unique and sportiest in the country.

A million dollar home building program is now in effect and homes of infinite charm are being erected for the future residents of San Jose.

The Administration Building—another architectural gem —is now completed.

Besides these accomplishments, now comes the announcement of the construction of another superb hotel to be called The San Jose-Vanderbilt. Work will begin shortly after January First on this hotel.

The San Jose-Vanderbilt will be an additional link in the Vanderbilt chain of hotels which comprises The Bon Air-Vanderbilt, Augusta, Georgia, The Condado-Vanderbilt, San Juan, Porto Rico and The Hotel Vanderbilt, New York City.

San Jose was sponsored and developed by a group of men representative of the highest type of business men of the country. It was their aim and ideal to make San Jose a composite of the best and most modern systems, devices, improvements and ideas that enter into suburban communities.

The fulfillment of every promise made and the splendid record of accomplishment are only two of the many factors that have gained the confidence of discriminating people who have purchased locations for their homes in San Jose.

There is ample opportunity for you to purchase desirable locations now at most advantageous prices and make an investment that is safeguarded by the steady and consistent progress of Florida's Super-Development.

## SAN JOSE ESTATES

220-222 W. FORSYTH STREET                                           JACKSONVILLE, FLORIDA

Jacksonville sat on its hands during the early years of the 1920s boom. Finally, several notable subdivisions took root, like San Jose Estates on the St. Johns River. But it opened just as the land boom was about to crest. Another period community of note was Venetia.

teners from afar who heard the program and could name some of the tunes were asked to telegram their answers to the Chamber. For doing so they received a free subscription to the development's newspaper, *The Venice News*.[23] In nearby Sarasota, the Chamber of Commerce joined hands with radio station WJBB to broadcast a popular program to northern prospects entitled "Voice of the Tropics" that featured music played by the Melody Kings and the Sarasotans. The ready-made city of Fulford By-the-Sea, north of Miami, owned radio station WGBU, which also used the airwaves for promotional messages. Each night it played the development's theme song, "Dreams of Fulford By-the-Sea."

Having reached out-of-state prospects, promoters and developers usually had to cajole prospective purchasers to visit Florida to inspect a setting or an investment opportunity. Whereas many parties came down under their own power, often a prosperous development would pay for all transportation and accommodation costs, including a free train, bus, or ship ticket along with a hotel room and meals. Ransom Olds, inventor of the Oldsmobile motorcar and founder of Oldsmar (37,000 acres big) on the northern fringe of Tampa Bay ("Oldsmar for Health, Wealth and Happiness"), conveyed prospects from the Midwest in chartered Pullman railway cars, as did his 1923 successor, Harold Prettyman. Free passage aboard a Miami-bound ship from eastern seaboard cities was proffered by the promotional department of Coral Gables in conjunction with the Clyde-Mallory Line, whose vessels tied up at NE 10th Street. Busses then brought prospects to the Mediterranean Revival utopia. Prospects arriving Miami that wished to view Fulford By-the-Sea had only to board the developer's private motor vessel at Miami's Elser Pier, which then proceeded to Snake Creek (Uleta River) where comfortable busses stood at the ready.

Many ready-made cities ended up purchasing their own fleet of buses to transport

In this postcard scene the sales force at Oldsmar gathers for a group portrait. (No women are present.) The setting was situated on the north shore of Old Tampa Bay, but the building of the Gandy Bridge (between St. Petersburg and Tampa) practically doomed the setting.

prospects, such as Hollywood-by-the-Sea, Boca Raton, Miami Shores, Fulford-By-the-Sea, Hialeah, Venice, Temple Terrace, Davis Islands, and Davis Shores. The fleet operated by Coral Gables included nearly one hundred luxury coaches that were painted in an unmistakable shade of pink. "Prospects were collected practically anywhere and were transported to Coral Gables entirely free of charge, afterwards being given a royal time for two or three days while they were being shown around the city as the guests of the Corporation. Many of these runs extended to over 500 miles—the longest running between Coral Gables and Montgomery, Alabama, a distance of 881 miles. (This journey was performed three times weekly in both directions.) In addition, occasional runs were made from points as far distant as New York, Chicago, and even San Francisco, covering anything up to four thousand miles."[24]

Another ploy used by the larger developments was the establishment of branch offices in major American cities, such as Atlanta, Chicago, Boston and New York. Here, walk-in traffic could meet with the developer's representative, obtain literature, review blueprints and conceptual sketches, and conduct business. Staffers could also assist prospects with travel plans to a development and, in many cases, supply complimentary transportation and accommodation tickets and vouchers.

Often the visit of a famed personality would reap dividends for a developer. This is exactly what happened when inventor Thomas Edison visited the ready-made city of Venice. Publicity articles were quickly prepared and, together with photographs, found their way into nationwide newspapers via the wire services. When President Warren Harding visited Cocoa Beach during the land boom, real estate developer Gus Edwards presented the nation's chief executive with a deed for a free ocean-front lot.[25] The developers of Whitfield Estates in Sarasota went so far as to hire world-famous golfer Bobby Jones to help sell property.[26] To jump-start sales at the 1,200 acre Croissant Park development in Fort Lauderdale, located south of the New River, developer G. Frank Croissant hired cartoonist Sidney Smith, creator of Andy Gump, to personally greet sales prospects. (Croissant himself won a nationwide contest in 1916 as "America's Greatest Salesman." Previously he had developed Calumet City, Illinois, for Henry Ford. After building Croissant Park, the developer tackled Croissantania, north of Fort Lauderdale.) Coral Gables employed William Jennings Bryan, the silver-tongued former United States secretary of state, who cajoled buyers daily for almost two years. He was paid a reputed annual salary of $100,000—half in cash, half in land. Bryan's orations were delivered to prospects in bleacher-type seats around that community's famous Venetian Pool. Here, Bryan was fond of reminding attendees that "Miami was the only city in the world where you could tell a lie at breakfast that would come true by evening."[27]

Staging marketing and publicity events also stimulated real estate sales during the Twenties boom, such as boat rides and races, fishing tournaments (the tarpon tournament at Venice drew nationwide attention); airplane and blimp rides, stunt flyers and wing-walkers; exhibitions by sports celebrities (Olympic swimmer Helen Wainright swam around Davis Islands for $10,000); band concerts, tennis and croquet tournaments, free golf lessons, and less exhilarating competitions involving dominoes, checkers, chess, lawn bowling, horseshoe pitching and shuffleboard. Visitors to Miami's Coral Way Park received a complimentary bag of grapefruit for stopping by, while hundreds of would-be investors at Lauderdale-by-the-Sea were given a free fish fry and a sight-seeing boat ride. A bathing beauty contest helped stimulate building lot sales at the aforementioned Croissant Park in Fort Lauderdale. Prospects requesting literature about the aforementioned setting of Oldsmar, on northern Tampa Bay, received a publicity package in the mail containing an Annual Pass (printed on card stock) which allowed the bearer to drive upon all local roads and occupy any seat in that community's public park. And one cannot overlook the Postcard Week contest, a publicity stunt undertaken by competing Florida communities. The cards themselves bragged about a community's attractions; prizes were awarded to who mailed the most to out-of-state friends and visitors.

In summary, Florida's developers and promoters utilized a variety of techniques during the Twenties boom in order to reach and close sales prospects and investors. Whereas most conducted their affairs with integrity and within the framework of the law, there were the usual exceptions such as when lot sales were fraudulently peddled through the mails, when homes were poorly sited or shabbily constructed, or when infrastructure was promised but never installed. Chapter 7 explores some of those indiscretions and what the state and federal governments did to remedy the issues, though it is safe to say it proved impossible to curb all of the abuses and punish every bad actor.

# 4

# More Communities of Note

Ten minutes to half an hour in any spot in this state would convince the most skeptical eyes and ears that something is taking place in Florida to which the history of developments, booms, in-rushes, speculations, and investments yields no parallel.

—*New York Times*, 16 August 1925

Once again we explore a group of communities that played a unique role in Florida's land boom of the Twenties. The selective list includes developments that either had been established before the real estate phenomenon and as a result of it came of age, or were conceived as a direct result of that building and migration frenzy. Books about each could easily be written and in many cases superb ones have. Space limitations here permit only a brief account of each, but in no way should this marginalize or diminish their fascinating story or significance.

## Coral Gables

If one Florida community embodied the best of all things during the fabled Twenties land boom it was assuredly the Miami suburb of Coral Gables. No other ready-made city that decade so convincingly achieved the ideals of its developer and planners, or lived up to its lofty and captivating slogan "Where Your Castles in Spain Are Made Real!"

The prime mover behind Coral Gables was Pennsylvania native George Edgar Merrick (1886–1942), a giant among American developers whose memory is still cherished and revered. Perhaps no greater cameo of the man and his vision was that penned in 1926 by author Rex Beach: "This is a story about a dreamer and his accomplishments; about a man whose eyes made pictures when they were shut; a man who beheld a stately vision and caused it to become a reality. At heart, he was a writer, a poet, an artist; but fate, with curious perversity, decreed that he should write in wood, steel, and stone, and paint his pictures upon a canvas of spacious fields, cool groves and smiling waterways. His dream was to build a City Beautiful, without blot or blemish, without ugliness or dirt; a city of majestic size but of perfect harmony. A city planned with reverence and with care, and built after the old Grecian ideal that nothing is so sacred as the beautiful: *that was his vision.*"[1]

The Merrick family moved from Massachusetts to South Florida in 1899. George, the

60

son of a Congregational Church minister, was then thirteen years of age. His parents were tired of the cold northern clime and had purchased, sight-unseen, the 160-acre Gregory homestead situated in the back country of Coconut Grove, a purchase that more or less depleted the family's life savings of $1,100.

Almost immediately family members began clearing parts of their newly-acquired spread, and before long the fertile soil yielded cash crops of guavas and vegetables, products that George and his brother sold door-to-door in Miami from a mule-drawn cart. What profits the agribusiness produced were plowed back into planting more crops along with grapefruit trees. When not physically laboring, George buried himself in books, particularly poetry, and dreamt of one day leaving Florida and pursuing a writing career.

The grapefruit groves, which began to bear fruit in 1907, helped to generate a modest but steady income for the family. Gradually more help was hired to manage the groves and vegetable fields of S. Merrick and Son. Later, George went off to Rollins College in Winter Park, an institution founded by Congregational Church folk from New England. Shortly afterwards the Merrick clan moved from its wooden cabin into an attractive columned house built largely of limestone rock that had been designed by George's artistic mother. The family dubbed their new abode "Coral Gables"—today a museum on Coral Way.

George left Rollins after two years of study and, at his father's behest, enrolled at the New York Law School in Manhattan—a precursor of the Columbia University School of Law. However, George's father took ill which necessitated George returning home to run the family business. Though still desirous of a writing career, he quickly grasped the vicissitudes of capitalism and began to take business risks. He acquired more property and planted more grapefruit groves. In one apocryphal moment—the date lost to the sands of time—he began embracing the vision of one day building and developing a planned community.[2]

Gradually the Merrick plantation became the largest producer of citrus and vegetables in Dade County. George also sold acreage and, like his thrifty father, plowed profits back into the business and accumulated additional real estate. And to learn more about the realty business, he went so far as to open his own real estate office in Miami, even joining Realty Securities Corporation in that city as vice-president. In the latter capacity he honed his organizational and executive skills and helped launch several area subdivisions, including North Miami Estates and Riverside Heights.

Merrick's knowledge of community planning grew as did his appreciation of the City Beautiful movement which emphasized beautification, aesthetics, order, and Utopian ideals. He also began touring planned communities within and outside Florida, including Shaker Heights in Cleveland, making careful note of mistakes that other developers had made. Back home he began subdividing his real estate holdings and in doing acquired first-hand knowledge of street planning, landscaping, fountains, parks, amenities, and what construction techniques and materials were best suited for sun-baked Dade County. According to the noted historian Arva Moore Parks, these dozen or so infant projects—such as Twelfth Street Manors at the corner of Flagler Street and Douglas Road—were really "a dress rehearsal for the big event."[3]

Although he avoided the limelight, Merrick became a commissioner of Dade County and ardently supported the construction of new roads like the South Dixie Highway (US 1), the Tamiami Trail, the County Causeway to Miami Beach, the Ingraham Highway along the coast, and the Miami Canal Highway. (Several of these roadways would later benefit his ready-made city.) Merrick, who married in 1916, built a home on Coral Way that he and his wife christened Poinciana Place. Two years later, he resigned from Realty Securities Corporation and devoted himself to enlarging the family business and solidifying plans for a ready-made city. He also became a published author.

Merrick began carving out his City Beautiful dream in 1922, using three thousand acres. To help perfect his vision, he drew into his inner circle nephew Denman Fink, a nationally-known artist, illustrator, and muralist from New Jersey, who translated the developer's Spanish vision into a planned community having impressive entrances, plazas, tile-roofed homes, fountains, tree-lined boulevards, parks, golf courses and obelisks. As Merrick stated in an interview, "Just how I came to utilize the Spanish type of architecture in Coral Gables, I can hardly say, except that it always seemed to me to be the only way houses should be built down here in these tropical surroundings. I made a trip to Mexico and Central America and was more convinced than ever of the possibilities offered by the adaptations of the Spanish and Moorish type of architecture. The gleaming white coral rock, the palm trees, tropical flowers and verdure seemed to me to provide a natural setting with which Spanish architecture alone would harmonize."[4] Fink's drawings were elegantly conceived and quickly incorporated into newspaper advertisements.[5] (Fink also created the famed Cream of Wheat cereal ads as well as the orange, green and white color scheme for the University of Miami where he later became head of the art department.)

Also part of Merrick's inner circle was Frank Button, a regarded landscape architect, whose creativity was already on display at the Biscayne Bay estate of Charles Deering, called Vizcaya. For architectural assignments, Merrick engaged H. George Fink, a first cousin, who lately worked at Miami Beach for developer Carl Fisher. Another important player became Edward "Doc" Dammers, a shrewd real estate operator, whose engaging sales methods could win over the most recalcitrant of prospects. Dammers, who later became the first mayor of Coral Gables, would conduct his early lot auctions for Merrick from the back of a mule-drawn wagon, cajoling purchasers with free china and knick-knacks.

The original plan for Coral Gables occupied just a small slice of the present-day city, bordered by Sorolla on the north, Bird Road on the south, Red Road on the west and Anderson Street on the east. Whereas Denman Fink rendered drawings for the advertisements, Merrick himself would often edit and embellish the copy. On the first day of sales, 28 November 1921, some five thousand people appeared. Profits realized were immediately reinvested and more land was acquired. Merrick also hired the noted architect Phineas Paist as his "color expert," thereby assuring that all homes and buildings within the ready-made city met specific appearance and construction criteria. In time, Paist would become the supervising architect for the Coral Gables Corporation.[6] Interestingly, the early coral rock bungalows in Merrick's setting rapidly gave way to homes and buildings having a Spanish flavor faced with stucco and tile roofs. Further, the original business section of Coral Gables was moved from County Club Prado to its present location east of LeJeune Road, where Denman Fink conceived an impressive Commercial Entrance at Alhambra Circle and Douglas Road.

In 1923 the inviting Coral Gables Golf and Country Club clubhouse opened. Further, a $5 million new development plan was announced, numerous "spec homes" were built, the

attractive Granada entrance was completed, a finance plan for home buyers was
rolled out, an impressive sales facility
opened, and an elementary school started
beckoning students. Merrick also unveiled
the attractive Granada Section that year,
as well as the 180-acre Douglas Road tract.

While both residential and commercial progress intensified in the new community, landscape architect Frank Button
was busily at work overseeing the planting
of hundreds of trees, tropical shrubs and
flowers. More sections of the growing city
opened—Country Club, Crafts, and
Cocoanut Grove. (Country Club Section,
which opened in early 1924, was Merrick's
most elaborate undertaking at that point
and would eventually boast a luxury
hotel.) Millions of dollars were being
spent on local and nationwide advertising
to assure a steady supply of purchasers.
Merrick's publicity machinery also began
chartering trains directly from New York,
Philadelphia and Washington, D.C. And,
nearly one hundred thirty-passenger touring busses were purchased from manufac-

George Merrick, creator of Coral Gables and perhaps
the most brilliant developer of the Twenties land
boom, believed in having a cadre of key internal players
and advisors. A true executive, the master is seen posing
here for the camera in his usual confident manner.

turers such as Mack and Fageol. Painted an unmistakable shade of pink, they collected future
purchasers from distant points both within and outside the state.

Between October 1923 and March 1924, Merrick would sell over seven million dollars
in property, build more than six hundred homes, pave more than sixty-five miles of roads,
complete eighty miles of sidewalks, plant more than 50,000 trees, and install a street lighting
system that covered 238 miles. Sharing credit for the success story was the nationwide sales
force of Doc Dammers that consisted of some 3,000 persons.

One of the more memorable moments in "Gables" history took place in December
1924, when the famed Venetian Casino complex opened to the public—today known as the
Venetian Pool. Built on an unsightly quarry, the superb facility had been designed by Denman
Fink to the highest standards of architectural beauty. It featured green lagoons, shady por-
ticos, vine-covered loggias, fountains, painted murals, carved balustrades, ornamental iron-
work, barrel tile roofs, waterfalls, diving platforms, tea rooms, a dance floor, dressing rooms,
and massive stone Spanish-inspired towers—the only structure of its kind that is today listed
in the National Register of Historic Places. Shortly after its opening, Merrick hired the
famed orator William Jennings Bryan—the "Great Commoner"—to lecture crowds daily
at the pool about the wonders of South Florida and the attractiveness and stability of a
Coral Gables investment.[7]

That same year finishing touches were applied to yet another Gables landmark, the Alhambra Water Tower, while in 1925 the DeSoto Fountain (on Granada Boulevard) was turned on. To house the flood of visiting prospects from around the country, several small hotels opened such as the Cla-Reina (1924), the Antilla (1925) and the Casa Loma (1925). Merrick, meanwhile, was busily acquiring more land for his Biscayne Section (on Biscayne Bay) that would one day embrace his Tahitian Village. Later, in 1926, he opened the stunning Colonnade Building to house the ever-expanding Coral Gables Corporation, this at the corner of Coral Way and Ponce de Leon Boulevard—the columned edifice today helping form the Westin Colonnade Hotel.

Among many Coral Gables milestones, one achievement that bordered on the fantastic was the construction of one of America's most beautiful hotels—the Miami-Biltmore. Plans for a luxury hotel were first announced by Merrick in early 1924. In fact, one of his staff architects had previously visited Spain and conceived an impressive complex that would be crowned with a replication of the Giralda Tower that stood atop the Roman Catholic cathedral in Seville. But financing and building such an undertaking would require a highly experienced hotel partner. In time, Merrick befriended the famed Canadian-born hotelier John McEntee Bowman, who had access to big money and possessed a proven record as head of the Bowman-Biltmore Corporation.

Bowman and Merrick concluded their negotiations between February and May in 1924, with the latter being named president of the Miami-Biltmore Hotel Corporation. The noted architectural firm of Schultze and Weaver of New York City, whose previous work included several Biltmore facilities at Los Angeles and Atlanta, would design the new edifice.

In November 1924, Bowman and Merrick formally announced that their $10 million hotel would be built on one hundred and fifty acres on Anastasia Avenue. Conceived largely in Spanish Revival architecture, the property would boast 400 rooms, a country club, service building, two 18-hole golf courses, polo fields, tennis courts and a monstrous 150-by-225-foot swimming pool—for many years the largest in the world. News of the project was flashed across the country. Groundbreaking took place in spring 1925, and construction proceeded at breakneck speed. On 14 January 1926 the landmark building (then the tallest structure in Florida) opened, its breathtaking interior exhibiting one magnificent detail after another: exquisite hand-painted frescoes on barrel-vaulted ceilings, travertine floors, imposing marble columns, leaded glass fixtures and carved mahogany furnishings. Both the Atlantic Coast Line Railroad and the Seaboard Air Line Railway rushed socialites and captains of industry from the Northeast to Miami aboard their "Miami Biltmore Specials."[8] (Grandly restored, the world-class hotel is now operated by the Seaway Hotels Corporation.)

About a month after the Miami-Biltmore Hotel opened, Merrick unveiled his much anticipated jewel of Tahiti Beach. The enclave was part of the developer's last big purchase for Coral Cables, the Biscayne Bay Section. He had acquired the tract in March 1925, and by doing so extended the southerly reach of Coral Cables directly to Biscayne Bay. So confident of its potential was Merrick that he began billing Coral Gables in promotional literature as the "Miami Riviera with 40 Miles of Waterfront: America's Finest Suburb." (Just twenty miles of waterfront actually existed, after all canals were measured, but publicity men counted both sides of the waterway!) At Tahiti Beach, Merrick envisioned yet another luxury hotel, a casino, yacht club, fashionable waterfront homes, and a broad sandy beach. Eager to see the vast new section developed, Merrick agreed to let other developers help construct the Biscayne Bay Section, provided of course that their real estate products conformed to the rigid construction and appearance guidelines of the city.

Almost immediately after acquiring the Biscayne Bay Section, Merrick ordered canals to be dug from Biscayne Bay to where the Miami-Biltmore Hotel would one day stand. When the colossal edifice opened for business in January 1926, no fewer than twenty-five Italian gondolas and gondoliers were at the ready to ferry patrons from the hostelry down to Tahiti Beach via the Coral Gables Waterway. At Tahiti Beach, guests and visitors could partake of what author Les Standiford called "an oceanfront experience."[9] Though still uncompleted, the setting consisted then of Polynesian-styled thatched huts, a clubhouse with dining room, and a band shell with a dance floor. Sadly, the 1926 hurricane would demolish much of the setting. Later the area became a public beach until 1970, when it was redeveloped as a luxury enclave called Cocoplum.

Whether Merrick and his adjutants wished to acknowledge it or not, the Twenties land boom had crested by the time the 1926 hurricane struck. Much of the real estate mania and hokum of recent years had lost steam owing to a decreased number of buyers, partly because so many Americans now turned to the stock market for rewarding investments. Despite the trend, progress at Coral Gables was still being reported. One of Merrick's long-cherished priorities was establishing a collegiate seat of learning, and to this end he offered the University of Miami a personal pledge of $5 million along with 165 acres of land for a campus site (in the new Riviera Section) together with conceptual drawings prepared by Denman Fink and Phineas Paist. The University's Board of Regents accepted Merrick's benefactions in April 1925. In October of the following year the institution opened with nearly eight hundred students, not in the magnificent Merrick Building originally planned but in the nearly-completed Anastasia Hotel on University Drive.

In the same month that Merrick announced his educational gifts, Coral Gables formally became a Florida city with a mayor and city commissioners. Previously, it was Merrick who controlled the community's development through his Coral Gables Corporation, power that he had to ultimately relinquish. Almost immediately after the city was created, a trolley line opened between downtown Miami and Coral Gables proper, an enterprise well documented by historian Seth Bramson.[10]

To keep buyer interest buoyed in Coral Gables, the American Building Corporation of Cincinnati announced in fall 1925 that it would erect one thousand homes in Coral Gables for $75 million. Various themed villages were envisioned, including a French Country Village, Dutch South African Village, Chinese Compound Village, Florida Pioneer Village, an Italian Village, French City Village, and a French Normandy Village. Eleven other themed villages were never constructed (Javanese, Spanish Bazaar, Spanish Town, Neapolitan Baroque, Tangier, Persian, Mexican, Tangier Bazaar, African Bazaar, Persian Canal and Venetian Canal). Unfortunately, only seventy-five of the 1,000 projected homes were ever built, the land boom's decline severely curbing any further construction.

George Merrick—creator of one of America's most desirable and livable cities—received an honorary bachelor's degree from Rollins College in 1927. That year the magnificent Coral Gables Coliseum opened. At this point Coral Gables could boast 3,000 homes, eighty apartment buildings, seven hotels, 122 offices and store buildings, two hos-

One of the spectacular edifices that arose in Coral Gables during the land boom was the Colonnade, designed by Phineas Paist and Walter DeGarmo. It initially housed the sales headquarters for the ready-made city. The edifice is now part of the Westin hotel chain (courtesy Florida Memory, State Archives of Florida).

pitals, twelve schools, eight churches, imposing entrances, plazas, and a trolley system. In 1928, the last major edifice of the boom would open its doors: the stunning Coral Gables City Hall designed by Phineas Paist, which still stands and is used for municipal purpose.

Unfortunately, the finances of the Coral Gables Corporation (and those of Merrick himself) were steadily deteriorating. Loan repayments and bond interest could not be made, creditors were up in arms and cash was becoming increasingly scarce. According to the 16 April 1928 issue of the *New York Times*, the Coral Gables Corporation had now been taken over by a group of financiers from New York and New Orleans, despite the Corporation having between 600 and 700 creditors and approximately $29 million of debt. (There were no liquid assets whatsoever.) Later that year, in July, three unpaid creditors forced the newly-acquired Corporation into an involuntary bankruptcy. A receiver was appointed and meetings were quickly held with bondholders. A reorganization plan evolved and the chaos of the times began to subside.

How George Merrick felt after losing control of his development, moreover being removed from the Coral Gables City Commission, will likely never be known. For several years afterwards, he and his family operated a popular fishing camp in the Florida Keys that was, sadly, pummeled by the 1935 hurricane. Undeterred, Merrick went on to chair the Dade County Planning Board (1935–1939) and became postmaster for Miami in 1940. Two years later the king of Florida developers died. As one chronicler lamented, "Saturday afternoon,

March 28, 1942, was a sad occasion for the family, the friends, and associates who gathered by the hundreds at the Plymouth Congregational Church to show their love and respect for George Edgar Merrick. Men and women of all walks of life came to pay tribute to the backwoods' farm lad who became one of the area's most outstanding citizens. His mortal remains lie interred beside those of his parents in Woodlawn Park Cemetery, but his memory lives on in the hearts of his friends."[11]

On 18 April 1942, the *New York Times* reported that Merrick—who once refused $80 million for his real estate holdings in Coral Gables in 1925 (today's money: $1.05 billion)—left an estate valued at a mere three hundred dollars, consisting of "equity in an automobile and a salary balance due from his job as Miami's postmaster." The article went on to say that the renowned developer had used his remaining fortune and income to help satisfy claims growing out of the fabulous land boom of the Roaring Twenties.

## Miami Shores

Competition is one of the touchstones of free markets, and it was certainly present in Florida during the Twenties land boom. Not even George Merrick—doyen of ready-made cities—was immune from rivals. In fact in late 1924 a real challenger to Merrick's model city emerged in the northeast sector of Dade County called Miami Shores, "America's Mediterranean on Biscayne Bay." Interestingly, much of the competing city would be designed by Kiehnel and Elliot, the very same firm that conceived the elegant Coral Gables Congregational Church and the Coral Gables Elementary School. Aware that a serious competitor was afoot, Merrick shrewdly placed a "full page advertisement [in Miami newspapers] welcoming the new development, then increased his own advertising and promotional events."[12]

Hugh Anderson, the leading light behind Miami Shores, had come to the Magic City from Chattanooga in 1910. The handsome, twenty-nine-year-old bachelor became associated with the old real estate firm of Tatum Brothers, into whose family he would one day marry. Early on he showed a penchant for dealing in high-end real estate projects. Around 1920, he helped form the Venetian Islands Company, a subsidiary of Biscayne Bay Improvement, whose goal was to create a chain of man-made islands between Miami and Miami Beach and connect them with a new causeway (Venetian Way) along the route of the "old" Collins Bridge. Although the proposed causeway had not been built by 1922, the islands themselves were "still raw after having been lifted from the Bay bottom. Lots were selling well at $5,750 apiece."[13] Soon, the new terra firma would sport homes having splendid Mediterranean Revival architecture.

With the success of Venetian Islands assured, Anderson partnered with other developers, such as Roy Wright, and together they formed the Shore Land Development Company—later the Shoreland Company—to create a ready-made city north of Miami proper on Biscayne Bay. Organized in January 1924, the master plan for Miami Shores called for no fewer than nine thousand building sites, nearly six miles of bay frontage, four miles of inland waterways, and ten miles of roadways. Even a new causeway to Miami Beach was envisioned, as well as a golf course, country club, yacht club, a business district, apartment

# Moonbeams across the Bay

### In front of your ideal Southern Home at

# MIAMI SHORES

### America's Mediterranean

The man who loves the water and his boat will appreciate Miami Shores. Ten miles of water-frontage — all of it accessible by yachts — superbly developed with every city improvement provided, and all costs included in the first purchase price—located on spark-ling Biscayne Bay—*That Is Miami Shores!*

For social recreation—our beautiful $1,500,000 club house to be erected on the shores of Biscayne Bay.

For golfing—our two splendid golf courses, one on the mainland and one on the Miami Shores Island.

For investment—remember Miami is located on all the main high-ways leading from the North to the center of Miami. Remember that 50 per cent of it is already included in the city limits of Miami. Remember that it is within a few minutes' ride of Miami Beach and the ocean via the Miami Shores causeway. Remember that Miami Shores has under way a 12-month program calling for the expenditure of $35,000,000 in building and development.

Write for full information.

# MIAMI SHORES

## America's Mediterranean

##### 125 E. Flagler Street, Miami, Fla.

**Considerable hoopla and ballyhoo preceded the opening of the ready-made city of Miami Shores. Many felt it would surpass Coral Gables. Unfortunately, the community came alive just as the Twenties real estate phenomena was cresting, and the initial enterprise would ultimately fail.**

buildings, hotels, a school, churches, a railroad station, along with parks, plazas and imposing entryways! In all, the development was projected to cost some $200 million.[14]

In order to create Miami Shores it was essential for Anderson's firm to acquire approx-imately 2,800 acres of land around and near the northern section of Biscayne Bay. As one observer noted, the overall plat "had an extensive bayfront and was crossed by the West

Dixie Highway, the railroad, the East Dixie, and the designated route of a new "federal aided" highway. Into the plat was gathered much of old Biscayne—the Moore pineapple plantation, the Brooks homestead, the starch mill property, Fred Kennedy's store and post office, and the land which had belonged to such early pioneers as the Hunts and Barnotts. Graves had to be moved from at least three small cemeteries, and there may have been other graves, grown over and forgotten."[15]

Other land purchases that Anderson consummated included nine hundred acres of pineland and mangrove swamp along Biscayne Bay (at Arch Creek) between NE One Hundred and Fifteenth Street and One Hundred and Twenty-Seventh Street, with the East Dixie Highway on the west and the Bay on the east. Anderson ordered extensive plans prepared for bulkheading and filling the swamp and for deepening and widening Arch Creek which ran across the tract. Canals were planned as well, including one with wide, double boulevards—the "Grand Concourse"—that would have a canal down its center. (This would lead to the new causeway to Miami Beach, at this point only a mile and a half away.)

The Shoreland Company additionally envisioned a chain of islands in Biscayne Bay running north from the aforementioned Venetian Islands development to the proposed Miami Shores causeway that would, in effect, give a north-south, center-of-bay boulevard where the islands were to be ultimately connected. (The chain was never built, but pilings outlining one of them were visible for years just off the 79th Street Causeway, often referred to as Pelican Island.) One mangrove swamp island, lying across the Bay from Miami Shores, was actually bulkheaded, filled, and named Miami Shores Island—today called Indian Creek. A hotel, exclusively for women, also appeared on the grandiose master plan, as well as a 350-room, ten-story luxury hotel that a Detroit company would develop at a cost of $2 million, located on the Bay at the mouth of Arch Creek—the Atlantic Ocean to be visible from its upper floors and balconies.[16]

The first subdivision to be sold at Miami Shores, called the Bay View Section, was comprised of some 4,000 lots. Improvements and infrastructure were fairly well advanced when the sale began. A seawall had been built on the Bay, about a hundred yards from shore, though it still awaited fill, which meant that some of the more expensive lots in Bay View were still under water. The Shoreland Company, which had offices on East Flagler Street in downtown Miami and in the Bay View Section, set the sale for 4 December 1924. Seventy-five well-dressed salesmen had orders to be at all times "dignified" and not to accost passers-by like "panhandlers." Though some salesmen had private cars to take prospective buyers to the property, the Shoreland Company purchased ten new Cadillac sedans which they lined up on East Flagler Street near their office. Within sixty minutes after the sale opened, all the lots facing West Dixie Highway were sold, and before nightfall some had been re-sold by the original purchasers at a good profit. Sales that one day amounted to $2,509,170 (today's money: $32.9 million).[17]

The next sale, occurring on 3 September 1925, consisted of some 1,500 building lots in the Arch Creek Section of Miami Shores. Here, the recently pumped-in sand had hardly settled, some lots were again underwater, and certain canals and boulevards were still a paper dream. But that hardly stopped frenetic buyers. The sales office of Shoreland in Miami opened at 8:30 a.m. but had to close two and a half hours later. In fact, for five days they remained closed as the response had totally overwhelmed the firm. In some cases the same lots had been inadvertently oversold to two or more purchasers causing a nightmare of paperwork. According to the *Miami Daily News* on 4 September 1925, the one-day sale brought in the full value of the property listings: $33,734,350 (today's money: approximately $295 million!). Of that amount, $11,319,650 had to be refunded to buyers owing to the oversubscriptions. Another newspaper remarked that "three-fourths of the purchasers had not even seen the property they contracted for—they accompanied their binder checks with memoranda empowering the officers of the company to select their lots for them."[18] Developers in South Florida were awe-struck by the news.

Despite auspicious and lucrative beginnings, the fact remained that Miami Shores had been hatched just as Florida's land boom was cresting. "The rows of dominoes were precariously poised," said one local resident, and "one too many defaults would trigger it and the ripple effect would be total disaster. A gnawing of anxiety was masked by the upbeat advertising and dazzling new plans."[19] Nevertheless, the Miami Shores Orchestra continued to give free concerts at its East Flagler Street headquarters which, in turn, were broadcast over radio station WQAM, each program beginning and ending with the development's theme song: "On Miami Shores." (Interestingly, the song became one of the biggest hit tunes in America, second only to the Missouri Waltz.)

As 1925 closed, a glittering theatre complex opened in Miami Shores at Arch Creek comprised of an antique Spanish village of shops, bazaars, and cafes, "all in hopes of sustaining the forward motion a bit longer." Pueblo Feliz—the "Joyful City"—was an extravaganza of music and dancing that featured a pageant production about the history of Florida,

*Miami Shores will have the Finest Country and Yacht Club in the South*
*The illustration shows the elevation facing Biscayne Bay*

**Part and parcel of community sales literature were artist sketches of amenities. This one, for a stupendous country and yacht club facility at Miami Shores, no doubt dazzled sales prospects. It was never built.**

called Fountania. A twenty-piece orchestra provided music along with a pipe organ. The theatre itself, which sported a high ceiling beamed with pecky cypress, had pew-like, cushioned seats, a stage sixty feet wide, and a seating capacity of 1,500. Among the celebrities who attended performances was Ziegfeld Follies producer and Broadway impresario Florenz Ziegfeld, Jr., along with his movie star wife Billie Burke. Sadly, the popular tourist attraction was ripped asunder by the 1926 hurricane followed by a disastrous fire.[20]

Early in 1926 it was reported that "approximately fifty homes had been completed in Miami Shores, another fifty were under construction, and an additional one hundred were being planned. The commercial building program was well in progress, sidewalks and roadways were continued to be laid out, and landscape work was also advancing."[21] One project centered on placing 400,000 cubic yards of fill on the low prairie that had been part of the old Hunt homestead, in order to bring it up to grade—an area today part of the Miami Shores Golf Course. Despite these achievements, the cash drain upon the Shoreland Company had taken a huge toll. Then, the 1926 hurricane struck. "Dredges sank, road machinery was ruined, there was no money for payrolls, and employees drifted away."[22]

Fast running out of cash, Hugh Anderson obtained several bailout loans, notably a large one from the J. S. Phipps estate in New York City, a family fortune linked to Carnegie Steel. Though the treasury of Anderson's firm was temporarily refreshed, the company later defaulted on its obligations and declared bankruptcy in 1927.[23] In the following year, to oversee and complete their recently acquired assets, the Phipps interest formed (through its Bessemer Properties division) an entity called New Miami Shores Corporation which, in 1931, became Miami Shores Village. Today, with its attractive commercial district, parks, and plethora of Mediterranean Revival-styled homes, the setting remains one of Florida's most inviting and attractive suburbs.

And what of Hugh Anderson—the one-time hotel clerk through whose hands later passed tens of millions of dollars? The wavy-haired guru had no choice but to declare personal bankruptcy in 1937, disclosing in court papers that his liabilities totaled $8.5 million while his assets amounted to a mere four hundred dollars.[24] In brief, Anderson had become yet another casualty of the not-to-be-forgotten Twenties land boom.

## Hollywood-by-the-Sea

Our selective survey of noteworthy boom-era communities heads further up the Gold Coast to Hollywood, better known in the Roaring Twenties as Hollywood-by-the-Sea. Its millionaire progenitor was Joseph Wesley Young, Jr., a Washington state native that had demonstrated his real estate mettle—before coming to Florida—in Indianapolis and Long Beach, California. From the get-go, "JW" wished to create in the Sunshine State a ready-made city for everyone, "from the opulent at the top of the industrial and social ladder to the most humble of working people."[25]

While promoting several subdivisions in the Allapattah section of Miami, Young began to formulate ideas for his Dream City. Translating his vision into working plans fell to Rubush and Hunter, an architectural firm based in Indianapolis where, years before, Young had earned the friendship of Miami Beach developer Carl Fisher. According to author Kenneth Ballinger, "Young's smartest move was to induce Frank C. Dickey, then a Miami councilman and former United States engineer in charge of Miami harbor, to join him. Streets, sewers, sidewalks, light and water plants and other public works costing between $15,000,000 and $20,000,000 would be built [at Hollywood] under Dickey's direct supervision."[26]

Having selected a suitable tract near water, Young wanted his Utopia to have "a wide boulevard extending from the ocean westward to the edge of the Everglades, with man-made lakes paralleling each side of the roadway. One end of each lake would empty into the Intracoastal Waterway; the other would serve as a twin turning basin for private yachts."[27] Surveyors began locating Hollywood Boulevard in May 1921, a one-hundred-foot wide thoroughfare which then was the widest in all of Florida. Young felt that the impressive east-west artery would capture the attention of motorists navigating the nearby north-south Dixie Highway, who would then turn in to investigate. The ploy heightened when Young completed the almost-impossible-to-miss Hollywood Hotel in early 1923 near the ocean end of the artery, near Circle Park. (The facility later became the Park View Hotel.) According to Joan Mickelson, Hollywood's preeminent historian, an open-air sales pavilion was erected along Hollywood Boulevard where motorists and prospects stopped and received a high-energy sales presentation along with "a sandwich, an apple, pie, and coffee."[28]

Like many other period developers, Young embraced many of the concepts and ideals that formed the City Beautiful movement. For example, he insisted on zoning regulations, parks, and a central business district, a friendly network of lighted streets, dedicated spaces for schools, churches, a golf course, and country club. As Hollywood city archivist Richard Roberts relates, "Unique in Young's city plan was the incorporation of three large circles of land located along his planned principal boulevard. These circles became the sites of a ten-acre park (originally named Harding Circle and later renamed Young Circle), the City Hall complex (originally named City Hall Circle and later renamed Watson Circle), and a military academy (Academy Circle). Academy Circle, now Presidential Circle, is the current site of a focal commercial structure."[29] Roberts also confirms that it was Young who named Hollywood after the Los Angeles suburb and christened several streets after United States presidents.

Young's first property purchase had been a one-square-mile tract of pineland obtained from Dania resident and farmer Stephen Alsobrook. The cost was $175 an acre. An existing building thereon was converted to company offices. Young also formed the Hollywood Land and Water Company, whose myriad departments and subsidiaries would oversee all future land acquisitions, construction details, sales, utilities, road building, etc. Surveyors wasted little time in staking out the city's Central Section followed by the Little Ranches Section, the Lakes Section, and finally the beach area.[30]

The first homes in Young's tailor-made city included a mix of bungalows, cottages, and Colonials, though eventually the architectural style of choice became Spanish Mission and what is now known as Mediterranean Revival. Many of the latter residences were sheathed in white, buff, or pink stucco, and had tile roofs. Independent contractors constructed these early homes, but Young's holding company began offering products of their own beginning in 1924. Interestingly, the first permanent structure at Hollywood-by-the-Sea was not a home at all but a garage, conceived in the Spanish Mission style no less, by architects Rubush and Hunter that housed the developer's trucks that serviced a limestone rock pit. Since many of

Young's construction workers were African Americans, the developer established an all-black residential section called Liberia—now Atlanta Street.

According to one account, "During the early days of development in Hollywood, 1,500 trucks and tractors were engaged in clearing land and grading streets. Two blocks of pavement were laid each day. A large power plant was installed, and when the city lights went on for the first time, ships at sea reported that Miami was on fire! Radio alarms and the red glow in the sky brought people to the rescue from miles around."[31]

Eager to promote his planned city, Young spent a small fortune on a national advertising program. Further, he purchased twenty-one touring busses that went about collecting sales prospects from such distant points as New York and Boston. Free travel and accommodation trips were offered with no obligation to buy. Upon arriving in Hollywood-by-the-Sea, "prospects were driven about the city-to-be on trails blazed through palmetto thickets; so desolate and forlorn were some stretches that many women became hysterical, it is said, and a few fainted. Society leaders and titled personages of Europe were given choice lot sites to induce others to purchase lots nearby. Men prominent in business, politics, and the arts were hired to stimulate sales, either by pep talks or personal contacts. Every salesman had his 'bird dogs' who met trains and busses, or talked to passing motorists at filling stations, restaurants, and hot dog stands, or they roamed at large rounding up prospects. Auctions were popular, both for the Grand Opening and whenever sales lagged. Patrons were often attracted by blaring bands, free banquets, vaudeville shows, and the drawing of lottery tickets."[32]

To accommodate travelers and prospects coming by train, Young convinced the Florida East Coast Railway to halt its trains at the burgeoning setting. In fact, Young even financed and erected a splendid station in the Spanish Mission style in 1924. (The impressive structure was demolished forty years later to straighten 21st Avenue.) Young's high-profile prospects were taken aboard his $200,000 yacht, the *Jessie Faye*. The appearance of celebrities and bluebloods, along with every other imaginable city development and event, were played up by the *Hollywood Reporter* newspaper, another Young endeavor that the developer had launched in 1922.

In a brilliant move in 1924, Young had nearby Lake Mabel surveyed as a possible deep-water harbor. A year later he purchased 1,440 acres around its bay and, before long, the Tropical Dredging and Construction Company (a Young subsidiary) had nine dredges on the scene along with 300 trucks and seven steam shovels. It was here that Young did create a deep-water seaport for, initially, vessels in the European, Cuban and South American trade. To add credence to the undertaking, Young engaged General George Washington Goethals, of Panama Canal construction fame, but the aged army officer never got geared up to Boom tempo and ultimately departed without having added much to the harbor. By a legislative act in 1927, the City of Fort Lauderdale jointly issued bonds with Hollywood—some $4.5 million worth—for the dredging and reclamation project which, in the end, created a thirty-five-foot deep harbor, a large turning basin, as well as a channel two hundred-feet wide. Warehouses, gasoline tanks, and storage sheds lined the waterfront; docks and piers, the largest 1,200 feet long, projected into the harbor. Amidst speeches and cheering crowds, imposing "Port Everglades" opened the following year—today the second busiest cruise ship port in the world.[33]

Previously, in 1925, Young's contractors oversaw construction of the Hollywood Boule-

**Among the important first buildings at Hollywood-by-the-Sea was a public school. Like several structures in the ready-made setting, it was built with Spanish Mission elements (courtesy Florida Memory, State Archives of Florida).**

vard Bridge across the Intracoastal Waterway, thereby allowing residents and tourists direct access to the Atlantic Ocean. By early the following year, Hollywood-by-the-Sea could boast "2,420 dwellings with approximately 18,000 people, thirty-six apartment buildings, 252 business buildings and nine hotels either completed or under construction. The city had grown in size to include 18,000 acres, six-and-a-half miles of oceanfront, with an assessed value of $20,000,000."[34] No wonder the neighboring hamlets of Hallandale and Dania wished to be annexed to prosperous Hollywood, a petition that the state legislature and Hollywood city fathers ultimately approved.

Not to be overlooked were the fabulous projects Young spearheaded along Hollywood's renowned beachfront. Of note was the two-mile long, thirty-foot-wide, pink cement "Broad Walk" which began at Johnson Street and opened in March 1923. (Today the 2.5 mile walkway and bike path is one of the finest beach boardwalks in America.) Then there was the famed Hollywood Beach Casino bathing pavilion, completed in 1924 at a cost of $250,000, which touted 824 dressing rooms, eighty shower baths, a shopping arcade, and an Olympic-sized swimming pool. But the jewel at the beachfront opened in February 1926—the $3-million, seven-story Hollywood Beach Hotel that contained five hundred rooms with private baths and the world's largest solarium. Young's publicity machine wasted little time in issuing double-page color ads in national magazines that depicted the imperial structure.[35]

Other noteworthy edifices that arose in Young's dream city included the popular Hol-

# *Follow the Sun — to Hollywood --*
## *Golden Days and Glorious Nights*
### *at Florida's Most Beautiful Hotel*

DOWN where winter is summer—on the coral shore 'twixt Palm Beach and Miami —rising like a palace out of fairyland, is Florida's most entrancing retreat from the snow and freezing winds of the north —Hollywood Beach Hotel.

Right on the ocean, looking forth on tropical beach and sea, it is the center of life as you dream it. Balmy breezes blow through your rooms. You don bathing suit and go straight to the broad beach with its gently rolling surf.

Spacious chambers with gorgeous decorations and furnishings — conveniences and refinements, matchless amidst the most luxurious appointments, single out this magnificent hotel for your comfort and delight. Delicious tablefare, freshened with vegetables, fruits, butter, milk, and eggs from the hotel's own farms, intrigues your appetite.

Every outdoor sport and recreation invites you—golf on two excellent courses, horseback riding, tennis, motor boating, aquaplaning, deep sea fishing, and bathing on the peerless beach. Every night dances, recitals, concerts make it a favorite rendezvous in Florida's brilliant social playground.

Florida Enchantment at its best is here. Turn your back on winter and catch up with the sun at Hollywood. Write, and complete information and rates will be sent promptly.

Hollywood Beach Hotel, Hollywood, Fla., *New York Office, Canadian Pacific Bldg., 342 Madison Ave.*
*On Dixie Highway — Two Railroads — and Inland Waterway*

# HOLLYWOOD *Florida*

### Florida's all-year seaside city . . A place to live

JOSEPH W. YOUNG
*Founder*

The fabulous Hollywood Beach Hotel was one of the last major projects overseen by that community's developer, Joseph Young. The hostelry dripped with luxury; its guest list came from all corners of the globe. Colorful ads for it ran in nationwide newspapers and magazines.

lywood Beach Golf and Country Club (Seventeenth Avenue and Polk Street); the twenty-four classroom Hollywood Central School and the Hollywood Hills Inn (at the western end of Hollywood Boulevard, at the city's remotest circle) together with many handsome business buildings, beautiful churches, and sumptuous homes.

Sadly, disaster struck on 18 September 1926. A deadly hurricane pummeled Hollywood-by-the-Sea with frightening winds and rising floodwaters. Thirty-seven persons perished, countless trees were uprooted, roofs on buildings were blown off, and many homes were completely destroyed. Young led the rebuilding effort as head of the Hollywood Relief Committee. But not even the Hollywood Municipal Band, which played rousing marches and other inspirational music as the rebuilding took place, could totally eradicate the pain. The huge task of rebuilding coupled with the financial losses inflicted caused thousands of Hollywood residents to abandon their new homes and return to northern cities. Consequently, the population of Hollywood declined precipitously from 18,000 to approximately 2,500 persons. Property values also dramatically fell. As a result of the turmoil, residents of Hallandale and Dania seceded from Hollywood, refusing to pay taxes to what was now a bankrupt municipality.[36]

Despite the setbacks, new residences were eventually built in the westernmost reaches of Hollywood, an area that became known as Hollywood Hills, where the Highway Construction Company of Ohio was toiling away on new homes. But by February 1927, after the hurricane and the collapse of Hollywood's real estate market, Young had been failing to meet his financial commitments to the Ohio firm, as well as to other lenders. Despite his never-ending efforts to promote the new Port Everglades, Young's financial condition had been steadily deteriorating, to the extent that he lost control of his myriad holdings. Nevertheless, the ever-popular developer continued to live in his Dream City until April 1934, when he collapsed in his Hollywood Boulevard home and died of heart failure at age 51.[37] Another brilliant and successful developer of the famed Twenties land boom had gone to his reward.

## Boca Raton

One of the great stories of the 1920s land boom involved the transformation of a quiet farming settlement called Boca Ratone. In time the rustic setting became one of the real garden spots of Florida, one whose beauty and attractions continue to mesmerize visitor, tourist and home seeker alike.

Spearheading the metamorphosis was Addison Cairns Mizner (1872–1934), the best-known architect in Florida during the Twenties and one of the greatest in America at that time. Mizner's contributions to society architecture became legendary, to the extent that many of his innovative ideas and techniques are embraced this day by architects, builders and clients. Though Mizner's vision for "Boca" was breathtaking, his tailor-made city fell short of completion for it was launched just prior to the land boom's collapse and almost from the get-go became mired with internal dissension and financial irregularities. Nevertheless, Mizner is still greatly revered in Boca as well as in posh Palm Beach where our story begins.

Palm Beach is situated on a long narrow strip of land that is separated from the Florida mainland by a long narrow body of water called Lake Worth and, as one wit noted, "by a sudden increase in living expenses. On the mainland side of Lake Worth is the rising young city of West Palm Beach, which has the same sort of climate that Palm Beach has, but the air of the latter place is somehow different. At Palm Beach one has the feeling that he is breathing the very same air that the world's greatest bankers and society people are breathing, whereas over in West Palm Beach one doesn't know or care who has been breathing the air."[38]

When Mizner first arrived in Palm Beach, his six-foot, 250-pound frame was in a debilitated state. He had come to the tropical enclave as a house guest of Paris Eugene Singer, whom he had befriended in New York City. Cleveland Amory, America's social historian extraordinaire, notes that Singer was one of twenty-five children belonging to sewing machine tycoon Isaac Merritt Singer. Eight of Isaac's children were legitimate; Paris, the 23rd child—born in and named for the French capital—was not. Nevertheless, Paris would inherit a large share of his father's fortune. He owned several international homes including a non-descript bungalow in Palm Beach—the era of Spanish and Mediterranean styled mansions not yet in vogue. Exhausted and ill like Mizner, Singer journeyed from New York to Palm Beach with his compatriot, whereupon Singer was "carried off the train on a stretcher."[39] The date was 3 January 1918.

Mizner, a Californian by birth and one of eight children, ultimately acquired an undying passion for Spanish architecture, especially of the sixteenth and seventeenth centuries. When Mizner was thirteen, his father (who had run unsuccessfully for the California governorship) became a special ambassador to the five republics of Central America, an opportunity that furnished the future Florida developer with an incredible exposure to society, the moneyed class, foreign culture, and prominent dignitaries. He subsequently became fluent in Spanish, sharpened his painting skills using watercolors, and relished being a student of landscaping and history. Eventually, he attended the ancient University of Salamanca in Spain, yet failed to obtain there an architectural degree—a deficiency that his detractors in later years were quick to point out. Upon returning to San Francisco, he served an apprenticeship with a local architect and became his business partner. Eventually convinced that his years of training were over, Mizner began advertising himself in 1895 as a full-fledged architect in that city.[40]

Unfortunately, the budding architect never achieved a thriving practice and, seeing his personal finances deteriorate, he exited California and cast his luck in the Klondike gold rush. He would stake out a successful claim near Dawson—a town he helped lay out—though much of the fortune he made was cleverly confiscated by government authorities. He then left for Hawaii to paint. Samoa beckoned next, then Australia where he became, of all things, a prize fighter. The wanderlust hardly subsided, and before long Mizner began exploring the Philippines, Siam, and India, after which he returned to San Francisco. By now a world traveler, moreover a "resort sport" and bon vivant, Mizner began investing in a successful coffee venture in Guatemala, a country from which he also successfully exported antiques and objects d'art.

Mizner moved to New York City in 1908 where, on Park Avenue, he opened a small architectural office. His affable personality and cultured ways delighted those he encountered, including members of the "Newport crowd." He also befriended the illustrious society architect Stanford White, which led to Mizner's firm receiving several small commissions. "I worshipped him," Mizner later confessed, "for he was my God."[41] But the First World War affected Mizner's practice and those of countless other architects. His personal health also began to falter. (He had been mugged in New York City, had battled ulcers, and continuously dealt with a chronic leg injury of prior years.) At the behest of Paris Singer, the sickly pair eventually departed New York and headed to Palm Beach in the company of a nurse.

Mizner's friendship with Singer grew, even proving fortuitous. Singer would later admit that he got "caught up in Mizner's verbal and artistic daydreams and visions."[42] At that moment, Palm Beach was still dotted with inferior, non-tropical homes together with a monstrous wooden hotel (the Royal Poinciana, built by Henry Flagler); a beach club, and a casino. So much more could be achieved at the setting, thought Mizner. Singer eventually suggested a collaboration so as to "restore Mizner's health and his own spirits."[43] Thus, what eventually became known as the Everglades Club was born.

Paris Singer ultimately erected off Worth Avenue a convalescent hospital for wounded American officers returning from the First World War. Previously he had paid for hospitals in France and England, but Singer loved America and felt that one was needed in a warm clime. The sewing machine heir proposed that he bankroll and operate the facility in Palm Beach, which he dubbed the Touchstone Convalescents Club. Mizner, in turn, would conceive the Spanish-inspired building and attendant villas and oversee the myriad construction details. For services rendered, Mizner would receive a $6,000-a-year retainer for life. Construction commenced, but the Armistice—signed in November 1918—meant that few if any soldiers would come to Palm Beach. Singer then recast the project into an exclusive social enclave—the Everglades Club.

Because the First World War had placed strict embargoes on domestic building supplies and created shortages of European labor and craftsmen, Mizner formed his own materials firm, Las Manos ("The Hands"), whereupon he recruited and trained local workers in old-world building techniques. By taking over a blacksmith shop, his firm (financed by Singer) began producing ornamental iron grills and lighting fixtures, and he built kilns in order to produce period roof, floor, and wall tiles. (After Mizner hit his stride as a society architect, he outright purchased the facilities from Singer and expanded them.) What became Mizner Industries became one of the largest manufacturing facilities in Palm Beach County, additionally producing cast stone columns together with window and door surrounds, hollow building blocks, Spanish-styled furniture, antiqued pecky cypress for room ceilings; lamps, candlesticks, railings, balconies, door latches, hinges, along with fountains, urns and handmade pottery.

The completed Everglades Club touted a splendid dining hall, private rooms, apartments (including an opulent one for Singer himself), servants' quarters, kitchens, and eventually tennis courts and a golf course. The outside of the main building featured a tower, cloistered patios, and a courtyard. For some, Mizner's creation had somewhat the appearance of a Spanish mission church with a bell tower. Returning wounded officers were, of course, invited to stay as guests, but the real clientele of the establishment became the moneyed class of America that wintered in Palm Beach. The doors opened 25 January 1919 with twenty-five charter members, all of whom Singer personally approved.[44]

That Mizner's architectural creation aroused serious interest in Spanish architecture cannot be disputed. In fact his collaboration with Singer opened the way for a flood of Palm

Beach commissions—from fabulous mansions to inviting villas and commercial buildings. Equally impressive was the Mizner client list. First to commission him were Eva and Edward Stotesbury of Philadelphia, for whom, in 1919, he conceived their marble hall and columned Spanish palace on 42 acres that extended from Lake Worth to the Atlantic Ocean. *El Mirasol* ("The Sunflower") boasted no fewer than thirty-seven rooms, six patios, a tea house, an auditorium, a swimming pool lit from the underside, a private zoo, and a forty-car garage. In 1923 Mizner completed perhaps his finest Palm Beach mansion—*Playa Riente*—for Oklahoma oilman Joshua Cosden, which *Vogue* magazine hailed as the finest private residence in America in the early 1920s.[45]

As acclaimed author Ida Tarbell states about Mizner, "Calls for houses flowed upon him," so much so that architect is thought to have had one hundred commissions in hand by 1925.[46] (Other period Palm Beach architects meeting success included Marion Syms Wyeth, Maurice Fatio and Julius Jacobs.) Another Mizner client was Harold Vanderbilt (who bought Mizner's 1925 home *El Solano* that was eventually owned by musician John Lennon), along with Dr. Willey Lyon Kingsley (his *La Bellucia* sold in 2009 for a Palm Beach record of $24 million); John S. Phipps (of the Pittsburgh steel family), Anthony Drexel Biddle, Jr., Edward Shearson (*Villa Flora*); Rodman Wanamaker (heir to the Wanamaker department store fortune whose estate *La Guerida* became President John F. Kennedy's "Winter White House"), along with dozens of other social leaders or would-be social leaders.[47]

Of far lesser scope were two Mizner projects conceived for the Worth Avenue shopping district: Via Mizner and the Via Parigi, two roofless winding courts that were bordered by shops displaying exotic wares, patio restaurants, and open air cafes. Outside stairs led to second floor apartments and studios, their casements opening upon iron-grilled balconies. Tropical trees, shrubs and vines contributed to the "Old World" atmosphere.

Interestingly, Mizner had begun practicing architecture in Florida without a license. In fact he had been practicing without one in New York, though to prove his qualifications there his lawyer eventually obtained for him a "License of Exemption." With a growing reputation in Palm Beach, Mizner found himself unable to avoid the Florida State Board of Architecture. The transplant finally appeared before that august body and "came prepared with such a wealth of research and background material—stacks of his own sketches and paintings together with blueprints by his associates—and rendered such a verbal demonstration of his qualifications, that he was given a license on the basis that he had passed a Senior Examination."[48]

With his reputation and moreover his personal wealth soaring, Mizner now turned his creative attentions to a long-held dream: that of creating a tailor-made city embracing everything Spanish-Mediterranean that he so ardently believed in and fantasized about. Before long the instrument for that vision became a little farming community some twenty-five miles south of Palm Beach called Boca Ratone—the "e" eventually being dropped by the Mizner publicity machine. Beginning in April 1925, news of Mizner's grandiose project began to appear in the national media as the "Dream City of the Western World," about seven months before the Florida land boom would crest.[49]

In brief, Mizner envisioned Boca as a cosmopolitan world community. Prior to the public announcement, his partners and investors of the newly-formed Mizner Development Corporation had acquired two miles of beachfront at the Boca Raton inlet, together with roughly sixteen thousand acres of undeveloped "high land"' directly in back of the ocean frontage. Among those identified with the entity were Paris Singer, the Duchess of Sutherland, Jesse L. Livermore (the "Great Bear of Wall Street"), composer Irving Berlin, utilities magnate Clarence Geist, business woman Elizabeth Arden, Rodman Wanamaker, Harold S. Vanderbilt and William K. Vanderbilt II. Mizner personally persuaded the former U.S. Senator from Delaware, T. Coleman du Pont, to become board chairman. Officials of the newly-incorporated Boca Raton wasted little time in appointing Mizner as town planner.

The centerpiece of Mizner's dream city would be a colossal beachside hotel having one thousand rooms and hundreds of private apartments. According to sales literature, *Castillo del Rey* ("King's Castle") would be the world's "most complete and artistic hostelry." Other elements of Boca Raton would include parks, two eighteen-hole golf courses, a polo field, a casino (even though gambling was illegal in Florida); a radio station, water tower, two railway stations, an industrial quarter, a neighborhood of Spanish-styled homes, together with miles of newly-paved streets that would sport lush tropical landscaping. Through the heart of the setting would be located the 2.5 mile long Camino Real, a one-hundred-sixty-foot-wide grand boulevard modeled after Rio de Janeiro's Botafogo Canal, that could accommodate some twenty lines of moving traffic—ten on each side of the waterway.

"It is my plan," Mizner told his salespeople, "to create a city that is direct and simple ... to leave out all that is ugly, to eliminate the unnecessary, and to give Florida and the nation a 'resort city' as perfect as study and ideals can make it." It was rumored that the Mizner Development Corporation would spend some $100 million during its initial years. Sales offices were subsequently opened in Miami, New York City, Philadelphia, Pittsburgh, and Chicago.[50]

Raising capital for the grandiose endeavor proved to be no easy task. Mizner's initial strategy to finance construction costs was to publicly sell stock in the Mizner Development Corporation, borrow funds from banks and investors, and utilize proceeds from the sale of building lots. The precise amounts garnered from each source have never been learned, as financial records of the corporation have largely vanished. However, we do know that the Mizner syndicate generated $2 million on the first day of selling lots in May, 1925, while another $2 million was raised before that month ended. In fact, within six months of the project's launch some $30 million had been collected (today's money: $394.4 million).[51]

Exactly how this large amount was ultimately spent also remains something of a mystery. Certainly some of the funds went towards the costs of infrastructure and the construction of certain projects, notably an administration building (modeled after El Greco's home in Toledo, Spain) and the building of a small elegant hotel (the Cloister Inn) to accommodate visitors, tourists, and sales prospects. We know that Mizner sold company stock to several area banks and bankers, which paved the way for him and his Corporation to obtain large, quick loans. (Many were later revealed as being unsecured; others were secured with bogus collateral). The close affiliation with area banks also allowed certain bankers to play their own insider games and become enriched, events that Florida author Raymond Vickers expertly chronicles in a scholarly book.[52]

Essential to Boca's success would be an aggressive marketing campaign, and for this assignment Mizner turned to a Hollywood, California, figure named Harry Reichenbach,

# The Dream City of the Western World

## The Culminating Achievement of an INSPIRED ARCHITECT

ART AND NATURE unite to create the world's most beautiful and distinctive resort of wealth and fashion in the newly conceived and now actually building BOCA RATON. BOCA RATON is just twenty-six miles south of Palm Beach, where the tempering waters of the Gulf Stream almost literally wash the strand—where Florida's blue skies are most smiling—where her balmy airs are most caressing.

The Riviera, Biarritz, Mentone, Nice, Sorrento, the Lido, Egypt all that charms in each of these finds consummation in BOCA RATON.

Art assures her ascendency in BOCA RATON through the creative genius of Addison Mizner. The same artistic hand that designed and built the resplendent clubs, the glittering casinos and the imposing estates of Palm Beach now gives the world its most beautiful resort of international finance, society, the professions and the arts. BOCA RATON is Addison Mizner's culminating achievement.

Every structure of public or semi-public character in BOCA RATON shall issue from under Addison Mizner's own hand. Every building of whatever character shall be approved by him in plan and design. Thus BOCA RATON shall ultimate in a municipal entity as to plan—a completed picture as to effect—a perfected architectural unity of enduring stability and surpassing beauty.

Social supremacy and financial solidarity are assured to BOCA RATON by the wealth and standing, the character and achievement of its proprietary sponsors.

These men and women of world-standing in society, finance and affairs know that the best of democracy is the flower of genuine aristocracy. They therefore invite men and women of substance and standing to participate in their unique undertaking.

## Mizner Development Corporation
### Developers of BOCA RATON Florida

Some of the best community advertisements of the Twenties in Florida were issued by the Mizner Development Corporation—the progenitor of Boca Raton. This compelling example was seen by Americans in coast-to-coast newspaper ads.

the so-called "Father of Ballyhoo." A highly regarded press agent and stunt arranger for films, movie stars, and notables, Reichenbach was known to Wilson Mizner, Addison's brother. The ambitious advertising and publicity program that Reichenbach rolled out became a classic in hyperbole, though it eventually proved controversial. (Examples of his work are reproduced in *Boomtime Boca* by Susan Gillis. See Bibliography.)

Wilson Mizner, it should be noted, had relocated from New York to Palm Beach once

# PLATTED AREA IN PERSPECTIVE OF THE
# MIZNER DEVELOPMENT

**Sales brochures for Boca Raton often included this perspective of the ready-made setting. Unfortunately, the city was launched late in the land boom, the initial project collapsed and what ultimately evolved differed from this proposed plat.**

his brother's star began to rise, the brothers having botched a strip development in nearby Boynton Beach in 1924, called the Mizner Mile. Regarded as a playwright, wit, con artist, cardsharp, drug addict, gigolo, scoundrel, and something of a crook, Wilson readily admitted that he possessed no prior financial experience or business acumen. Yet, his brother named Wilson treasurer of the Mizner Development Corporation and, overnight, the sibling began controlling millions of dollars. (Wilson once publicly remarked that Addison's building schemes at Boca were nothing more than a platinum sucker's trap!) Wilson's behavior, along with his improper business methods, disturbed certain board members, so much so that the aforementioned Coleman du Pont resigned as chairman on 24 November 1925. In the following week, three more prominent directors resigned, including the New York speculator Jesse Livermore. In addition to having issues with both Mizner brothers, the resigned directors resented their names being used in advertisement endorsements for Boca, for such could easily give rise to personal liability.[53]

News of the resignations quickly went over the wire services. Coleman, himself, wrote a letter to the *New York Times* explaining his position. The resignations immediately cast a dark shadow over Boca and the Mizner Development Corporation. Addison Mizner responded by saying that the resigned directors had merely disagreed with certain management and business policies of the corporation, whereupon he rounded up a new board and reorganized the corporation. But the death knell had been sounded. Just as the resigned directors had predicted, the Boca dream began facing serious financial difficulties, the land boom started to fizzle, and sales prospects started to vanish.[54]

Despite the setbacks, several signs of progress were still being made at the resort city. For example, the 200-room Cloister Inn—built in just twenty-two weeks—opened on 6 February 1926, its public rooms having to be filled with personal furniture and antiquities owned by Addison Mizner himself. At the gala inaugural ball, guests danced to Grant Clarke's tune "In Boca Raton." Today the eastern wing of the edifice helps form the splendid Boca Raton Resort and Club.

Also of note was the opening of the Dunagan Apartments on De Soto Road, while thirty Spanish-inspired new homes were completed in the nearby neighborhood of Old Floresta. Additional streets were paved, while jetties were built and inlets dredged. But the colossal, $6 million Castillo del Rey hotel at ocean side—hyped at the launch of Mizner's dream city—never opened for it was never built. Neither was Mizner's million-dollar island castle in Lake Boca Raton or the grandiose station for the Seaboard Air Line Railway. And only a half-mile of the twenty-lane Camino Real highway had been completed, its palm-lined canal then nothing more than a muddy ditch. Watching the reversals from Palm Beach was Mizner's companion, Paris Singer, who himself was trying to develop a new resort community on Singer Island where he, too, found the going rough.[55]

The curtain now went up on the final act. In May, 1926, Addison Mizner left for his annual antique buying spree in Europe, principally in Spain. But while abroad he was notified by cable to cease all purchasing, that the last of the Mizner Development Corporation funds were gone. Back in Florida, the Corporation's creditors, vendors, and defrauded lot buyers began filing lawsuits. By July the stockholders voted to turn their corporation over to Central Equities of Chicago, a firm headed by the famed Dawes brothers. For a 51 percent controlling interest, Central promised to inject capital, collect all remaining monies from the sales of lots and receive a percentage of net profits. So much for promises! Central, it turned out, was secretly run by two former vice presidents of Mizner Development Corporation who, according to the scholarship of Caroline Seebohm, "applied lot sales to their own accounts, put a meager $100,000 into the corporation, and from then on abandoned their responsibilities."[56] Mizner's dream city floundered anew, more lawsuits mounted, and finances—what little was left—plunged. Although a weakened Mizner managed to deal with the roller-coaster ride, the master managed to find some refuge in his architectural practice. But where was the Boca project headed?

Into the financial morass walked a white knight: Clarence Henry Geist, a public utilities magnate from Indiana who once had been a Mizner supporter and a board member of the Mizner Development Corporation. In March 1927, several creditors filed an involuntary bankruptcy proceeding against the Mizner Development Corporation. The case wound its way through court proceedings and eventually the assets of the Corporation (some fifty homes, the Cloister Inn, and some 15,000 acres of land) were put on the auction block. In October, Geist placed a $5,000 bid and agreed to assume all outstanding liabilities of the Corporation, which ran into the millions. Geist was the only bidder. But the bankruptcy judge thought the cash figure too low and eventually got Geist to raise his bid to $71,500. Mizner, standing on the sidelines, said it was "like the death of a diseased child, as it had to come ultimately."[57]

Geist spent a small fortune on transforming the Cloister Inn into the private, 450-room Boca Raton Club, which opened in 1930. He also financed a modern water treatment plant, paid for an elegant railroad depot where trains of the Florida East Coast Railway could halt, and dredged the Boca Raton Inlet so club members could dock their palatial steam yachts.

By now the Twenties land boom in Florida had petered out. Nevertheless, the firm of Addison Mizner, Inc., was still undertaking architectural commissions. In fact the master even managed to visit his native California. Addison's brother, Wilson, also went there and, among other endeavors, became a partner in the famed Brown Derby in Los Angeles. Finances, though, haunted the legendary architect, especially after Mizner Industries went bankrupt. Fortunately, the benefactions of friends made difficult times somewhat more tolerable. Addison Mizner died of a heart attack at his Palm Beach villa on 5 February 1933. In court papers filed in West Palm Beach the following year, the visionary of Boca—through whose hands had passed tens of millions of dollars—had left an estate valued at a mere $2,500.[58]

No account of Boca can close without mentioning some of the other developers who found the environs ripe for projects. In June 1925, just as Mizner's utopian dream was picking up speed, George Harvey, a real estate developer from Boston, announced his Villa Rica development—a 1,400-acre modern city within the Boca Raton city limits. Spanish-styled homes were featured along with a fancy railway station and a hostelry called the Villa Rica Inn. That fall, other county developments were hatched including Del-Raton (north of Villa Rica); Del Boca (to the west and south of the city); and Boca del Faro (south of the city on the Broward County line). Del-Raton Park also joined the list, a $3 million "American Venice." (It was actually located within Delray Beach but rode the Boca wave of publicity.) Another regarded developer was G. Frank Croissant of Chicago, who unveiled Croissantania, a 2,360-acre tract north of the Mizner plat and west of the Dixie Highway. Still other developments included Boca Raton Heights, Boca Vista, and Boca Centrale. As previously noted, this inviting quarter of Florida continues to be a most desirable community for visitor, tourist and homeseeker.[59]

# Sebring

One of many Florida locations that was dramatically transformed by the Twenties land boom was Sebring, the seat of Highlands County. Situated in the "Scenic Highlands" or "Ridge country" of the state, Sebring is known for its low rolling hills, extensive citrus groves, and shimmering blue lakes. "On summer afternoons, towering cloud formations pile up in the eastern heavens to frame the landscape, frequently blurred by distant rain storms."[60]

George Eugene Sebring (1859–1927), a wealthy china and pottery manufacturer from Sebring, Ohio, enjoyed hunting in Florida and eventually owned a home in Daytona Beach. But after visiting what would one day become Sebring, he became enamored of the setting's development possibilities and subsequently acquired some 9,000 acres so as to create a lakefront town on the eastern shore of Lake Jackson. The tailor-made town site that evolved would be patterned after the mythological Grecian city of Heliopolis—the "City of the Sun"—with streets radiating from a central park which itself represented the sun.[61] A civil engineer from Winter Haven produced a plat of the town site in April 1912. Together with his son, George and Orvel Sebring formed Sebring Real Estate and the Sebring Development Company to market their new property.

Work on the model town and winter oasis commenced later that year, a few months before the Atlantic Coast Line Railroad built through the new setting en route to Moore Haven from Haines City. Although the freezes of 1917 killed many area citrus groves, they were soon replanted, and life continued in Sebring at a leisurely pace until the famed real estate boom of the 1920s. In fact, so great did the influx of human traffic become during that extravaganza, that the infant community actually hired an official greeter, "who spent his days in the streets and parks shaking hands with visitors. He never greeted the same person twice."[62]

An impressive, pastel-colored brochure about Sebring was released by the Sebring Board of Trade in 1920, just as the land boom was getting legs. The sixty-page promotional piece teemed with photographs, testimonials, poetry, maps, and local facts. It also elaborated on Sebring's inviting and health-giving climate, the town's excellent drinking water, the fertility of her soil, the variety of affordable homes, and the scenic roadway that spun around the perimeter of Lake Jackson. Sports activities were also emphasized in the publication and honeyed words flowed about Sebring's hotels, businesses, parks, churches, railway communication, city sanitation, and farming lands.

Of special note in this elaborate brochure was the ease and affordability of growing citrus in Sebring. "Seven hundred and ninety dollars will buy a Home Orange Grove, size 50' by 150', right in town, with city water, and within from 750 to 3,000-feet of Lake Jackson and from 1,000 to 1,800 feet of the business district. Each grove contains eighteen trees, one each of an alligator pear, lime, tangerine, the balance each one-half orange and grapefruit. The trees are two-year buds. They will begin to bear within four to five years. When the tree is six years old you can expect a heavy crop. Sebring oranges sold in New York City in April, 1920, for $10.40 a box. The grove of one of our neighbors averaged twenty boxes to the tree."[63]

Sebring underwent a formidable transformation during the land boom. In addition to

**Sebring was built around the inviting waters of Lake Jackson. George Sebring and his colleagues issued a sumptuous brochure during the infant hours of the Twenties land boom, even before such became a staple item for all other Florida communities.**

receiving a multitude of new residents, the city itself undertook many physical improvements, the outlays for such later becoming, according to one author, "a bitter lesson in municipal economics."[64] So great was the list of improvements that when the land boom bubble burst in 1927–1928, there was no necessity to execute further public projects for several decades.

Though the Sebring Board of Trade had issued its fancy brochure to attract newcomers, tourists, and farmers, it was not until 1924 that the local papers really began calling attention to the vast land transactions that were going on, the fabulous profits being made, or the construction of million dollar hotels in the area. For the next three years, according to local historian and author Allen Altvater, "an epidemic of a peculiar mania infected everyone, even the most conservative and sober-thinking persons. Bankers, who were the more cautious investors, were caught up in the disease. One Sebring bank was so carried away that its principals started planning a new six-story office building and had gone so far as to have stationery and checks printed with the architect's rendering of the proposed structure."[65]

As the year 1924 closed, the population of Sebring had tripled because of northerners invading the town, most of whom had brought large sums of money to be gambled on the future of Sebring and the state. As Altvater further relates, "as soon as they qualified to vote, they literally 'took over' the government of the city. Every meeting of the city council was besieged by developers begging to have their subdivisions taken into the city so they might have the benefits of public utilities and the use of the city's credit for street paving and other activities. All this required the floating of bonds to finance the improvements. All the bond elections were carried off by lop-sided majorities with little thought being given as to how the principal and interest payments would be met."[66]

Interestingly, real estate mania would permeate Sebring for three solid years. "At its zenith, some two hundred real estate brokers and promoters were busily plying their trade in the area. Twice that number were real estate sales people while still more were so-called 'binder boys' and 'bird dogs.' The population of Sebring had soared from about 850 persons to more than 4,000. Whereas early residents and settlers looked upon Sebring as their permanent home, most of the northern crowd just wanted to invest, turn a profit, and move on. Many of the newcomers also insisted on more entertainment and recreation, often at

Among the many commercial buildings erected on Sebring's downtown circle was the attractive Hainz Building. The 1927 structure housed several businesses and offices. It has since been renovated and continues to serve a useful purpose (courtesy Florida Memory, State Archives of Florida).

city expense. Further, many families decided to purchase a motor car during the land boom, even luxury vehicles, which prompted additional road and street building. The purchase of speed boats became popular, too. The consumption of alcoholic beverages increased, with a number of night clubs surfacing on the town's outskirts. Aggressive new business folk formed a Chamber of Commerce to outdo the stodgy Board of Trade; they issued their own fifteen-page promotional brochure in 1925 calling Sebring 'The Orange Blossom City.' This influx of new peoples also meant more children. School space doubled during the boom, and to accommodate additional teachers the city even erected a dormitory."[67]

Thanks to the research efforts of Allen Altvater, we also learn that the storm of real estate transactions placed severe demands on the facilities of the county administration, so much so that Sebring commissioners made preparations to build a permanent court house at a cost of approximately a quarter of a million dollars. "With foresight, the City of Sebring exercised its option during the boom to purchase the utilities plant from private owners for $84,000."[68] In four years its capacity was increased from 150 KVA to 2,000 KVA in order to meet the demand for electricity. (The steam powered generators were replaced by ones that were diesel powered). New wells had to be dug for the town's water supply and a new elevated storage tank was constructed, 125 feet high. New water lines were installed about the town. More fire trucks were purchased, additional firemen were hired and a new fire house opened in 1927. A single man police force gave way to five uniformed officers with cars. Similar expansions were also needed in the Streets and Parks Departments. On top of this, commissioners also approved plans for a new incinerator during the boom years, together with a new pier into Lake Jackson, a municipal golf course, a sanitary sewer system and the hiring of a city engineer. To pay for these myriad improvements, Sebring ended up selling $3,608,000 in bonds.[69]

During the course of the land boom a significant number of new homes, subdivisions, commercial buildings, churches, hotels, etc. were constructed in Sebring. Whereas it is not possible here to enumerate every achievement, the reader has only to consult Stephen Olausen's marvelous work, *Sebring, City on the Circle.*[70] In it, the author catalogs every significant edifice in Sebring, especially those adorning its historic circle park in the downtown district. (Much of Olausen's research was used to obtain designations with the National Register of Historic Places.)

Among the many jewels detailed in Olausen's work are the Sebring Real Estate building on North Ridgewood Drive; the Dingus Building, Buckeye Building, and the Circle Theatre on North Circle Drive; the George Sebring Building and the Nan-Ces-O-Wee Hotel on North Ridgewood Drive; the Lakeview Place Subdivision (conceived with Spanish-inspired homes); the stunning Marjorie Rambeau residence on Jasmine Way; the Lake Jackson Recreational Pier (dubbed "The Little Coney Island"); the Ivey and Sunrise Garden apartment buildings on Lakeview Drive NE; the Sebring Hotel (corner of Oak and South Ridgewood avenues); the massive Harder Hall Hotel on Golfview Drive (completed 1928) on the western shore of Lake Jackson; the Central Fire Station on North Mango Street; the Highlands County Courthouse on South Commerce Avenue; the First Presbyterian Church (Late Gothic architecture), which opened its doors in 1926; and the Lake Sebring Casino on Lake Sebring Drive, completed 1926.[71]

One of the more fortuitous events occurring in Sebring during the land boom was the arrival of the Seaboard Air Line Railway. Whereas the city had been served for many years by a local branch of the Atlantic Coast Line Railroad, in early 1925 the town became an important stopping point on a major eastern trunk carrier.

For many years the Seaboard system lacked a connection with the burgeoning east coast of Florida. To remedy the problem, President S. Davies Warfield authorized the construction of a new 205-mile line from its mainline at Coleman (below Wildwood) to West Palm Beach via Auburndale, Winter Haven, Avon Park, Sebring, Okeechobee and Indiantown. A bond issue was floated, and construction of the new route—hailed as the largest new railway construction project in America for years—commenced in 1924. The work proceeded at breakneck speed, and in Sebring alone some twenty-five homes had to be moved or razed to accommodate the railway's right-of-way. The line was completed on January 21, 1925, and four days later Warfield inaugurated a new passenger train over the route from New York: the Orange Blossom Special. Packed with dignitaries, investors, bankers, and shippers, the inaugural run of the "OBS" stopped in Sebring where a momentous reception was staged, whereupon the various passenger train sections departed for West Palm Beach. (Two years later the line was opened to Miami.) A splendid Spanish-styled depot was built in Sebring by the Seaboard, designed by the architectural firm of Harvey and Clarke in West Palm Beach, which still stands and today serves Amtrak passengers.[72]

As the land boom began to fade into history, Sebring bravely faced the consequences of over-expansion and the loss of many residents. Despite fewer tax revenues, the city prudently managed its affairs though painful decisions had to be made. Budgets were dramatically cut, city personnel were discharged and municipal bond interest was occasionally skipped. Fortunately, the city's utility operations furnished much-needed cash. After the boom, many local businesses went belly up. Banks closed too, often leaving depositors penniless.[73] George Sebring, whose generosity affected so many lives, went to his reward in 1927, just as the land boom came to an end. Fortunately, he did not have to witness the severe economies and hardships that townsfolk had to endure during the subsequent years of the Great Depression.

# 5

# Railways and Highways

Florida!—with its tropical sunshine, its endless mileage of bathing beaches on
the Ocean and on the Gulf—the gentle breezes crossing innumerable Central
Florida lakes laden with the aroma of the orange blossom—yachting and motor
boating in waters mirroring the colors of the tropics—polo—golf—tennis—
racing at Hialeah, Pompano, and other courses—all amid scenes of unsurpassed
and beautiful surroundings, is without equal in this or any country.
—President S. Davies Warfield, Seaboard Air Line Railway, 1927

## Railways

Odd as it may seem, the Twenties land boom in Florida launched a railway revival
within the state as a result of the various companies trying to accommodate the unprecedented levels of passenger and freight traffic, opening up new territory, or invading the
domain of a competitor. As a result of these combined endeavors, the all-time record for
railway mileage in Florida was established that decade as well as for the frequency and level
of train service to, from, and within the Sunshine State.

As Florida author Kathryn Abbey once stated, "transportation and settlement always
go hand in hand; the former makes possible the latter, while the latter creates demand for
the former."[1] This certainly applied to the land boom story. After all there was no sense in
real estate magicians and promoters marketing Florida to the nation-at-large if a deficient
transportation network did not exist here. Although automobiles and road building played
a significant role during the Roaring Twenties, statistics confirm that railroads transported
the lion's share of freight that decade and a substantial percentage of all travelers.

During the First World War America's railroads were controlled by a government agency,
the United States Railroad Administration. The "USRA" advertised railroad transportation
and even issued a special guidebook about the routes and attractions located in the southern
states—today a prized collector piece. After the war ended the various carriers were returned
to their actual owners in March 1920, often in a worn condition owing to the crush of
wartime traffic.

Almost immediately Florida's railroads resumed their marketing of the Sunshine
State to the tourist, homeseeker, fruit grower, manufacturer, and industrialist. The various firms also resumed building up traffic in their respective territories, expanding their
in-state routes, attracting new freight customers, buying new equipment, and modernizing

facilities, initiatives that—in many instances—had been sidetracked by the war years.

Prior to the First World War railway traffic to and from the Sunshine State had moved on a seasonal schedule, passing through the northern gateways of which Jacksonville was the largest and most important. "Citrus fruit and vegetables usually began to move to northern markets in October, continuing until about the first of May. Heavy southbound passenger business to Florida began in the fall and reached its height by the latter part of February, only to shift at that time to the heavy movement of passengers heading to northward until the latter part of April."[2] Thus, the really busy season for Florida's railways ran from October to May, the remainder of the year being marked by lighter business along with train service being reduced to a minimum.

These patterns only changed slightly during the war years, though some schedules were consolidated in order for the compa-

UNITED STATES RAILROAD ADMINISTRATION

America's railroads were under Federal control during the First World War, but the United States Railroad Administration continued to advertise the wonders of Florida to the nation.

nies to handle wartime traffic. Of consequence to the land boom was that a new category of traffic appeared during the war years themselves: passengers that heretofore had gone to southern Europe for their winter season but could not as a result of the hostilities. Instead, countless such persons came to Florida, and what they saw and enjoyed was favorably communicated and remembered. Consequently, after the war, "increasing numbers of new people started coming into Florida yearly; towns and winter resorts began growing and improving; and, new areas were reclaimed and set out in citrus fruits and garden products."[3]

According to *Railway Age* magazine, the first "abnormal" activity that Florida rail officials detected started in 1920, when a growing interest in real estate became apparent and an unusually large amount of construction was begun in the vicinities of Miami, West Palm Beach and points north along the inviting east coast. "This activity marked the beginning of what later became known as the land boom period."[4]

A plethora of real estate projects were hatched in South Florida between 1919 and

1923. Large and lavish hotels were constructed as well as apartments, office buildings, theatres, churches, places of amusement, and many new homes. Further, towns and cities began to issue tax-free municipal bonds to pay for roads, bridges, causeways, parks, streets, sidewalks, auditoriums, piers, canals, schools, incinerators, sea walls, libraries, even cemeteries. Industry expanded too. New manufacturing plants sprang up about the state, or existing ones were enlarged, especially those that produced lumber, hardware, windows, roofing materials, cement, tile, steel beams, crushed limestone, and concrete block. At the same time a large amount of new road construction was being undertaken by the state, counties, and cities. When building supplies, raw materials, and products could not be manufactured or obtained locally, they were outsourced and sent to Florida destinations in railroad freight cars.

When the Twenties land boom had gotten legs there existed in Florida thirty-two separate railroad companies which operated some 3,700 miles of track. However, just three companies really dominated the scene: the Atlantic Coast Line Railroad, which in 1920 operated in Florida 1,791 miles of track; the Seaboard Air Line Railway (1,036 miles); and the Florida East Coast Railway (764 miles). Together, the so-called "Big Three" controlled more than eighty percent of all the railroad mileage within the Sunshine State.[5]

Without question this trio of firms would witness a dramatic increase of revenues and profits between 1920 and 1924. However, in 1925, as the land boom roared out of control, traffic and income exceeded their wildest expectations. That summer the normal lull in traffic did not manifest as people from every section of the United States poured into Florida as never before. This influx of humanity also placed an unprecedented demand upon housing, hotels, apartments, restaurants, boarding rooms, and every kind of public utility, especially in South Florida between West Palm Beach and Miami. There simply was not sufficient capacity.

So great did these demands for public utility become that life itself became difficult for many of the newcomers and tourists. As one participant remarked, "Many people not equipped for 'gypsying' had to sleep out in the open. Until the lower-priced hotels reopened, the overflow also spent nights in railroad stations. Public utilities were overburdened. Electric light plants, insufficient last winter, were being enlarged and trying to run at full tilt at the same time. Cooking was done by electricity; but lucky were those who had oil stoves and candles, for electric current was cut off without warning in certain towns for as much as twelve hours at a time. Antiquated telephones, cranked by hand, and overworked telegraph offices furnished little in the name of quick communication. Inundated post offices were bad enough. Worse was the brackish artesian water. Worst of all were the recurrent ice famines. Ice plants were being rebuilt. On several days no ice could be obtained without a physician's prescription, which entitled one to only fifteen cents' worth. Florida was not to blame. She did her best. But no better prepared than San Francisco for the earthquake was Florida for that dramatic midsummer horde of dusty, trusting, hopeful pilgrims."[6]

In addition to transporting record numbers of passengers and freight during the height of the land boom, the Big Three also had to move the state's huge citrus and vegetable crops to market, as well as deliver countless incoming carloads of building supplies and materials. "Enormous orders placed by merchants, the heavy movement of building and highway materials, coupled with one of the largest crops in the history of Florida, together placed an enormous burden upon the Big Three which became increasingly difficult to carry."[7]

With no let-up in sight and business owners thinking that the land boom would not end any time soon, Florida business brokers and dealers began ordering supplies far in excess of their actual requirements, all of which began a wild speculation in all classes of commodities. Almost overnight, trainloads of building supplies, materials, and merchandise were ordered without advance notice to the carriers and were shipped to the Sunshine State without a specific destination, changing hands many times en route, and often reaching a locale where no service tracks or unloading facilities existed. "This caused end-customers to leave the freight in railroad boxcars, which ended-up occupying every available foot of track, tying up cars urgently needed elsewhere and literally choking the very movement of trains."[8] Further complicating the scenario were the thousands of empty refrigerated cars (essential for the annual movement of vegetables and citrus to northern markets) that started to appear in the state. Lastly, railway labor shortages began to surface in addition to delays caused by summertime flooding and bad weather.

To untangle the huge mess, traffic experts from around the country were brought to Florida to resolve the issues. Based on their input, the Big Three had no choice but to impose an embargo on 31 October 1925—a first in state railroad history. Immediately, all incoming and outgoing freight traffic was halted except for certain foodstuffs, agricultural products, livestock, petroleum, fertilizers, and a few other essential commodities. Eventually the prohibitions would also extend to household goods, bottled drinks, even chewing gum! When the embargo was first called some four thousand railroad cars were stranded in the huge rail yards at Jacksonville—railroad nerve center of the state—while another ten thousand cars were ordered held at outlying points such as Atlanta, Washington, D. C., St. Louis, and New Orleans. Gradually the congestion eased, and the last sections of the embargo were lifted on 15 May 1926. By then, though, the land boom was fast running out of steam.[9]

In order to meet the traffic demands during the land boom years, it was also essential for the Big Three to undertake aggressive construction and expansion programs. Whereas such would have normally been staggered over a period of several years, time was now of the essence and, more often than not, the myriad projects gave way to hurried plans and rushed construction methods. "Every available resource was thrown into the work, and in spite of unprecedented difficulties encountered through the severe congestion of traffic and the shortage of labor and materials, the Florida roads pushed their work at a remarkable rate, opening one unit after another to meet the traffic burden which, with increasing force, was being placed upon them."[10]

Statistics confirm just how great the traffic demands were. Between 1921 and 1925, freight traffic on the Big Three increased by almost one hundred percent. Also, revenue passenger miles—total number of revenue paying passengers times the distance travelled expressed in miles—of the three railways stood at 866,156,080 in 1921 and climbed to a whopping 1.26 billion miles four years later. Further, the combined operating expenses of the Big Three rose to over $140 million in 1926, from just $100 million in 1921. In that same timeframe their total combined net income shot up to $34 million from $7 million. Even more impressive were the outlays for additions and betterments: in 1921 the combined amount was $4,959,671 versus $43,299,768 in 1926.[11] Such outlays went for new lines in

Florida, second tracks in busy corridors, enlarged and improved facilities, the installation of passing tracks and yards, extensive ballasting of track and heavier rail, new and heavier bridges, freight and passenger stations, enlarging or building new shops and engine terminals, and installing miles upon miles of automatic block signals so as to expedite traffic in and out of the Sunshine State.[12]

No company was better poised to capitalize on the land boom than the Florida East Coast Railway—the "FEC." Based in historic St. Augustine, the company's single-track main line descended the state's east coast and served every important community along what company literature hailed as the *American Riviera*. In addition to its 522-mile route, between Jacksonville and Key West, the FEC also operated eight branches that totaled an additional 233 miles. In 1920, when the land boom dawned, FEC revenues amounted to $13,701,191; net operating income stood at $1,826,169.[13] If one impediment plagued the FEC at that time it was the lack of capacity owing to a single-track main line. But as we will see, even this handicap would vanish as the era of "effortless riches" unfolded.

Under President William Beardsley, the FEC began a multi-year program of improvements beginning in 1920. Installation of heavier steel rail began, new passenger and freight stations were erected along its route and the railway's principal yard facilities were expanded and modernized. Further, suspect wooden bridges were reinforced with steel beams, new passing tracks were installed and orders were placed for a bevy of new engines and cars. Even a new headquarters building complex was begun in historic St. Augustine—today owned by Flagler College.[14]

In 1923 Beardsley relinquished the presidential post to William Kenan, Jr., another Flagler confidant whose sister, Mary Lily Kenan, became Henry Flagler's third wife in 1901. When Flagler died twelve years later, Mary stood to inherit her husband's $100 million-plus estate provided she could outlive the trust fund that her husband had established. She did not, and after Mary Lily's passing in 1917 most of the Flagler estate, which included the Flagler fortune in trust, then passed to her brother, William, and two other sisters. Thus, the Kenan family would obtain a proprietary, fiduciary, and majority stock interest in the Flagler System of railroads, steamship lines, a chain of impressive hotels, and several land companies.[15]

William Kenan, whose fortune would one day help found the Kenan-Flagler School of Business at the University of North Carolina, subsequently made a host of strategic corporate decisions. Not the least of these was getting his fellow FEC directors to approve, in 1923, the construction of a new double-track steel drawbridge for the railway's St. Johns River crossing in Jacksonville and to make extensive renovations to the company's shops in New Smyrna. That same year the Interstate Commerce Commission sanctioned the FEC to extend its Okeechobee Branch (from Okeechobee to Lemon City, near Miami) and to construct a "belt line" around Miami proper between Little River and Larkin (South Miami).

Decisions of greater import would occur a year later in 1924. Eager to possess its own route into Miami proper was the Atlantic Coast Line Railroad, another Big Three player, which the FEC met and interchanged traffic with at busy Jacksonville. That year, Kenan received a buyout overture from Henry Walters, the patrician chairman and principal stockholder of the "Coast Line." Walters knew that the FEC was experiencing growth pains and that it lacked deep pockets. Kenan, who regarded Walters as both a mentor and a father figure, ultimately concluded that the Flagler System must remain intact, as its founder (Henry Flagler) and his sister (Mary Lily) would have wanted. Thus, instead of selling the railway Kenan embarked upon a large and costly round of capacity and modernization projects.

To finance these endeavors, Kenan's board proceeded to issue trust equipment certificates so that the FEC could acquire a fleet of Mountain-class steam locomotives (they burned oil, not coal) along with a number of switching engines, steel passenger cars, two hundred boxcars, one hundred ballast cars, and twenty cabooses. More importantly, the FEC decided to issue $45 million of mortgage bonds, the bulk of which would go to fund the installation of a second main-line track from Jacksonville to Miami.[16] Remaining proceeds from the bond issue would permit the FEC to further advance its Okeechobee Branch down to Pahokee (its muck lands were producing fantastic yields of fruit, vegetables, and sugar cane); help pay for the aforementioned eighteen-mile belt line around Miami's north and west sides; enlarging Bowden Yard in Jacksonville; and allow construction of several new stations such as at Daytona. (A new station at Hollywood was also erected but funded by that city's founder, Joseph Young, Jr.)

Business results in 1925—the land boom's zenith hour—greatly pleased Kenan interests. Revenues and profits soared as never before just as several improvement and capacity projects came to fruition. For example, the new thirty-mile "Moultrie Cut-off" opened, which eliminated the westerly, main-line track swing through East Palatka. Also, the massive $2.4 million drawbridge over the St. Johns River opened, the busy Okeechobee Branch was pushed past Pahokee to Belle Glade and the Miami Belt Line was completed between Hialeah

The Florida East Coast Railway station at Hollywood was paid for by the city's developer, Joseph Young. The first train stopped at the Spanish Mission structure on 6 April 1924. Sadly, the impressive building was razed in 1967, in the name of progress (courtesy Florida Memory, State Archives of Florida).

and Larkin. Work now commenced on the new Miller Shops complex near St. Augustine, while in that same city another addition was begun to the company's new headquarters building. Lastly, the railway spent another $4 million on additional locomotives and rolling stock.[17]

Florida's land boom began petering out in 1926, the year which the FEC enjoyed both record revenues ($29,427,460) and net operating income ($5,167,479). That same year the long-awaited second main-line track opened with a state-of-the-art signal system between Jacksonville and Miami. Further, the impressive Miller Shops opened its doors, as did the aforementioned addition to the company headquarters building. And, just as in the previous year, orders were again placed for even more engines and cars.

Unfortunately, this euphoric state of affairs that was driven by the land boom rapidly deteriorated in 1927. Real estate buyers and investors started to vanish; real estate construction greatly slowed; and thus FEC revenues substantially declined. In fact, the railway would experience that year its first financial loss of the decade. Later, in 1929, a mere $13.4 million in revenues would be recorded—a far cry from the record set three years earlier. The only bright spot that year was the completion of the Okeechobee Branch to Canal Point which furnished a handy connection to the big Atlantic Coast Line Railroad.[18]

Though the Twenties land boom in Florida eventually vanished, what did not disappear was the debt load of the FEC or its obligations to service all of it. The downward pressures eventually proved too much and, in 1931, the firm slipped into receivership—a scenario that founder Henry Flagler would no doubt have found disturbing.

Reaping even greater rewards during the land boom era was the Atlantic Coast Line Railroad. Based in Wilmington, North Carolina, the Coast Line served six southeastern states with nearly 5,000 miles of track, a figure that jumped to 13,333 miles when controlling interests in other railroads were included. The company's 600-mile main line track—impeccably maintained and double-tracked in 1925—stretched between Richmond, Virginia, and Jacksonville, Florida. Significant secondary routes existed within the Sunshine State, not the least of which was the artery between Jacksonville and Tampa by way of Sanford, Lakeland and Plant City. In 1920, when the land boom more or less began, the Coast Line's gross revenues amounted to $25,304,074. That same year the company transported some ten million passengers, moved 17.3 million tons of freight and employed nearly twenty-five thousand workers. Without question it was a firm to reckon with.[19]

By its own admission the Coast Line became completely overwhelmed in 1925 with land boom traffic. As Chairman Henry Walters stated in the company's annual report that year: "Your Company has watched the rapid growth of Florida and, as far as possible, has anticipated the transportation needs of the State by large and substantial improvements of your property. No one, however, could have foreseen the phenomenal growth and development that has taken place there in less than a year's time, thrusting suddenly upon the railroad such a volume of business that it was unable to give normal service and resulting in a congestion of traffic which could only be overcome by drastic measures."

Ever since 1902, when the company obtained the Plant System of railroads in the South, the Coast Line had undertaken annual improvement projects throughout its Florida territory. When the land boom surfaced, the modernization and capacity programs naturally intensified. New steel rail was installed on major routes within the state, its busy freight yard at

Lakeland was enlarged and a number of new stations were erected, such as at Lake Wales, Frostproof, Avon Park, and Richland. Improvements were also carried out in the early 1920s at the yard and terminal facilities at High Springs and Sanford. Work on two important taproots—the Haines City Branch and the Tampa Southern Railroad—also commenced.

The Coast Line's so-called Haines City Branch had been completed between Haines City and Goodno (via Sebring and Lake Placid) just before the United States entered the First World War. After the war, construction resumed and by 1921 the track had reached the growing agricultural and timber setting of Immokalee, by way of Sears and Felda. Tri-weekly train service to the remote setting then commenced.

In an effort to tap traffic in soil-rich Manatee County, the Coast Line began construction of its Tampa Southern subsidiary between the neighborhood of Uceta (East Tampa) and Bradenton, this

Henry Walters, the distinguished chairman and principal stockholder of the Atlantic Coast Line Railroad, was a highly regarded transportation executive. Much of his fortune helped found the Walters Art Museum in Baltimore, one of the nation's finest.

in 1920. In the following year the track was pushed further south to Palmetto, whereupon the company's contractor created the Ellenton Belt Line and a spur track to Senanky where citrus and vegetable growers abounded. Sarasota, a city that was profoundly affected by the Twenties land boom, became the next objective, and in 1924 rail service to that splendid Gulf coast community commenced. To confirm the setting's growing importance, the railroad would erect here an impressive passenger and freight depot designed in the Spanish Mission architectural style.

When the Roaring Twenties commenced, the Coast Line was operating four popular passenger trains to Florida from New York City: the ACL Express, the Havana Special, the Palmetto Limited, and the seasonal but famous Florida Special. In the winter tourist season of 1920–21, the Everglades Limited was added to meet traffic demands as was the Everglades—an all–Pullman passenger train. Still later, the Florida West Coast Limited was put on as well as the Florida East Coast Limited. In fact so great did the crush of passenger traffic to Florida become that the firm even revived a ghost of the past: the West Indian Limited. By the time the land boom peaked in 1925–26, nine Pullman trains were running between New York City and Jacksonville—five ran the year round; four were put on just during the winter tourist season. Other carriers, in conjunction with the Coast Line, furnished service from Chicago and other key Midwestern points. Some of these famous trains included the Florida Seminole, the Southland, the St. Louis–Jacksonville Express, the Floridan, Flamingo, and three popular passenger trains known as the Dixie Express, the Dixie Flyer and the Dixie Limited.[20]

One region of the state somewhat deficient in railroad transportation during the early land boom years was Southwest Florida. For example, the territory below Fort Myers was completely devoid of railway service. Area businessmen, including millionaire Barron Collier (for whom Collier County is named), had been agitating for more rail service and went so far as to obtain a charter from the legislature to incorporate the Fort Myers Southern Railroad. The Coast Line, eager to seize an opportunity, acquired the "paper" corporation, whereupon its work forces began laying track south of Fort Myers to Bonita Springs where the "iron horse" arrived in 1925. Laborers then began grading and spiking rails further south to the inviting Gulf setting of Naples, where the Coast Line erected a brick and wood station on the outskirts of town near today's Naples airport.

In that same year another Coast Line contractor installed rails on the Moore Haven and Clewiston Railroad, between its namesake settings, in order to tap the area's lucrative vegetable and sugar cane traffic. (The little carrier connected with its owner, the Coast Line, at Moore Haven). About the same time yet another Coast Line contractor resumed work on the aforementioned Haines City Branch, south of Immokalee to Deep Lake where the aforementioned Barron Collier owned extensive grapefruit groves and vast tracts of pine timber.[21] Collier's little fourteen-mile Deep Lake Railroad transported these and other products south of Deep Lake to his company town of Everglades City.

Demand for even more railroad transportation increased as the land boom intensified. In response the Coast Line decided to extend its Tampa Southern taproot from Sarasota southeasterly to Southfort, near Fort Ogden. Its so-called Fort Ogden Extension would connect the Tampa Southern to the ACL's busy Lakeland-Fort Myers-Naples route at Fort Ogden. In another strategic move, and in an effort to expedite trains out of Florida originating on the Gulf coast, the Coast Line began its Perry Cut-off between Perry and Monticello which, when completed, gave the railroad an alternate route out of Tampa to southern Georgia that bypassed the busy Jacksonville yards and shortened the rail route between Florida and the midwestern states.

The Coast Line would enjoy record revenues and profits in 1926 owing to the frenetic events in Florida. That year the company inaugurated train service between Bonita Springs and Naples, and from Immokalee down to Deep Lake. Further, construction began on a huge new yard and shop complex at Uceta, which eventually would employ over one thousand Floridians. In 1927, Coast Line trains began using the newly-opened Perry Cut-Off and the Fort Ogden Extension, while the Fort Myers Southern Railroad was completed beyond Naples to Collier City—today Marco Island—in order to serve island local residents and a clam cannery.[22]

Whereas Florida's land boom had, by 1927, ground to a halt, the Coast Line decided to purchase Barron Collier's Deep Lake Railroad and extend its Moore Haven and Clewiston line past Clewiston to Canal Point (meeting the Florida East Coast Railway in the process) where another big processing plant of Southern Sugar Company existed. The Coast Line rebuilt the flimsy Deep Lake Railroad in 1928, whereupon it inaugurated train service to Everglades where it also erected a Spanish-inspired passenger and freight station was erected. (Today the depot helps form a restaurant.) Everglades itself became the ultimate southern point of the sprawling Atlantic Coast Line Railroad system. On at least one occasion, the company's wealthy and revered chairman, Henry Walters, whose fortune made possible the famed Walters Art Museum in Baltimore, would visit the remote locale.

The remaining "Big Three" player, the Seaboard Air Line Railway, also flexed its muscle during Florida's historic land boom. Based in Norfolk, Virginia and Baltimore, the company's main line track ran inland from that of the Coast Line, the latter always regarding the Seaboard as something of an interloper. Nevertheless, the Seaboard undertook numerous expansion and modernization programs in Florida in order to capitalize on the extraordinary traffic demands of the 1920s. Orchestrating its aggressive strategy was the Seaboard's chairman and president, Baltimore banker Solomon Davies Warfield. Warfield had always been enamored of the Sunshine State, and frequently at his side during the land boom years was Florida governor John Martin.

Since before the First World War, Warfield wanted to connect both the east and west coasts Florida by rail and invade South Florida to Miami. To achieve this goal, the Seaboard first chartered the Florida, Western and Northern Railroad which, when completed, would connect Coleman (below Wildwood, on the Seaboard mainline) with West Palm Beach by way of Auburndale, Avon Park, Sebring, Okeechobee and Indiantown. Another project would connect Tampa with West Palm Beach. All this construction required fistfuls of capital; however, financiers did not see eye-to-eye with Warfield, and without their funds he could not execute the dream. He then hit on a novel plan: issue bonds with an incentive.[23]

To create the bait, the Seaboard acquired some 160,000 acres of undeveloped land in and near Indiantown at a very low figure. Bonds in the subsidiary rail company were then issued upon the value of the land *after* it would get the railway and when the property was ready for cultivation and development. Stock in the land company that Warfield formed was given to the buyers of $7 million worth of bonds, as a bonus. The scheme worked. Warfield then hired Jefferson Construction Company of Charleston, South Carolina, to build the 204-mile line in rapid fashion between Coleman and West Palm Beach, the route in many places being straight as an arrow including one section that was fifty-four miles long. The line passed through the live oak hammocks of Sumter County to Polk City whereupon the right-of-way cut through the beautiful "Ridge country" of the state where countless citrus groves existed. To accommodate the route through Sebring, some twenty-five homes had to be relocated. Mile after mile of prairie lands were next encountered, after which the single track passed by endless stands of longleaf pine. Harvey and Clarke, an architectural firm in West Palm Beach, designed the stations along the new route, including a splendid edifice in their own city (still in use) that touted Spanish Baroque details.

Nine months after construction began, on 25 January 1925, the Seaboard's new line to West Palm Beach opened. To celebrate the occasion, Warfield inaugurated a new passenger train for the occasion, the Orange Blossom Special, which he packed with five hundred dignitaries from throughout the country. The success of the new line proved immediate. The bonds, with land and the completed railroad behind them, rose in price on the New York Stock Exchange, from $102 to $197, which paved the way for an even bigger securities issue that would soon be announced.[24]

Shortly after the route to West Palm Beach opened, the Seaboard finished up two smaller projects: the Valrico Cut-Off and the Gross-Callahan Cut-Off. The former branched

**When the Seaboard Air Line Railway opened its line into West Palm Beach in 1925, communities all along the route rejoiced. A big public outpouring occurred at Lake Wales when the Orange Blossom Special passenger train nosed into town from West Lake Wales (courtesy Florida Memory, State Archives of Florida).**

from the Seaboard mainline at Valrico (east of Tampa) and proceeded in a southeasterly fashion for Welcome Junction, where Seaboard rails already existed to Mulberry, Bartow, and Lake Wales. (At West Lake Wales the Cut-Off intercepted the newly opened extension between Coleman and West Palm Beach.) By building the Valrico Cut-Off, the Seaboard could now offer service directly from Tampa to West Palm Beach, in essence creating a cross-state route. The other shortcut, which linked Callahan with Gross, gave Seaboard trains a quick exit out of Florida that bypassed the congestion at Jacksonville. Still another project of note was completed in 1926, when a nineteen-mile gap was closed between Brooksville and Inverness.

Warfield's initiatives in Florida naturally attracted press attention, and among those

The Seaboard Air Line Railway opened its line through Opa-locka, en route to Miami, on 8 January 1927. Ads proudly announced the event in area newspapers. A huge reception and Arabian skit was staged for dignitaries aboard various sections of the Orange Blossom Special.

that became enamored of his achievements was Clarence Barron, president of Dow Jones Publishing, publishers of the *Wall Street Journal*. In fact, Barron wrote several favorable articles for that newspaper about the Seaboard, including one on 26 February 1925 that was entitled "Florida by the Air Line." Interestingly, the story led many northern investors to believe that Warfield was actually creating an airline company, an industry whose stocks were then in vogue. Quite unexpectedly the stock value of the Seaboard Air Line Railway began to rise!

Revenues on the Seaboard jumped to $62,864,711 in 1925, a substantial increase over the previous year thanks to the heavy freight and passenger traffic associated with Florida's land boom. Warfield now boldly unveiled his biggest Florida project ever: the Seaboard All-Florida Railway. In brief, the new subsidiary would extend the newly-opened West Palm Beach line southwards down to Miami, and additionally create a new line in Southwest Florida from Fort Ogden (Hull) down to Fort Myers and Naples. After obtaining permission to build the two routes from the Interstate Commerce Commission, the Seaboard floated a $25 million bond issue without a land company behind the bonds. Investors responded, whereupon Warfield hired the nation's largest railroad contractor—Foley Brothers of St. Paul, Minnesota—to execute the two big construction projects.

The sixty-six-mile line from West Palm Beach to Miami, via Fort Lauderdale, Pompano, Boca Raton, and Opa-locka, was finished in December 1926, along with a short branch at Miami to the Seaboard's new switching yard and locomotive facility at Hialeah. Another appendage, 28 miles in length between Hialeah and Homestead, was opened in April 1927. Although the new line from West Palm Beach pleased residents along the route, along with shippers of freight, not so enamored of the project was the Florida East Coast Railway, which regarded the Seaboard as an intruder into its sacrosanct territory.

Groundbreaking ceremonies for the extension to Fort Myers and Naples took place in the "City of Palms" (Fort Myers) in February 1926. The sixty-nine-mile taproot would commence at Hull (Fort Ogden), a way station on the Charlotte Harbor and Northern Railroad subdivision of the Seaboard. The track largely proceeded through palmetto scrub land to Fort Myers, crossing the Coast Line route to that city at a remote hamlet called Gilchrist. At Estero, some fifteen miles below Fort Myers, another Seaboard subsidiary (the Naples, Seaboard and Gulf) would advance the track to Bonita Springs and Naples proper. Warfield declared Naples as "a most attractive place with beautiful beaches, the latitude approximately that of Miami, and one of the best situated winter resorts on the west coast."[25] The Seaboard chairman also envisioned Naples as one day becoming a deep-water commercial port—something that its well-to-do residents of today would no doubt vehemently oppose! Land for the "West Coast" extension was secretly acquired, and when the Seaboard announced its plans to build the route, the Coast Line, which already served some of Southwest Florida, was no doubt shocked.

Whereas many streams and rivers had to be bridged on the extension to Miami, the greatest engineering challenge on both coasts was crossing the wide Caloosahatchee River at Fort Myers. Here, a long low-slung drawbridge had to be installed. Harvey and Clarke, the aforementioned architectural firm in West Palm Beach, designed a stunning $75,000 Spanish-styled station at Fort Myers along with a commodious freight building on Michigan Avenue (both still standing and commercially used) as well as a fourteen-track switching yard with an electric coaling tower. Another splendid station in Mediterranean Revival style arose in downtown Naples, on 5th Avenue South, which today has been thoroughly restored and serves as a museum and arts center.

To capitalize on the agricultural production of Southwest Florida, the Seaboard installed two branches from its Fort Ogden–Fort Myers–Naples extension: a thirty-mile appendage from Fort Myers eastwards over to the citrus and cattle lands of LaBelle via Alva, Buckingham and Floweree, and a nine-mile westerly branch from South Fort Myers that was to connect with the old cattle dock at Punta Rassa—where today's causeway to Sanibel Island begins. The latter, though, was only completed as far as Truckland, in Iona (the most frost-free zone in the continental United States) where truck farming flourished.

North of Fort Myers, at Tamiami City, the Seaboard track intersected the rail operations of McWilliams Lumber Company. Succeeded by Dowling-Camp in 1929, the latter's logging trains utilized the Seaboard track down to Fort Myers, then easterly over its LaBelle Branch to the pine timberlands near Alva. At Hickey Creek, portable logging spurs of the company penetrated area forestlands, its workers actually residing at the remote setting in modified boxcars. (Today Hickey Creek is an inviting Lee County park.)

After the new east and west coast extensions of the Seaboard were completed, Warfield staged what many regard as the greatest railway opening ceremony in American history. Over 700 hundred dignitaries from ninety cities and eighteen states would attend the event— most of them important Seaboard shippers, investors and bankers. For several days, beginning on 5 January 1927, Warfield pampered the delegation aboard five, completely separate sections of the company's famed Orange Blossom Special passenger train, first down the west coast, then the east. Stops were made at most every community, where guests were greeted by cheering crowds, flag wavers, and band music. Florida Governor John Martin rode the lead train with Warfield, and both delivered brief addresses to the well-wishers. Nearly five thousand persons would greet the Warfield delegation at Miami's Palm Park.[26]

Not only did the Seaboard construct new lines in response to Florida's spectacular land boom, but it also acquired, by sale or lease, existing firms like the Charlotte Harbor and Northern, the East and West Coast Railway, the Tampa Northern, the Tavares and Gulf, the Gainesville and Gulf, the Tampa and Gulf Coast, and the Georgia, Florida and Alabama Railroad. Other projects it undertook in the 1920s to meet the heavy traffic demands included the laying of a second main line track in busy sections of Florida and installing miles of automatic block signals. Further, several engine and yard terminals were enlarged, and orders were placed for many new locomotives and cars.

Naturally these expansionary and improvement measures came at a great price. Even though the Seaboard enjoyed record net income in 1926 ($17,771,852), in the following year—after the land boom had crested—profits plummeted to a mere $31,576! That same year the company's revered but controversial president died. The drop in revenue and profits, together with the cost of servicing all its new debt, proved too much for the Seaboard to bear, and the firm consequently slipped into bankruptcy during the early years of the Great Depression. Warfield's faith in Florida, though, never flagged, and even upon his deathbed he was justifying the Florida investments to a confidant.[27]

Oddly, the railway renaissance that flourished in Florida during the Roaring Twenties ended not on the peninsula but in the Panhandle, specifically in distant Pensacola where real estate hysteria that decade hardly prevailed. The event involved the St. Louis–San Francisco Railway, nicknamed "The Frisco," a big and profitable carrier that serviced Midwestern America with over 5,600 miles of track. Although the firm tapped many river ports within its territory, it did not service an actual ocean port. The impediment nagged at Frisco management, especially after the company obtained an entrance into the coal, iron, and steel belt of Birmingham, Alabama. Fortunately, an opportunity soon presented itself in the Sunshine State.

Pensacola possessed the best deep water port on the Gulf of Mexico. For decades, the Louisville and Nashville Railroad practically monopolized that location, but another player—albeit much smaller—was the Gulf, Florida and Alabama (G, F and A), whose underlying companies included the rail lines of Southern States Lumber and the Gulf Ports Terminal Company.

The G, F and A main line stretched between Pensacola and Kimbrough, Alabama, by way of Cantonment and Muscogee. Most importantly it owned a valuable shipping dock at the Pensacola waterfront. But owing to poor finances and management, the G, F and A went bust only to re-emerge as the Muscle Shoals, Birmingham and Pensacola Railroad. Despite a new name and new owners, business remained sluggish, and in 1925 the Frisco managed to acquire the little entity for a mere $305,000.

Now came a big challenge: connecting Kimbrough, Alabama, with the Frisco system at Aberdeen, Mississippi. Frisco construction engineers tackled the project with gusto, and within two years a 152-mile connector track linked the two firms. The Frisco also rebuilt the existing line into Pensacola proper with brand-new crossties, rails and fresh ballast. New stations and freight platforms also appeared, and every suspect trestle and bridge was replaced in anticipation of the new traffic.

Amidst considerable pomp and ceremony, the Frisco opened its Pensacola line on 27 June 1928, well after the land boom craze. A special train with dignitaries arrived in Pensacola from Frisco headquarters in St. Louis. The City of Pensacola rolled out the carpet and even declared a citywide holiday. Storefronts were gaily decorated and grand opening festivities were staged, including a parade, a colorful boat regatta on Escambia Bay, and a sumptuous evening banquet. And on that note a prosperous American railroad giant became part of Florida during the frenetic years of the Roaring Twenties.[28]

## Highways

The Age of the Automobile began well in advance of the First World War, though it grew by leaps and bounds after the Armistice had been signed in 1918 and gasoline rationing was abolished. Aficionados know that the earliest of motorcars were steered with a tiller. By adding a rear door, the so-called tonneau became a "touring car." Springs and pneumatic tires made the going easier, while canvas tops and side curtains shielded drivers and passengers from foul weather. By the end of the war, "the average speed of cars had so increased that the public demanded a hardtop limousine, sedan, and cabriolet, hitherto the privilege of the rich."[29]

Bad roads in the pre-war era—both in Florida and elsewhere—proved to the biggest obstacle in making cars popular, not price. Eventually, though, well-travelled roads became macadamized, though many in rural America still offered only dirt, gravel, or sand surfaces. In heavy rain, ruts and potholes became commonplace and often made a pleasant journey in the country almost unbearable.

Henry Ford introduced his famous Model T in 1908. Six years later he unveiled his assembly line of mass production. Within months, he then shocked the world by announcing his workers would receive a minimum wage of $5 a day. Morale lifted at Ford, production soared. In 1916, Ford sold over a half-million Model T's, which were nicknamed "tin Lizzies" or "flivvers." Two million were produced in 1923, and in 1927—when production ceased in favor of the Model A—a whopping fifteen million units had been manufactured. Initially, the Model T had cost $825 for the two-seat runabout. By the time the Florida land boom reached its peak in 1925 it was priced at $260.[30]

In brief, Henry Ford revolutionized American life. He emancipated the farmer and factory worker, and allowed them to "roll to Florida for the winter. Filling stations and service garages sprang up along main roads. But none of these things were possible without good roads."[31] The Ford Motor Company would sell more "flivvers" than all other cars combined, but plenty of competition developed near the Model T's price range such as the Dodge and the Maxwell. "Over 2,000 different makes of autos have existed in the United States. But one-by-one the little plants—Metz, Moon, Stanley Steamer, Winton, and hundreds more— all went broke or they were absorbed."[32] Florida passed its first laws regulating motorcars in 1908. That year some 700 car owners paid the tag fee of two dollars.

Convinced that the motorcar was here to stay, the Florida Legislature established a State Road Department in 1915 with five board members and a Commissioner—William Cocke, a highway engineer from Richmond, Virginia, who was paid an annual salary of $3,000. Governor Park Trammel wasted little time signing the Act. Congress passed the Bankhead Act in 1916 that allowed federal funds to aid state highway construction, and in the following year Florida reconstituted its newly-formed highway department with broader powers. Prior to these initiatives the construction and maintenance of roads and highways in the state was largely in the hands of counties and cities with no coordinated system.

"Beginning in 1919 the newly formed department was given its first big necessary funds for carrying out a comprehensive program. Road construction advanced until, during the land boom period, expenditures reached as high as $18 million annually."[33] Though some funds came from Federal sources, most were derived from a tax on gasoline: three cents in 1923, four cents in 1924, and five cents in 1929.

The early automobile roads in Florida were made of dirt, clay, vitrified brick, lime rock, crushed shell and, sometimes, compacted straw! During 1922, partly owing to the demands of land boom traffic, the Department began construction of its first major project: a sixteen-foot-wide, forty-three-mile-long concrete highway from Lake City to Jacksonville—the ninth longest hard-surfaced road in America. When the $1.2 million appropriation for the work proved inadequate, Federal aid was obtained and the highway opened in 1923. (It was later extended west of Lake City to Tallahassee and Pensacola.) That same year voters in Duval County approved an outlay of three million dollars to improve its overall system with eleven new roads and two major bridges. But even with this outlay, Duval still could not match Polk County which, for years before and afterwards, had the highest regarded road system in the entire state.[34]

That a huge number of people came to Florida by car in the Twenties is something of an understatement. It has been estimated that one-and-a-half million persons arrived in the early 1920s via all modes of transport. Between 1920 and 1925, the population increased four times faster than any other state. At the peak of the real estate craze, in 1925, some 2.5

million people came into the state.[35] Not only were highways into Florida jammed with motorcars, but so was the network of roads within the state.

In his book *The Truth About Florida*, author Charles Fox supplies some interesting statistics about the density then of motorcar traffic. Many boom-era travelers drove through Jacksonville and crossed the St. Johns River toll bridge en route to downstate destinations. In August 1925, the Board of County Commissioners hired surveyors to tabulate license plates and the passenger count in each vehicle stopping to pay tolls. In that one month alone—again, the land boom's zenith year—604,667 southbound cars paid the toll and generated revenue of $34,976. Of those cars, 12,500 had out-of-state plates. Most were from Georgia, the passenger count being 7,892. North Carolina came in second with 855 cars (3,406 persons) followed by Alabama (838; 2,536), Indiana (836; 3,245) and South Carolina (788; 3,149). Two cars, with four passengers in each, came from Idaho and South Dakota.[36]

Another tabulation of motorists took place in Lake City, where a large number of cars also entered the state. As one commentator noted, "Automobiles from states north of Florida whip southward through the streets of Lake City at the average rate of two and three and even more a minute, and continued so to whip for the greater part of the year 1925. Boy Scouts, requested to keep a check on incoming automobiles, found that the southbound cars averaged seventeen hundred a day through Lake City; and they further found that the average number of persons in each car was three and eight-tenths. It is being ultra-

So-called "Tin Canners"—motorists who came to Florida with some of their worldly possessions—helped form the tide of humanity that arrived for the Twenties land boom. Most stayed at camps, such as this one located at De Soto Park in Tampa.

conservative, therefore, to state that in 1925 there were at least 4,000 persons entering Florida daily by automobiles. It is equally conservative to say that another 3,000 entered the state by train each day, and that the number entering by boat was 200. When the proper mathematical computations are made, it can be seen that the United States has been so swept by Florida fever that at the most conservative possible estimate the number of outlanders who entered the state during the year of the big rush was over two and one half million."[37]

If anyone remained skeptical about the number of motorcars that came into Florida during the boom, they had only to study the consumption rates of gasoline for the state. Just for the first two months of 1926—as the land boom began to wind down—the American Petroleum Institute reported that Florida had the highest consumption rate of gasoline in the entire nation—52.6 million gallons against 29.1 million in the same months of the previous year, a gain of eighty percent and accounting for four percent of the total amount of gasoline consumed in America. Oddly, faraway Oklahoma ranked second.[38]

There were approximately five thousand miles of hard-surfaced roads in Florida in 1925, forty-nine different routes being maintained by the state. Governor Cary Hardee—who opened the famed Gandy Bridge connecting St. Petersburg with Tampa—supported road building in the early Twenties, but the greatest advocate of highway construction proved to be his successor Governor John Martin, who once said that more road building was an absolute must, "from one end of the state to the other, before the people now living were in the cemetery."[39] The state road department advocated new roads having a minimum sixty-six-foot wide right-of-way, though many aggressive supporters pushed for a width of one hundred feet. "One may drive over the roads at a higher speed than is permitted by law in any other state. Forty-five miles an hour is the legal limit on the open road, under the statute of 1925, and no municipality may impose a limit of less than twenty-five. The principal motoring hazards in Florida arise not from dangerous railroad grade crossings but from roving razorbacks and range cattle, and the fact that anybody may drive a car, no driving license being required."[40]

Three highways that eventually proved extremely popular with boom-era motorists were the Dixie Highway, the Tamiami Trail and the Conners Highway.

Promulgated by Indiana politicians and businessmen in 1914, the Dixie Highway was conceived as a north-south tributary to the even longer transcontinental Lincoln Highway. Among its chief promoters was Carl Fisher, the future developer extraordinaire of Miami Beach. Initially, Fisher called the route to Miami the Hoosier Land-to-Dixie Highway. Others wanted to dub it the Cotton Belt Route. But ultimately the Dixie Highway was agreed upon. How much Fisher himself invested in the project—if any—has not been learned.

Contrary to legend, the "Dixie" was not a new highway per se; rather, it was "a new route that was cobbled together from a network of existing roads."[41] Construction projects either filled in any missing links or supposedly improved those sections needing rehabilitation. State and local monies usually funded the actual work; Federal aid would only match what the states themselves could raise. "Governors of interested states and the founders of the Dixie Highway movement held a preliminary meeting in January, 1915 to form an association to build the road and plot a route." That April a formal gathering occurred at the "Good Roads Conference" in Chattanooga, where three thousand persons attended. The state governors got control of the project and organized a Board of Directors. The mission became simple: build a highway from Chicago to Miami in the most direct manner possible.[42]

A distinctive red and white marker sign, emblazoned with the capital letters "DH," would identify and guide motorists over the proposed Dixie Highway. The Association's publication—Dixie Highway—kept subscribers abreast of ongoing construction and progress. "So many important cities wanted a part of the highway that Carl Fisher suggested a compromise: there would be two Dixie Highways, running parallel to each other, called the eastern and western divisions."[43]

Considerable discussion evolved over final design and location details. In the end, the Dixie would enter Florida at two points: Jacksonville and Tallahassee. Once within the state, the route was projected to either utilize existing roads or some purpose-built section. A period map of the Association depicts the Western Route beginning in Sault Ste. Marie, Michigan, and heading southwards to Indianapolis, Nashville, Atlanta, and Macon, whereupon it entered Florida at Tallahassee and then on to Gainesville, Orlando, Arcadia, Olga, and thence under Lake Okeechobee to the east coast. (A connector would link Chicago with Indianapolis.) The Eastern Route, also beginning in Sault Ste. Marie, descended for Cincinnati, Knoxville, Savannah, thence to Jacksonville.

On 9 October 1915, the "Dixie Highway Motorcade," consisting of some one hundred vehicles led by Carl Fisher in a Packard touring car, left Chicago for Miami, its daily progress making good copy for almost every local and national newspaper. At Jacksonville, the cars proceeded down the "Coastal Highway" which itself had been cobbled together and opened in 1911. Supposedly the worst portion of the latter existed between Daytona and Cocoa Beach, the Fisher entourage having to expend some fifteen hours alone to reach Cocoa from Jacksonville. Interestingly, at West Palm Beach local car owners couldn't resist joining the fun, and by the time the motorcade reached Miami—thirteen days after departing Chicago—nearly one thousand vehicles could be counted. Fisher was appropriately feted, of course, for days on end. (The sole woman making the entire trip was later interviewed by Marjorie Stoneman Douglas, her very first article for the Miami Herald newspaper.)

Owing to traffic demands in Florida, several connectors eventually linked the two Dixie routes, such as the North Florida Connector: Tallahassee to Jacksonville; the East Florida Connector: Hastings to Orlando; the Central Florida Connector: Kissimmee to Melbourne; the Scenic Highland Highway: Haines City to Okeechobee; and the South Florida Connector: Arcadia to West Palm Beach.

The name Dixie Highway still appears on certain Florida maps and on signs in various locales. For example, in some South Florida communities the Dixie Highway (or Old Dixie Highway) parallels the Federal Highway (U.S. Route 1), which is sometimes just a block away. The so-called Hastings-Espanola-Bunnell Road (also known as County Road 13 or the Old Brick Road) was also part of the old Dixie Highway. How many land-boom motorists used the Dixie is unknown, but the number was enormous. Even though the Eastern Route opened to Miami before the land boom began, construction details were still being carried out on the historic roadway—later known as U.S. Route 1—as late as 1926.

Another significant highway project begun before the land boom and completed just after that real estate hysteria—one wholly contained within the Sunshine State—was the fabled Tamiami Trail between Tampa and Miami. Today the "Trail" is really the southernmost

Sheet music was composed for many Florida settings and attractions during the 1920s. Even the Dixie Highway was crooned about, as this cover attests.

**The most difficult part of the Tamiami Trail to construct was through the fabled Everglades—the so-called "River of Grass." Even today the motorist encounters remote sections where wildlife, fish and 'gators abound.**

264 miles of U.S. Highway 41, which runs from State Route 60 in Tampa to U.S. Route 1 in Miami. Between Tampa and Naples, the Trail runs in a north-south direction; then it becomes a west-east road across the Everglades and becomes South Eighth Street in Miami-Dade County, only to end a short distance away in the downtown Miami district.

The Trail's story could easily fill a book. It was conceived about the time the Dixie Highway was just getting legs; chief among its proponents was Captain James Jaudon, a Miami real estate developer, who proposed a highway connecting the Atlantic coast with that of the Gulf. (His Chevalier Corporation owned considerable land in the Everglades—in the path of such a road—and Jaudon paid for many miles of the Trail west from Miami.) In 1915, a group of businessmen from Miami, Naples, and Fort Myers met with state officials in Tallahassee to discuss the feasibility of a cross-state highway from Miami to Tampa via Naples, Fort Myers, Venice, Sarasota, and Bradenton. Some wished to call it the Miami to Marco Highway; others, the Atlantic to Gulf Boulevard. But the name Tamiami Trail stuck—Tamiami being a contraction of the words Tampa and Miami.

Preliminary surveys of the Trail were made, the greatest challenge being the section west of Miami to Naples through the Everglades. Cities and counties along the proposed route usually formed Highway and Bridge Districts, whose bonds would supposedly fund construction costs in their respective locales. The work began in September 1916. Good progress followed, but halted as the nation entered the First World War. Afterwards, the work resumed, but ongoing funding then became precarious. To arouse the public's interest in the Trail, a group of civic-minded individuals formed the Tamiami Trailblazers. In spring 1923, their ten-car caravan departed Fort Myers with twenty-three Trailblazers and two Seminole Indian guides, the goal being to fix the Trail's exact route through the Everglades. The dangerous, three week odyssey that ensued would make national headlines.

In the meantime, advertising magnate Barron Collier of Everglades offered to finance the remaining construction work provided the Florida Legislature carve Collier County out of Lee County. Collier County was subsequently created in 1923, though squabbles ensued between Collier and Captain Jaudon over the Trail's exact route, the latter wanting it to penetrate his Everglades land holdings. The state, though, sided with Collier's recommendations, which gave rise to the famed "dog leg" (in the middle section of the Trail) that bypassed the Jaudon tract.

Advertising millionaire Barron Collier, for whom Collier County in Florida is named, helped finance the last portions of the Tamiami Trail. The executive was well known throughout America, and many of his local achievements endure to this day.

As author Doris Davis relates: "The following year, 1924, the Florida State Road Department officially recognized the project. The Legislature incorporated the Tamiami Trail as part of the State Highway System and assumed the responsibility for completing it. The job began with surveyors and rod men clearing the right-of-way, working breast-deep in the swamp. After them came the drillers, blasting their way through more than ninety miles of hard rock under the muck. Ox carts were used to haul dynamite. When bogged down, men would shoulder the explosives and flounder through the water. Giant dredges followed, throwing up the loose rock to provide a base for the segment of road that took thirteen years and approximately $13 million to pave across "America's Last Frontier."[44]

The Tamiami Trail officially opened to traffic on 25 April 1928. Collier himself led a long motorcade which began in Tampa and three days later ended in Miami. A fair was even held in Everglades City. The hardy Trailblazers were present, who related their hazardous experiences; Captain Jaudon gave an address on the Trail's history; and Governor John Martin spoke. Whereas countless motorists would use the Trail between Tampa and Naples during the land boom itself, that real estate phenomenon had long since passed when the Trail was opened throughout.

We conclude this chapter with a brief account of one of the less-known, yet interesting road achievements of the land boom era: the Conners Highway, which ran between Twenty

Unique in Florida's road annals was the building of the Conners Highway in the Twenties. Privately funded, the toll road ran from a point near West Palm Beach to Okeechobee City, via the eastern shore of "Big O." It connected both coasts before the Tamiami Trail fully opened.

Mile Bend (west of West Palm Beach) and Okeechobee. The highway's progenitor was millionaire developer William J. Conners of Buffalo, New York, a highly successful businessman and former Democratic State Chairman of the Empire State.

Conners and his wife first visited Palm Beach in 1917. After viewing the Everglades up close and realizing the potential of its rich mucklands and need of roads, Conners purchased some 40,000 acres east of Canal Point, near Lake Okeechobee, for agricultural purposes. At that moment one could only access the lake from West Palm Beach via the rough Okeechobee Road to Twenty Mile Bend, then by using a series of canals. Conners decided to build a 52-mile toll road from the "Bend" to Canal Point, and on to Okeechobee City (today, Okeechobee)—nineteen miles alongside the Palm Beach Canal and thirty-three miles along the eastern shore of the second largest fresh-water lake in America.

The Florida Legislature gave quick approval to Conner's project, likely because the promoter's fortune would fund the multi-million dollar cost. A considerable amount of construction equipment was needed for the work, including seventy-four trucks, six gas locomotives with portable railway track, rock crushers, fifteen steamboats, and seven land excavating machines. Engineers and laborers slaved around the clock, the monthly payroll being $40,000. Certain land owners at Okeechobee City, excited that they were getting the road, paid for the construction of a truss bridge, with an opening swing, over Taylor Creek.[45]

The two-lane, $1.8 million Conners Highway opened to traffic on Independence Day, 1924, in time for boom-era motorists to enjoy. The toll was $1.50 per car and driver; 50 cents for any passengers. The *Jacksonville Times Union* newspaper, in its issue of July 24, 1924, noted "that a crowd of about 15,000 people joined in the gala. There was even a barbecue which was held at a house that Conners had built for himself on the lakeshore by the toll booth." Considerable publicity preceded opening day, and Conners—no stranger to publicity—designed a colorful brochure that was dropped from airplanes!

Because the Tamiami Trail was still unfinished across the Everglades when the Conners Highway opened, motorists coming from, or going to, lower South Florida found the toll route a convenient way to reach the opposite coast. Years later the state would acquire the road and abolish the tolls. Today, the old toll route helps form U.S. Route 98.

# 6

## More Communities of Note

Florida is a great laboratory of town and city planning and building. Almost everything that is good and everything that is bad is to be seen there in the flesh.

—John Nolen, American city planner, 1926

Again, we explore several communities that played a unique role in Florida's land boom of the Twenties. The places selected had either been established before that real estate phenomenon and as a result of it came of age, or were conceived as a direct result of the building and migration frenzy. Each has an interesting story worthy of lengthier treatment than space allows here.

## Venice

The old maxim "three's a charm" might well apply to the creation of the City of Venice, Florida, another ready-made town that surfaced during the Twenties land boom. The so-called "City by the Gulf" still remains a Mecca for tourists, homeseekers, transplants, and retirees. In fact the inviting setting still has many of the same qualities that existed in the frenzied 1920s: a balmy climate, unlimited boating and fishing, a magnificent bathing beach, beautiful parks, many stunning Spanish-inspired homes, and an architecturally interesting downtown commercial district.

Creating a city at Venice had first been promulgated by the Sarasota-Venice Company, a development firm headed by the Chicago heiress and socialite Bertha Palmer. The Palmer family, which owned considerable real estate holdings in what became Sarasota County, proceeded to hire a New York City urban planner to conceive a resort setting for Venice. Charles Wellford Leavitt (1871–1928) had designed numerous projects in America, including the Lake Mirror Promenade in Lakeland. Leavitt rendered a plan in 1915 that contained a gridiron of streets, a hotel, civic center, golf course, yacht club, a school, church, stores, canals, and parks. But the cost of building the proposed project shocked Palmer interests and the dream slumbered.[1]

Next on the stage stepped Dr. Fred Albee (1876–1945), a renowned New York City surgeon who pioneered advances in bone grafting, orthopedics, and rehabilitative medicine. A Maine native, Albee fell in love with the Sarasota-Nokomis area while vacationing and eventually purchased a considerable amount of real estate, usually from Palmer family interests. The crown jewel of these acquisitions occurred in August 1925, when Albee took title to a 1,468-acre parcel where the City of Venice would one day arise. (He paid $185,000, or roughly $130 an acre!) When Albee's purchase was completed, the distinguished Harvard Medical School graduate and author would own no less than thirty miles of Gulf and bay front land in the Venice-Nokomis area.[2]

For advice and guidance on how to best develop his vast real estate holdings, Albee turned to an international giant in city and regional planning. John Nolen (1869–1937) helped establish urban planning degrees at Harvard and the Massachusetts Institute of Technology. Nolen knew Albee first-hand and once visited the latter's home in Nokomis. In short order, a staffer from Nolen's office in Cambridge, Massachusetts, was dispatched to inventory the surgeon's properties. The subsequent research allowed Nolen to prepare a comprehensive development plan which he called "Venice-Nokomis: The White City on the Gulf." Embedded in the plan was the future City of Venice, which Nolen called "Venice Beach." A conspicuous element of the "Beach" was a wide, central boulevard running from the Tamiami Trail highway westwards to the turquoise waters of the Gulf of Mexico, where Nolen envisioned a "pavilion" hotel. To market his new White City plan, Albee hired a Sarasota realtor, Roger Rice, whom he also named as the exclusive sales agent.[3]

Despite the sites myriad development possibilities, Albee accomplished little at Venice Beach except for erecting a three-story casino beach building that cost $35,000. As to why, Albee felt that the timing for creating a city was wrong, that the land boom of late was about to crest. Further, Albee's wife reminded him that the work required would seriously impact his medical practice and lecture schedule. The surgeon concurred, and for the second time a plan for building a City of Venice was scotched.

Shortly after making his decision, Albee sold Venice Beach to perhaps the most unlikely of all land boom players in Florida: the Brotherhood of Locomotive Engineers—the largest, most powerful and richest union in America that had some 90,000 members. Not only did the Cleveland-based Brotherhood acquire Albee's holdings, but they also purchased numerous other parcels in the greater Venice area until they had assembled a tract some three miles wide and seven miles long—about 30,000 acres. During the negotiations, Albee recommended that the Brotherhood retain the services of John Nolen for his planning expertise. Before all was said and done Nolen's firm would create some 140 drawings for the Brotherhood's Venice project, though not all plans were built. The old maxim "three's a charm" was about to play out.

Formed in 1863 while the Civil War gripped America, the Brotherhood of Locomotive Engineers had dedicated itself to "elevating the social, moral and intellectual standing of its members, promoting their general welfare, as well as guarding their financial interests."[4] Affordable life insurance was obtained for members and a pension program was established. Sobriety was especially emphasized as were devotion and loyalty to job and family life. On balance, the Brotherhood was conservatively and carefully run during its first sixty-three years of existence. Among its many members was the American folklore hero Casey Jones.

Warren Stone, an up-from-the-ranks railroader, became the grand chief engineer of the Brotherhood in 1902. Eight years later, under his leadership, the Brotherhood opened an impressive $28 million headquarters building in downtown Cleveland. By the end of the

First World War, the union's coffers held very high balances, so much so that Stone felt the Brotherhood should now operate in the world of finance and real estate. That decision, according to a Princeton University author, marked the arrival in America of "labor capitalism."[5] In rapid succession the Brotherhood formed a chain of twelve coast-to-coast cooperative banks as well as an investment firm and several non-railroad companies. A controlling interest in New York City's Empire Trust Company was even obtained. Then, in 1923, Empire Trust and the Brotherhood acquired the forty-story Equitable Building in Manhattan's financial district. Though the Brotherhood received laudatory press reviews for its expansionary measures—Stone's portrait would grace the cover of *Time* magazine in 1924— many of the Brotherhood's investments met with financial reversals.[6]

Stone died in 1925 and was succeeded by Warren Prenter, another up-from-the ranks railroader. Just before the transition of power occurred, an audit of the Brotherhood's financial condition revealed that about one million dollars of "doubtful paper" existed at its cooperative bank in New York City. When added to other Brotherhood investments that had soured, the union was facing a financial incubus of some four million dollars. To remedy the situation it was suggested to Stone and Prenter that a one-time venture in Florida real estate be undertaken, where stories of fast money and overnight riches were rampant. Advocating the "flyer" was George T. Webb, a shadowy union executive who was president of the Brotherhood's Cleveland bank. Webb proceeded to survey both coasts of Florida for a suitable opportunity and subsequently took an option, on behalf of the Brotherhood and without authorization, on a substantial tract of land at Venice. (Other reconnaissance work and minor purchases for the union had been previously carried out by Sarasota realtors Albert Cummer and Albert Blackburn.)

Webb told the Prenter administration that the various Venice parcels should be acquired, platted, and resold, and the profits applied towards erasing the financial incubus. Brotherhood executives, unsure of such a speculation, ultimately visited Venice and, though not completely enamored of the setting, they allowed the option to be exercised. But in the twinkling of an eye, Webb reversed course and began cajoling his Brotherhood colleagues into developing Venice into a "ready-to-wear" resort city replete with homes, shops, hotels, casino,

John Nolen, a giant among American city planners, conceived the City of Venice, Florida. He also put forward improvement projects for Sarasota, Clewiston and other locales, and additionally drew plans for many subdivisions during the Twenties.

golf courses, farms, and industry—a strategy that would be far more lucrative than just selling real estate parcels and bailing.

Although objections to Webb's proposal were strongly voiced, the Brotherhood's directors—without ever officially sanctioning a development project—allowed Webb's plan to move forward. As one Brotherhood officer later stated in testimony, "The one thing that I wish to make clear to this Committee—and it was reiterated time and again here in connection with the first purchase in Florida—that it was *not* to be a development proposition but a sixty or ninety day turnover. You will find today that there was never authority given by the Board for the *development* of the Florida proposition. The next thing we knew we were in a development."[7]

Shortly after concluding its Venice purchases, the Brotherhood discovered that the charter of its investment division could not take title to the parcels, which prompted the organization, in September 1925, of BLE Realty Corporation. That same month news of the big purchase broke in the state's leading newspaper, but the article was intentionally vague about how the Brotherhood would actually use the property, only hinting that perhaps a retirement community might be created for railway engineers. Elsewhere, the Brotherhood said it would spend some $40 million on developing Venice—a million a month. Official word on how that kind of capital were to be raised was equally vague, though rumors of

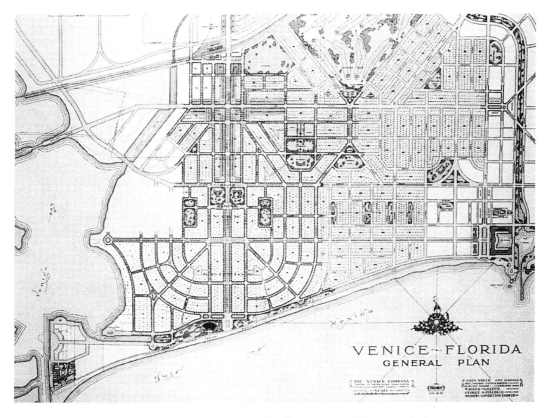

**Little has changed in Venice proper since John Nolen first submitted his General Plan. Venice Avenue still cuts through the community en route to the fabulous Gulf beach. Nolen later admitted that Venice was his culminating career experience.**

selling stock, issuing bonds and trust certificates, and obtaining loans from subsidiary operations were bandied about.[8]

One of the more commendable decisions made by the Brotherhood was to install proper infrastructure at Venice before any homes and commercial buildings arose, work that many Florida developers purposely avoided. This included the construction of streets with concrete bases, cast-iron water mains, underground lighting conduits, concrete sidewalks, and vitrified tile storm sewers.[9]

Southern Construction Engineers of Sarasota initially oversaw the foregoing work, but were later replaced by a prominent Washington, D.C., firm (Black, McKenney and Stewart) who placed more than one hundred engineers on the job. The latter surveyed the various parcels, prepared the plats, oversaw the draining of area swamplands, and located a canal to the Myakka River. The principal construction contract for the city was given to George A. Fuller Company of Chicago, who had previously built the Brotherhood's headquarters building in Cleveland. To house and feed its army of workers—many of whom were African Americans—the firm erected wooden dormitories along with a "Tent City" south of Hatchett Creek. The architectural firm of Walker and Gillette in New York City became the supervising architect, while Prentiss French, an up-and-coming young landscape architect, was hired to beautify Nolen's vision.[10] The controversial George Webb became the *de facto* BLE Realty official who oversaw everything at Venice. His opulent, Spanish-styled estate home— still standing—would eventually arise at 605 West Venice Avenue.

John Nolen submitted to the Brotherhood his pastel-colored "General Plan" for Venice in 1926. Nolen firmly believed that "Venice marks the beginning of a new day in city planning, not only for Florida but for all the country. Consider what this model city plan will mean to America—what it will mean to other cities yet to be built. It is the most complete plan we have ever attempted, and is being carried out faithfully to the last detail. Venice is now being laid out for fifty years ahead, so that there will be no overcrowding, no traffic problems and no architectural atrocities to mar the growth of a City Beautiful."[11]

Nolen's plan incorporated several "sections" (or neighborhoods) of the future city that featured curvilinear and gridiron streets. The city's principal artery, Venice Avenue, sliced through the community en route from the Tamiami Trail ("The Rialto") to the beachhead on the Gulf of Mexico, a throwback to his Venice Beach drawing. Nolen envisioned the artery terminating in an ornamental stone plaza, some 350 feet in diameter, modeled after the famous Plaza Michael Angelo in Florence, Italy. Venice Avenue ultimately measured two hundred feet wide in the residential quarter of the city and one hundred twenty feet wide in the business sector. An eighty-foot-wide "parkway" or bridle path went down its center. Citrus trees were planted on both sides of the parkway, while live oak trees and date palms marched alongside sidewalks. Still one of the most impressive thoroughfares in all of Florida, Venice Avenue alone cost $250,000 to construct.

All landscaping decisions at Venice were overseen by the aforementioned Prentiss French, who supervised a staff of twenty laborers. (Wages for the latter amounted to $3–$4 a day.) The landscape architect also oversaw a forty-acre nursery with shade buildings. In all, some three hundred different varieties of plants and tropical shrubbery were planted in the new city, some coming from such faraway destinations as Japan and Madagascar.[12]

Building lots in the first subdivision of Venice went on sale in November 1925. The Gulf View Section ran from the Seaboard Air Line Railway track to the Gulf of Mexico and included the business section of the city. Homes were sold with deed restrictions developed by Nolen: one dwelling per family, a single garage or greenhouse, no business enterprises within, no signs or fences, and the sale of homes could only be made to those of the Caucasian race. Domesticated cats and dogs were permitted, septic tanks were a must, and each dwelling had to have an underground garbage receptacle.

To ensure all homes blended architecturally, the supervising architects (Stewart Walker and Leon Gillette) insisted that all structures exhibit Northern Italian characteristics, such as tiled sloping roofs, stucco exteriors and colorful canvas awnings. (Prohibited were flat roofs, gaudy colors or unusually rough plasters.) All building plans had to be approved prior to construction. Residential lots in Gulf View ranged in price from $5,000 to $30,000 while commercial property could be acquired for $100 per frontage foot. The fanciest homes in Gulf View often touted heavy wooden doors, loggias, quatrefoil windows, massive fireplaces, courtyards and fountains, along with mini-balconies, iron-grilled windows, exposed wooden ceiling beams and tiled floors. Home owners often hung imported tapestries on interior walls and decorated rooms with antiques and heavy furniture.[13]

The public got a first-hand look at the Gulf View Section in February 1926. To usher in the crowds, special trains were run to Venice from Tampa, St. Petersburg, Orlando and other Florida points via the Seaboard Air Line Railway. Thousands attended the event including Florida Governor John Martin. A giant barbecue was even staged at the beachhead. Lot sales were conducted from the Venice Bathing Pavilion that Dr. Albee had originally erected. Visitors were also given access to the grounds of Fuller Construction, barracks, mess halls, and garages as well as the carpentry, machine and paint shops. Draglines and heavy equipment were on display too, and tours were made to Casey's Pass to see the huge hydraulic dredge.

Late in 1926, the second neighborhood in Venice opened: the Venezia Park District, which Nolen conceived around a trapezoid park framed by the intersecting streets of Nassau, Salerno and Sorrento. Homes in this area, like those in the Gulf View Section, were built by private contractors either on speculation or on a custom basis. Many of the homes built here, as well as in the Gulf View Section, are admired to this day.

By and large the Venezia Park and Gulf View homes were sold to middle and upper-income purchasers. However, this left most of the rank and file members of the Brotherhood with few or no opportunities to purchase a home owing to the high prices. Consequently, George Webb directed John Nolen to design a new neighborhood to satisfy the demands of railway engineers who wished to purchase "something" in what the Brotherhood billed as a retirement Utopia. Moderately-priced lots ($850–$1,600) with few deed restrictions became selling points for Edgewood, which Nolen located east of the Seaboard Air Line Railway track. One-story homes were advertised for $2,500. Country Club Parkway became the main north-south artery through the neighborhood, and in January 1927 Edgewood was formally annexed to the City of Venice.[14]

Newcomers to Venice who desired apartment life were not overlooked. In fact ten apartment buildings soon arose in the so-called Armada Multi-Family District. Conceived in what became known as the Mediterranean Revival style, they were erected by a Tampa builder at a cost of $38,000 apiece. Fancier still were the Worthington Apartments which cost $200,000 to build; the complex arose at the corner of The Rialto (the Tamiami Trail) and Palermo Place.

Once infrastructure was completed in the city, the construction of homes and buildings began in earnest. Almost immediately the wonders of Venice began to be advertised throughout the nation by BLE Realty's marketing arm, the Venice Company. Impressive ads and publicity articles about the "City by the Gulf" ultimately appeared in national magazines, travel and tourist brochures, booklets, in Brotherhood publications to their rank and file, and in the company-owned newspaper at Venice. Before long, visitors from around the country began to arrive in record numbers. Most were greeted by Venice Company sales personnel, who paraded them about the community in company-owned busses while reciting well-rehearsed sales scripts. But there existed one problem: hardly any overnight accommodations existed. Consequently, Venice Company staffers had to place sales prospects in homes and hostelries outside the budding city, often times in Sarasota—some eighteen miles distant—where several city hotels were situated.[15]

This shortage of accommodations prompted the Brotherhood to direct its architectural firm and contractor to find a solution—and fast. As a result the union announced in January 1926 that it would erect a $500,000 hotel at the intersection of Tampa and Nassau streets. Construction of Hotel Venice, conceived in the Italian Renaissance style, began in March and ninety days later the one-hundred-room, three-story building opened to guests. As the noted author and historian Janet Matthews relates, Hotel Venice quickly became a focal point of entertainment and promotion. Music and dancing occurred at the hostelry's Orange Grove Patio at nighttime, fanned by Gulf breezes. Electrically-lighted oranges even twinkled in the orange tree branches! Tea dances were staged in the afternoons and "women came with flowing georgette dresses."[16]

But the demand for space continued to escalate, so much so that that the Brotherhood began another facility shortly thereafter. Hotel Park View, which used the same basic plan as Hotel Venice, arose as another ninety day wonder on West Venice Avenue. (The building was later razed and replaced by the current Venice post office). Amazingly, the plea for more space continued, prompting construction of the $350,000 San Marco Hotel (today the Venice Centre Mall). Franklin Adams, president of the Florida State Association of Architects, drew plans for the ninety-two-room, three story building, which opened for business in December 1926. (Sixteen retail stores were located at street level). Area builders also put up smaller hotels. John Nolen's 1926 General Plan even included resort hotels at Casey's Key (the Venice Inlet) and at Rocky Point (near the Venice airport), though neither was built.

Much of Nolen's creative output, both in Venice and the multitudinous other communities he created or improved, embraced "Garden City" ideals. These precepts had been formulated in England at the turn of the century by Sir Ebenezer Howard. Hallmarks of the movement included small cities, an agricultural-industrial economy and protective greenbelts. Further, land uses were carefully defined. Specific areas would be set aside for homes, hotels, parks, schools, businesses and farms. Never did Nolen expect that Venice would be built in one fell swoop; rather, he anticipated that the city itself would unfold as the population expanded, perhaps to ten thousand inhabitants.

It was in the vicinity of Venice Avenue and The Rialto (Tamiami Trail) that Nolen platted the commercial or business district of the Gulf View Section. Once building sites had been prepared they were sold by the Venice Company. Building plans, like those for homes, also had to conform to the architectural guidelines of the day. Most commercial buildings were two story structures of block and steel with stucco exteriors. Many had large plate glass windows at street level set in either round arches or rectangular openings. Second floors often featured balconies and rounded arched windows. Canvas awnings, as found on many homes, were popular, and several buildings had recessed entranceways, decorative spandrels or twisted columns. The first commercial building opened in 1926. In time, a bank appeared as well as a general merchandise store and finery shops. By early 1927 the business sector could boast a pharmacy, grocer, a furniture store, an electrical company, tea room, hardware outlet, haberdasher, barber shop, a newsstand, and a five-and-ten-cent store. A Chamber of Commerce and a Venice Merchants Association were formed to promote local businesses.[17]

From the get-go, Nolen wanted the Seaboard Air Line Railway to move its track and station about a quarter mile east of its initial locations into Venice, believing that the coming and going of trains and the noise they generated would encroach on home and business owners. Brotherhood officials subsequently approached Seaboard president S. Davies Warfield about Nolen's request, which he quickly approved primarily because the union was willing to pay for all relocation costs and fund a new $48,000 station. The latter, today magnificently restored, opened in March 1927.[18]

Near the Seaboard track and south of the depot Nolen would plat an industrial park for Venice. Triangular in design, building lots ranged in price from $3,200 to $4,000. The initial group of industries attracted to the location included a building materials firm, a tile company, lumber yards, a brick works, a plumbing supply outlet, and a concrete products producer. In July 1926, the only permanent building in the city was Hotel Venice, but by year's end some 185 buildings were under construction or being completed, an investment of over $3 million. From a tiny hamlet, Venice quickly grew into a community of 3,000 people. In December 1927, Venice became a true Florida city with Florida Governor John Martin naming Edward Worthington its first mayor. All council members, including Worthington, were also Brotherhood development officials.

In 1926, ownership of BLE Realty Corporation shifted to the Brotherhood's Grand International Division. About this time certain union officials began questioning the activities of George Webb and the escalating costs of creating Venice. No financial plan had ever surfaced about the undertaking and heavy expenses continued to mount. Nevertheless, the union continued to fund the resort city and exert more pressure on sales and promotion personnel. To raise additional funds, a seven percent bond issue was floated, even though sales were less than desired. Although an advisory board within the Brotherhood prohibited any more land purchases at Venice, in the summer of 1926 another 20,000 acres made their way onto the union's books, increasing its holdings to 53,000 acres—nearly eighty square miles![19]

Despite its vast land inventory, the Brotherhood ended up developing only a small portion of its real estate portfolio. At the behest of the union, Nolen even furnished a "Regional Plan of Venice and Environs." One of its components called for the creation of a neighborhood outside the core city, principally for African American workers, which Nolen labeled

Harlem Village. It was never built. But one component of the Regional Plan that did meet with modest success capitalized on the agricultural possibilities of the area. It was called Venice Farms.

A huge variety of fruit and vegetables could be grown in the fertile soil of Venice, especially truck and vegetable crops that could quickly be brought to market in one hundred days or less. Two crops a year could be harvested, sometimes more. Nolen himself foresaw the day when the Venice Farms district would help feed the hungry city as well as provide foodstuffs for far-away Northern markets during winter months.

To reach Venice Farms, the Brotherhood constructed a twelve-mile, hard-surfaced road from Venice proper eastwards to the farming district. (It later became Venice Avenue East.) Dozens of five and ten-acre farm sites were platted. Each site was cleared, fenced, drained, plowed, and disked. Several artesian wells were also dug in the district for irrigation purposes, and a cover crop was planted for each new farm site beginning in May 1926, a month after sales began. A typical ten-acre parcel sold for $450 an acre, and was advertised as suitable for growing peppers, potatoes, eggplant, watermelons, squash, peas, beans, cucumbers, and strawberries. A small furnished farmhouse could be erected on the property for $2,500, while a chicken house and barn could be supplied to the buyer for an additional $1,000. Even a deep well could be dug, this for $500. A new Ford tractor could also be supplied at the same price. Thus, one could become a turnkey farmer for about $10,000.[20]

In addition to selling farm sites, the Brotherhood dedicated some eighty acres of land in the district for experimental vegetable farms, strawberry and poultry demonstration farms, and a model dairy operation. A farm board, organized by the Brotherhood, dispensed valuable farming information and assistance to the new farm owners, many of whom had no prior farming experience. The dairy operation, located six miles east of the resort city, was located on a 160-acre site that was fenced and cross-fenced into 25-acre plots. A large ventilated dairy barn accommodated one hundred cows. The barn was equipped with the finest milking equipment of stainless steel, the creamery and bottling operation regarded as the most modern one of its kind in all the southern states. Operations began with a herd of one hundred purebred Guernsey dairy cows.

The Venice Company wasted little time in issuing colorful and convincing brochures, pamphlets, and ads about the Venice Farm District. The farms themselves were sold in several promotions, the first one consisting of 1,500 acres. Later, the Brotherhood opened North Venice Farms (1,924 acres). In September 1926, *Florida Grower* magazine devoted an entire issue to the successes at Venice, which greatly aided sales.[21]

While Venice Farms gained traction, the Venice Company continued to promote its resort city. Its local rag, *This Week in Venice,* carried all the latest news, development information and gossip. The publication was later replaced with a slick publication called *The Venice News*, which often went to press with pastel color covers. One event greatly promoted in print was the annual tarpon tournament sponsored by the Venice Tarpon Club. Big cash prizes were awarded for the biggest catch, and in 1927 some 7,500 participants appeared, including many women. The visitation of famous personalities also made good copy for the aforementioned newspapers, especially when inventor Thomas Edison of Fort Myers visited Venice in March 1927.

To arouse further interest in the resort city, Brotherhood executive George Webb initiated discussions with Biltmore Hotel executive John Bowman about building a luxury hotel in Venice. However, the convoluted talks—Bowman wanted the union to buy Miami Biltmore bonds—eventually collapsed. Undeterred, Webb asked John Nolen to draw plans for the Rocky Point Section of Venice, near today's airport. Here, Nolen conceived a beachside building with dancing and dining rooms along with a "Sun Bake" tanning salon on its upper level. Nolen also submitted plans for an artists' colony at Lemon Bay that would consist of eighteen acres of home sites, including another ten for a casino. Two residential villages were also conceived just for citrus growers. Alas, none of the plans were built because the Twenties land boom was fizzling.

Despite the convincing ads and the positive publicity in nationwide newspapers and magazines, chinks were appearing in the Brotherhood's armor. The tremendous costs of creating Venice, and other Brotherhood ventures, were causing considerable turmoil in the boardroom at Cleveland. By the end of 1926, the terrific drain on funds prompted retrenchments. The union's New York City cooperative bank was sold that August, as were the stock investments in Empire Trust Company and the Equitable Building in New York City. In March 1927, the Brotherhood's legal counsel actually warned Prenter that the union was in a dangerous financial condition. "There has been no estimate of the amount needed for expenditures in the Florida venture ... no provision that it is properly financed."[22] Lawyers of the firm pressed for quick action, but radical changes did not occur until the Brotherhood held its triennial convention in Cleveland on 6 June 1927. Then, all hell broke loose. Tensions dramatically rose as the confidential report of the "Committee of Ten"—appointed to ascertain the true financial condition of the union—was learned by the press. As one author summarized, "The huge losses, errors of judgment, betrayals of confidence, nepotism, inefficiency, and extravagance that permeated the union's financial system, which had so long camouflaged itself as a great and glorious enterprise, were brought home suddenly to the bewildered delegates."[23] Prenter, bedridden with pneumonia, could not appear on the convention floor to answer charges of "laxity, carelessness, and indifference." Regardless, he and senior Brotherhood executives were soon stripped of their offices.

Alvanley Johnston, another up-from-the-ranks railroader, became the Brotherhood's new Grand Chief Engineer. The so-called Committee of Ten (later "Eight") was ordered to take whatever action necessary to rectify the mess, including the employment of outside experts. Quickly, they brought in Colonel Claudius Huston, chairman of Transcontinental Oil and future head of the Republican National Committee. Then, an outstanding cadre of Cleveland businessmen replaced the union's investment board. A plan to liquidate the bad investments evolved together with a compromise settlement with creditors. The actions resulted in an assessment against the Brotherhood for $5 million. To raise the huge sum, real estate was mortgaged and so-called "Loyalty Certificates" were sold to the union's rank and file, many of whom had seen their pension funds vanish like a soap bubble.

Meanwhile, a long and painful decline began at Venice. The Brotherhood's Venice Company went begging for sales prospects, unsold homes were locked, many residents moved away, and on moonlit nights street lamps were turned off to conserve money. Then, the inevitable lawsuits and a receivership became the order of the day, litigation that lasted into the 1940s. Though Venice became something of a ghost town, the beautiful "City by the Gulf" refused to roll over and die.

Decades would pass before Venice climbed out of its economic morass. An uptick occurred in 1932 when the Kentucky Military Institute moved its winter campus to Venice. Then, the revered Dr. Fred Albee bought the union's Park View Hotel and opened within it his famed Florida Medical Center. During the Second World War the U.S. Army established an air base at Venice, which introduced countless service folk to the area. Gradually, the town's appeal began to attract a new wave of retirees and transplants. New housing subdivisions appeared, mobile parks began dotting the landscape and the age of condominiums later arose.

And of the Brotherhood of Locomotive Engineers? After spending some $16 million on developing the City of Venice, the union exited the world of high finance and made a full recovery. Today it remains a potent labor voice in the transportation industry. As an aside, George Webb, once the majordomo of the Venice project, died in 1956, penniless in a Miami hospital. Friends took up a collection for a decent burial.

And of the renowned planner John Nolen? His able chronicler, John Hancock, notes that the path-breaking visionary ultimately completed more than 400 plans and urban designs before the start of the Second World War, including creations for eighteen regions and states, fifty-one cities and metropolitan areas, twenty-three suburbs, twenty-seven new towns, dozens of parks and parkway systems, subdivisions, housing projects, civic and commercial centers, colleges, industrial parks and airports. Nolen also became a consultant to every federal agency and program that dealt with the physical planning of towns, cities, regions and states.[24] Small in physical stature with a ruddy complexion and blue eyes, Nolen also found time to write numerous books and lecture extensively both here and abroad. Small wonder that, in 1978, city fathers of Venice would dedicate a bas relief statue of the great man—in John Nolen Park of course!

## Sarasota

Some twenty miles north of Venice lay another gemstone on Florida's Gulf coast—Sarasota. Although not created as a result of the Twenties land boom like the City of Venice, Sarasota nevertheless came of age during that real estate phenomenon. As Frank Stockbridge states in his popular 1920s book *Florida in the Making,* "Nowhere else on the West Coast, probably nowhere else in Florida, has there been so much real estate activity in so concentrated a territory as in Sarasota, beginning in 1924. In climate, in its curving expanse of water frontage around Sarasota Bay, the attractiveness of its outlying keys, and in the beauty of its harbor, the development of Sarasota started with exceptional natural advantages in its favor."[25]

First populated by Native Americans, what became the greater Sarasota area eventually attracted its share of pioneer families, homesteaders, farmers, and fisher folk. But as a community, Sarasota did not really get legs until the early 1880s courtesy of a Scottish land syndicate: the Florida Mortgage and Investment Company Limited. Sir John Gillespie of Moffat, Dumfriesshire, Scotland, emerged as the entity's prime mover while other prominent Scotsmen and landed gentry helped fill the directorate. To launch the colonization endeavor in Sarasota close to 60,000 acres were purchased from Philadelphia industrialist Hamilton

Disston. At that moment Disston's own syndicate, the Florida Land and Improvement Company, owned 2,500,000 acres of Florida land, 370,000 of which were situated in Manatee County.[26]

The plat for "Sara Sota" (as it was then spelled) had been drawn up in Edinburgh, the new colony being promoted as something of a tropical and agricultural paradise. As the popular author Jeff LaHurd relates, "For one hundred pounds sterling each family purchased a town lot in Sara Sota and a forty-acre estate outside of town, the site of which would be determined by a drawing."[27] After an arduous journey by sailing ship, train, and steamboat, the first wave of colonists arrived only to find their Utopia devoid of a pier, homes, stores and streets. One can only imagine how the party felt as they trudged down the wooden planks or waded ashore. Amazingly, a dusting of snow had fallen just a few weeks before.[28]

Many of the colonists became disillusioned and returned to Scotland. Others, though, stuck it out, buoyed by the arrival of J. Hamilton Gillespie, one of Sir John's sons who had been educated at Oxford and served in the British military. Keen to right the situation, Hamilton erected a hotel (the Desoto), built a pier, and—true to his Scottish roots—laid out a golf course, thought to be the first in America. But the dream of creating a thriving settlement proved elusive, and for years Sara Sota remained nothing more than "a restful fishing village with few ambitions."

All this began to change in 1910 when Bertha Palmer, a wealthy Chicago widow, visited the region after reading a real estate advertisement. In short order, she became enamored of the region's beauty, declaring the Bay of Sarasota to be more beautiful than the Bay of Naples, Italy. The Palmer interests went on to acquire some 90,000 acres of land for agricultural, ranching, and land development purposes. The heiress established a residence in nearby Osprey and proceeded to draw around her people of wealth and position—mainly from Chicago—who also came to Sarasota in the winter months for the salubrious climate and to make investments.[29]

Another turning point occurred in 1921, when Sarasota County was created from Manatee County. Prior to this legislative action, most every Sarasotan harbored disdain for its parent chiefly because it spent so little on local roads, schools and levied excessive taxes. But after an arduous battle the "divisionists" won the day, with Sarasota becoming the new county seat as well as its principal municipality. At that moment Sarasota County contained some 355,000 acres, 25,000 of which were farms and groves, "land as rich as the Delta of the Nile," claimed one sales brochure.[30]

Another Chicagoan who became awe-struck with Sarasota was Owen Burns, a well-heeled Maryland native of Scottish descent, who initially came to the area in 1910 to vacation and fish. Burns moved to Sarasota the following year, and for a reputed $30,000 acquired 75 percent of the incorporated town from J. Hamilton Gillespie. The purchase included hundreds of building lots, all the undeveloped tracts of the Florida Mortgage and Investment Company Limited, and the historic 110-acre golf course. An astute entrepreneur who was widely admired for his business acumen, Burns eventually organized the Sarasota Board of Trade, the Burns Transportation Company (which conveyed building supplies), and a construction company that, among other endeavors, helped beautify the city and its waterfront. Burns would also develop a number of commercial properties, notably in Herald Square, along with the imposing El Vernona Apartments (later called the Belle Haven). He additionally platted several subdivisions (such as Inwood Park and Washington Park); completed desirable residences in Burns Court, and acquired for development a portion of Cedar Point. The one-time owner of Bird Key also founded Sarasota's Citizens National Bank and built the first St. Martha's Parish church. Eventually he became a business associate of circus mogul/developer John Ringing, a relationship that ended bitterly.[31]

Perhaps the greatest endeavor of Burns was his spectacular El Vernona Hotel that opened Labor Day, 1925. Named for his wife, Vernona, the $800,000 landmark towered high above Broadway (today's North Tamiami Trail). Conceived by New York architect Dwight James Baum (1886–1939), a graduate of Syracuse University, the El Vernona was advertised as a Castilian palace. Guests entered the hotel's commodious lobby via a broad tiled piazza, whereupon they were immersed "into the soothing quiet of Andalusia's yesteryear." Antiques abounded, as did tapestries, lush curtains, floor tile from Tunis, and richly designed Spanish-styled furniture. Lanterns of hammered bronze and iron hung overhead. The building, constructed of concrete and fireproof, became a watering hole for the rich and famous.[32] (Demolished, the building has been replaced by today's Ritz-Carlton Hotel.)

Previously, the distinguished architect had designed for Burns—next to his hotel masterpiece—a Spanish-inspired office building complex from which both the developer and eventually the architect operated. Baum would also draw plans for a stunning Venetian Gothic estate for Mabel and John Ringling, which Burns built, that is today regarded as one of the great treasure houses of America. Another noteworthy edifice designed by Baum is the impressive Sarasota County Court House complex on Main Street, embracing Spanish Colonial Revival and Spanish Renaissance architecture together with Baroque and Rococo elements. If that were not enough, Baum conceived the Pineapple and Broadway/Belle Haven apartment complexes, as well as numerous private residences in Sarasota proper and ones on nearby barrier islands.[33]

Still another Chicagoan whose development hand greatly affected Sarasota in the Twenties was Andrew McAnsh, a one-time furniture manufacturer. Born in Scotland, McAnsh first came to Sarasota as a tourist, became enamored of its beauty, and was determined to capitalize on its future. His Mira Mar Corporation erected an attractive apartment building in 1922 (after sixty days of 24-hour efforts) along with a very popular hotel and auditorium, largely because the canny Scotsman had been able to extract from city fathers a ten year, tax-free existence for his properties along with free electricity and water. In fall 1925, McAnsh began the Mira Mar Beach subdivision on the north end of Siesta Key, and additionally built the Mira Mar Casino and purchased the Albee Road toll bridge to Casey Key.[34]

Prices of Sarasota real estate steadily rose during the land boom. More developers and players arrived, and newspaper stories about overnight riches became rampant. "Between 1924 and 1926," notes architect Michael McDonough, "the number of real estate firms in Sarasota increased from fifteen to more than two hundred." The author further notes that "the conception of Sarasota as a Mediterranean city was based on pure fantasy. It was a myth invented to influence a mass audience to buy real estate. Overnight Sarasota became an instant paradise with a ready-made history."[35]

For years, Sarasota had been ably served by the Seaboard Air Line Railway. But in 1924 the Atlantic Coast Line Railroad came to Sarasota and offered Pullman train service to northern markets. In the following year, Alpheus Griffin, a talented staff architect at the railroad's Wilmington, North Carolina, headquarters, conceived a noteworthy Spanish Mission-style station for Sarasota on South School Street. (Although that station was later demolished, a virtual twin went up on Peck Street in Fort Myers, which is today fully restored.) The elegant station was a strong visible reminder that Sarasota was in the throes of a growth cycle. As one chronicler waxed, "The golden age of Sarasota had begun."

As in most Florida communities, a host of subdivisions—nearly seventy!—surfaced in the Sarasota area during the land boom years. Of the more noteworthy was Whitfield Estates on Sarasota Bay, the first of many in Sarasota platted with a golf course. Developed by Forrest Adair, a prominent real estate dealer in Atlanta, design details were carried out by the Atlanta architectural firm of Pringle and Smith, which also conceived a fashionable Club House along with two estate homes. (The firm also designed the Sarasota Terrace Hotel owned by Charles Ringling of circus fame, as well as the American National Bank and Office Building.)[36]

Advertisements for Homecroft, a landlocked development located two miles from the Gulf and consisting of three hundred sixty building lots, touted homes that were constructed in the Mediterranean style. Developers of The Garden of Allah—whose main traffic thoroughfare bore the name Mecca Boulevard—offered four different styles of homes for the buyer. Sales brochures confirmed that "every improvement is unconditionally guaranteed and investors and homeseekers who buy in the Garden of Allah are assured of the completion of all these improvements." Other popular projects included Washington Heights ("Where prices positively will advance $500 to $1,000 a lot within a week"); Flora Terrace ("Where values inevitably soar because of the unsurpassed beauty of this marvelous tract of land"); Sorrento Shores ("Only nine miles south of the flagpole"); Indian Beach Estates; Mira Mar Extension on Sarasota Beach; Seagate ("Sarasota's most aristocratic suburb, a half-mile north of Sapphire Shores, on Indian Beach"); Pine Vista Estates ("Only twenty minutes from Five Points, where beautiful home sites can be purchased at the ridiculously low price of $3,650"); and Vamo, founded in 1928 on Sarasota Bay Inlet by the Webb family. Short-lived Pennant Park, developed by John McGraw, the famed manager of the New York Giants baseball team, was billed as "One of the most beautiful bits of homeland in the world," though it failed when the land boom went bust. Whispering Sands, conceived by architect Dwight James Baum, had been widely advertised in the media, yet remained a paper project. Out on Siesta Key, Gulf Bay Estates took root, a popular four hundred eighty lot subdivision proffered to the public by two Pierce-Arrow automobile dealers from Chicago and one marketed by realty magician C. Roy Kindt.

So intense did the real estate frenzy in Sarasota become in the Twenties that the City Council, together with its newly formed city planning commission, proceeded to hire the renowned civic planner John Nolen for advice and guidance. Nolen, who would achieve local fame by conceiving the City of Venice, recommended measures in Sarasota that would yield beautification and orderly growth. His detailed city, regional, and zoning plans were accepted by the Council in February 1925. Nolen felt that Sarasota's downtown district and its attractive bay front were the town's greatest assets. Overall, he recommended a grid system of streets, a relocation of railway tracks, adding schools, extending certain thoroughfares, building more parkways and creating a downtown waterfront park. Whereas it was impossible for the Council to fund all of Nolen's proposed improvements, several nevertheless were acted upon.

Some $19 million of real estate transfers were recorded in Sarasota in the first six months of 1925, a somewhat substantial sum for a town having a population of only 5,500 persons.[37] Naturally this wave of construction gave rise to many opportunities for architects and designers. Among those benefitting would be architect Thomas Reed Martin, who conceived nearly five hundred residences and commercial buildings including fifteen one-story stucco bungalows (with garages) in the Burns Court Historic District. Martin also drew plans for several fashionable homes along with ones for the Roth Cigar factory. M. Leo Elliot of Tampa conceived the Bay Haven and the Southside Schools, as well as Sarasota High School, the latter embracing Collegiate Gothic style. Alfred Clas was on the scene (the Crisp Building and Earle residence), as was Roy Benjamin who created the 4½ story Edwards Theatre. Lillias Piper, a prominent designer and decorator of New York City and Palm Beach, oversaw the El Patio Apartments. David Adler achieved local fame by planning the sixteen-acre Field Estate that contained several historic buildings, while Alex Browning and Francis James laid claim to the three-story Frances-Carlton Apartments that faced Sarasota Bay (complete with a domed observatory and mirador). T. Miller Bryan, together with developer Harry Rigby, oversaw nine buildings for the La Plaza Historic District in town. H. N. Hall designed the Sarasota Woman's Club building, and Fred Orr drew plans for the elegant Thomas home at 5030 Bay Shore Road.

Perhaps the most notorious developer in Sarasota during the Twenties boom was circus mogul John Ringling (1866–1936). Ringling's career is fairly well documented, especially his Florida years thanks to the scholarship of historian-author David Weeks.

Iowa-born Ringling had come to "The City of Glorified Opportunity" well before the real estate extravaganza of the Twenties got legs. But, like many, he was eventually sucked into the land boom's vortex. He had become a full-fledged millionaire owing to his financial interest in what became the Ringling Brothers and Barnum and Bailey Circus. His investment portfolio also included substantial or ownership positions in non–Florida real estate, along with ranches, cattle, oil wells, short-line railroads, and ultimately New York's Madison Square Garden. In 1925, his portrait would appear on the cover of *Time* magazine, the publication estimating Ringling's worth then at two hundred million (today's money: $2.6 billion).[38]

A one-time circus wagon driver and clown, Ringling reveled in the lifestyle of the rich and famous. He and his wife, Mable, maintained several other addresses along with yachts, private Pullman rail cars, luxury automobiles with uniformed chauffeurs, and a domestic staff, and they enjoyed international sojourns. Ringling also possessed a fabulous art collection (occasionally pledged to moneylenders) and the couple, who had no children, eventually built an opulent estate on Sarasota Bay together with a superb Italianate sanctuary to house the artwork. Ringling cultivated the company of moguls and luminaries, but we are also told that he rarely established close personal friendships—perhaps owing to his often imperious, coarse, and self-consumed nature. He spent lavishly in and about Sarasota, bestowed public benefactions and undertook daring development projects, sometimes—we are told—with financial legerdemain and ruthlessness. Ringling died in 1936. Regardless of his personality or behavior shortcomings, author Weeks reminds us that "the people of Sarasota and Florida were to inherit his entire estate."[39]

It was at the behest of friends that Mable and John Ringling first visited Sarasota—by yacht in 1910—after they were more or less snubbed by society folk in Tarpon Springs. A year later they purchased a winter home at Shell Beach (near the Sarasota airport) to supplement their Manhattan apartment and summer home in New Jersey that overlooked the Hudson River. In subsequent years, the Ringlings made large improvements to their winter abode ("Palms Elysian"), where they entertained family members and a few friends. Eventually the circus magnate would purchase additional acreage at Shell Beach for investment purposes.

Later, in 1923, Mable and John (mostly Mable) began planning an estate for their Sarasota parcel. The noted New York architect Dwight James Baum received the commission, and conceived for the couple a stunning $1.5 million Venetian Gothic edifice on Sarasota Bay. Built by Owen Burns and named *Ca' d'Zan* (Venetian dialect for "House of John"), the 36,000 square foot, fifty-six-room mansion opened in October 1925. Not only did the palatial mansion become the new Ringling winter home, but it would also serve to entertain prospective purchasers of Ringling-owned real estate.[40]

John Ringling believed strongly that Sarasota should never become a commercial maritime port, as did others in town. Rather, he envisioned Sarasota as a splendid resort community for society, captains of industry, bluebloods, and the moneyed class. To perfect his vision, he first acquired the defunct Yacht and Automobile Club at Cedar Point (now Golden Gate Point), which he converted and renamed Sunset Apartments. In addition to obtaining the Club's main building, the sale included numerous building lots. Owen Burns, who would begin forging a business relationship with Ringling, proceeded to dredge, fill, enlarge and erect a seawall around the setting, and for his efforts he acquired much of the Point's remaining acreage. Before long Ringling would make Burns his local agent and proxy, which proved especially helpful when the circus king was away on business, touring with the circus, or vacationing abroad. Although Burns and town fathers tried to convince Ringling that he should build a resort hotel at Cedar Point, he became convinced that one should only be built on one of Sarasota's barrier islands. This prompted Burns to build—on the mainland of Sarasota—his fabulous El Vernona Hotel.[41]

From the get-go, Sarasota's barrier islands greatly interested Ringling. Previously, in 1917, he had acquired St. Armands Key for development purposes, despite the fact no causeway or bridge existed between it and the mainland. But developing St. Armands and other barrier islands began to occupy much of Ringling's thinking. Accordingly, in June 1925, John Ringling Estates was chartered under Florida law with broad powers, from developing real estate to supplying electric power, from building hotels and golf courses to operating steamboats. Owen Burns was allowed to obtain a 25 percent stock interest in the firm. Over time Ringling's new corporation, or Burns, or all the parties would take title to land tracts on the barrier islands, together with some 2,000 acres on the southern end of Longboat Key. Exactly which party owned what was sometimes not manifestly clear.[42]

Owen Burns ultimately enlarged St. Armands and Coon Key, as well as the northern end of Lido Key and all of City Island. Infrastructure was installed in many locales along with "spec homes" and commercial buildings. To reach the keys from the mainland at Cedar Point, Ringling's new entity financed (and Owen Burns built) the Ringling Causeway—a wood and concrete structure with drawbridge, that the circus magnate personally opened

Dwight James Baum, who once worked with the legendary Stanford White, established his New York design firm in 1912. He conceived many projects in Florida, especially in the Sarasota area. He was distantly related to Frank Baum, creator of the *Wizard of Oz* books (courtesy Florida Memory, State Archives of Florida).

The El Vernona Hotel—pride and joy of Sarasota developer Owen Burns—was one of many magisterial hotels built in Florida during the 1920s. Conceived by Dwight Baum, it attracted a discriminating clientele. Eventually, John Ringling obtained ownership of the hostelry.

on New Year's Day, 1926. Afterwards, the causeway was opened to real estate dealers and their sales prospects, whereupon thousands of townspeople and visitors were allowed to view the island work of late. In the following year, Ringling magnanimously gifted the $750,000 causeway to the City of Sarasota, relieving his corporation of any future upkeep costs. When a municipal bond issue for a new recreation pier in Sarasota sputtered, it was Ringling who stepped in and purchased the remaining securities, again heightening the mogul's local image.[43]

It was at St. Armands that Ringling envisioned a master community of resort housing and shopping, a development that Ohio landscape architect and planner John Watson ably perfected for his superior. Causeway traffic from the Sarasota mainland fed into Harding Circle, named for the U.S. president whom Ringling desired as an island resident but who died before visiting. The famed Circle eventually sported Italian statuary that had been acquired by Ringling in Europe, together with an abundance of tropical landscaping. Exiting roads led motorists southwards to Lido Key and northwards to Longboat.[44]

The *pièce de résistance* of Ringling's barrier island endeavors would be a resort hotel, perhaps one like no other in Florida. News eventually broke that the Ritz-Carlton chain would erect one on the southern tip of Longboat Key—near today's Chart House Restaurant. However, the hotel chain required a good-faith deposit of $800,000 from Sarasota before the multi-million dollar edifice could be started. John Ringling's corporation subscribed $400,000 to the project and offered twenty acres of land for the hotel and an additional ten acres for truck and flower gardens. Sarasota, in turn, bonded itself for $400,000, but was only able to raise about half that amount. Nevertheless, construction commenced in March 1926, with an anticipated completion date of the following year.

Design details for the grandiose structure fell to the architectural firm of Warren and Wetmore in New York, who had conceived the chain's *magnum opus* in Manhattan as well as Grand Central Station. No detail would be spared on the Long Boat facility. Every court-yard, fountain, foyer, dining room and columned entranceway would embrace the finest of architectural details. But when Ringling began diverting funds for the hotel from the cor-poration, co-investor Owen Burns vehemently protested and ultimately brought legal pro-ceedings against the circus magnate. Progress on the hotel sputtered as the land boom fizzled, then it ceased. Not only was it never completed owing to finances—it was razed in 1965—but the manipulations and diversions ruptured the Ringling-Burns association.[45]

It should be noted that Ringling's older brother, Charles, was also on the Sarasota scene and established himself as an investor and capitalist. With John, the brothers would acquire nearly 66,000 acres of land in eastern Sarasota County, the so-called "Sugar Bowl" district where speculative oil drilling would one day occur. Like his brother, Charles had his own yacht, private Pullman rail car, and investment properties in downtown Sarasota including a bank and hotel. He and his wife, Edith, built a sumptuous $880,000 palace next to John's that utilized pink Etowah marble from Georgia; the landmark structure is today part of New College of Florida. Sadly, Charles enjoyed it for only six months before he passed away.

As the zany Twenties closed, the proverbial "Sword of Damocles" no doubt trembled over John Ringling. The myriad investments in Sarasota (and elsewhere) had required prodi-gious outlays of capital and the creation of burdensome debt. Added to this were the master's ongoing acquisitions of art, furnishings, and antiquities; the costs of maintaining a yacht

**One of many architectural gems conceived by Dwight Baum was the fabulous estate for Mable and John Ringling. The great treasure house of America fronts on Sarasota Bay. Ringling's nearby art museum also attracts visitors from around the world.**

and crew; funding trips abroad; and finding ways to finance a $1.5 million sanctuary that would house his art collection. (A superb Italian Renaissance building was completed for that purpose in 1929.)

With progress on the resort hotel halted over finances and litigation, the worst possible news now arrived: the fabled land boom of the Twenties was essentially over, just when many of Ringling's developments needed a steady stream of sales prospects and investors. Like most all Florida municipalities, Sarasota started to fall on hard times. To lift spirits, Ringling moved the winter headquarters of his circus to town in 1927 (at Beneva and Fruitville roads), but even this well-received act could not completely erase the economic doldrums of the city and county. Then the 1929 stock market crash occurred followed by the Great Depression.

Mable Ringling died two years after her stunning palazzo had been completed on Sarasota Bay. John Ringling was understandably devastated. The fortunes of Owen Burns also changed. His fabled El Vernona Hotel, badly run by a Ringling appointee, had been rendering zero profits. The hotel's mortgage had to be foreclosed, by financial friends of Ringling, whereupon the edifice was sold to Ringling himself which infuriated Burns even more. The lonely circus king would subsequently marry a rich widow, whom he later divorced at a cost of over $200,000 in attorney fees. Emily Buck Ringling then married the attorney.

With his health deteriorating, Ringling ended up pledging or selling many of his worldly assets to cover his financial defaults. At one point he even lost control of his beloved circus. After his death in 1936, more than one hundred lawsuits arose against the Ringling estate and its various entities, a tangled mess that took years and years to reconcile. Fortunately, John Ringling's long-held dream and directive would be fulfilled: that his stupendous estate on Sarasota Bay, his superlative art collection and the glorious sanctuary that housed it would survive intact. Today they are owned by the State of Florida for residents and visitors to forever admire and enjoy.[46]

# St. Petersburg

Another Florida city deeply affected by the Twenties land boom was St. Petersburg, the famed "Sunshine City" known far and wide for its broad avenues, sparkling beaches, salubrious weather, and moderate cost of living. Today boasting nearly 250,000 inhabitants, "St. Pete" is now the fifth most populated city in Florida, in fact the largest one that is not a county seat. Inviting green benches dotted the downtown district in the Roaring Twenties, their occupants incessantly chatting about one topic: real estate, real estate, real estate. Period literature extolled the fact that St. Pete enjoyed 361 days of sunshine each year. On rainy days, the *St. Petersburg Evening Independent* gave away free copies!

It was in 1875 that General John Williams, a Michigan farmer, acquired a considerable tract of land abutting Tampa Bay, his dream being to build a great city. Transportation facilities, though, were sorely lacking until Williams struck a deal with an exiled Russian nobleman, Peter Demens. In exchange for certain parcels that Williams owned, Demens terminated his Orange Belt Railroad at what would become St. Petersburg, assuring communication with the outside world. (His line from Sanford later became part of the Atlantic Coast Railroad.) According to local legend, the duo named their community by flipping a coin. Demens won the toss and christened the setting after his Russian birthplace, St. Petersburg. Williams, mindful of his Michigan roots, established St. Pete's first hotel—the Detroit—which the talented Demens built. Later, in 1892, St. Petersburg became incorporated, the State of Florida being a mere forty-seven years old at the time.

Before long, fish wholesalers opened shop on the railroad pier in St. Pete. The shipping channel was dredged, and improvements were made to the little port's facilities. A wealthy Philadelphia publisher, Frank Allston Davis, furnished residents and businesses with electric power beginning in 1897, then he acquired the local telephone utility. (F. A. Davis, medical book publishers, functions to this day.) A decade later, Davis opened St. Pete's first trolley line, acquired a large portfolio of real estate and founded nearby Pinellas Park.[47] America's first regularly scheduled airline service—St. Pete to Tampa—began operations in 1914, the population of St. Pete then being around 4,100 persons. With each passing year, even during the First World War, winter tourists and visitors began to multiply.

Despite the encouraging start, a bittersweet mood would permeate St. Pete in 1918–19. The country rejoiced when the Armistice was signed in November 1918, but that same year the business empire of F. A. Davis—the St. Petersburg Investment Company—failed. The news shocked the community. City fathers, convinced that certain components of the Davis empire could not fail, stepped into the fray and authorized the municipality to acquire many of the firm's assets by issuing bonds.[48] In fact, many municipal improvements made during the 1920s would be financed with even more bond issues—for water and gas works, sanitary and storm sewers, streets, water lines, parks, street lights, a recreation pier, and harbor improvements. Such indebtedness in 1923 stood at $3.7 million; by 1927 it reached $23.7 million.[49]

On the brighter side of 1919 was the fact that record numbers of "motor tourists" had begun to arrive. Henry Ford had put the cost of a motorcar in the range of most every American. This, coupled with the prosperity following the First World War, allowed countless northerners to come to Florida, many for the first time. Other tourists, homeseekers, and real estate investors arrived by train and ship. As one visitor observed, "As my train sped through the Carolinas and Georgia I looked out of the window and saw the highway crowded with cars—tin Lizzies, purring limousines, trucks, open touring coupes and motorcycles—some piled high with tents, farming tools, suitcases, pets, and children—a never-ending stream flowing to Florida in the summertime."[50] Many of these persons had pockets bulging with cash and the desire to invest in a vacant lot or winter home.

Among those also arriving by car were Tin Can Tourists, visitors who lived in or alongside their vehicles—thanks to a knock-down tent—for weeks or months at a time. Suitcases could be seen tied down to the running boards along with a take-apart stove. Beneath a false floor in the tonneau, the Tin Canners often stored kitchen utensils, a table, folding chairs and a water bucket. They congregated in camps and usually lived on canned food. A haven for them was established in St. Pete at Eighteenth and Second streets, called Tent City.

By August, 1920, some 120 Tin Can Tourist families were encamped in St. Pete, and to their delight the municipality freely furnished them with water, lights, toilet facilities, garbage collection, along with shower and bath facilities.[51] But the transients were sometimes ridiculed for their thriftiness, the popular jab being "They arrived with one shirt, a $20 bill, and never changed either." But St. Pete welcomed the Tin Canners as well as the manifold other tourists who took advantage of traditional accommodations in the city. Despite a sharp recession in America in early 1920, the economy of St. Pete suffered little thanks to this influx of humanity. Small wonder, therefore, that many observers felt that 1919 was the start here of the famed Twenties land boom.

There was no greater figure churning out St. Pete ballyhoo and hokum before and during the land boom than John Lodwick, who arrived in the Sunshine City from Ohio in fall 1918. Largely known in the Buckeye State for promoting sports events, Lodwick began his work as a freelance writer for the *St. Petersburg Times* and later worked as press agent for the St. Petersburg Chamber of Commerce. In his graduate degree thesis about the creative promoter and public relations expert, Nevin Sitler relates that Lodwick wanted "to create headlines and datelines displaying St. Petersburg, Florida in publications across the nation featuring Tampa Bay's beauty and ideal climate as a backdrop for every story."[52] One of the promoter's techniques was to interview and photograph out-of-state visitors, whereupon he would send the pictures and copy back to their hometown newspaper, the theory being that locals would read it and come to St. Pete to find out why one of their own found the setting so inviting. The technique worked.[53]

The year 1919 also marked the opening of a drawbridge between the mainland of St. Pete and Pass-a-Grille, on the southern end of Long Key. Spearheading the project was the flamboyant investor William McAdoo, who was attempting to develop much of St. Petersburg Beach.[54] The rickety wooden bridge (25 cent toll to get on the island, nothing to get off) was the first to connect the city center with the turquoise waters of the Gulf of Mexico. The setting of Pass-a-Grille had likely been named by fisher folk who stopped near the pass to cook their seafood meals—grille meaning broiling.[55]

As the Twenties unfolded, more and more tourists, visitors, and investors became interested in St. Pete real estate. This, in turn, gave rise to more real estate firms and salespeople, auctions, and developers. In fact, many employed in the industry began to prosper as never before. A keen observer of the goings-on was real estate mogul Walter P. Fuller, who not only witnessed and participated in the Twenties boom but actually published a colorful book about the era. "The story is one of the periodic epidemics of gambling that have swept this country three or four times each century; a something-for-nothing fever with more color and substance than most; a disease born of the intoxicating tonic of Florida sunshine and sand, but bottomed—believe it or not—on Henry Ford's famous $5 a day minimum wage and the millions of cheap cars that flooded our highways as a result. World War 1 and the sharp recession that followed also helped initiate the bubble."[56]

Fuller himself got his first taste of the "effortless riches" in 1920, when he purchased forty acres of land at the southwest corner of Gulf Coast Highway and Park Boulevard in Pinellas Park for $45.27. Four years later he and his partner sold the parcel for $40,000 cash! "A queer thing about booms is that after they run for awhile, in spite of the hoots and skepticism of the cautious and pessimistic, gradually the more conservative become convinced that here is 'a sure thing' and it's then the real fun starts."[57]

Although one might think that the sale of new and existing homes drove the Twenties land boom in St. Pete, it was actually the sale of vacant building lots. Fuller confirms this in his book after he examined real estate advertisements in the *St. Petersburg Daily Times* in

1925, the boom's landmark year. For example, the issue for Sunday, November 22, sported 134 pages, eighty-nine pages of which contained advertisements. Of that amount, nearly 75 percent (approximately sixty-seven pages) were real estate ads, 98 percent of such having full pages. A whopping 70 percent of all the real estate ads were for vacant building lots; 10 percent were for acreage; 2 percent were employment ads issued by real estate firms, developers and promoters; and 1.5 percent of the ads were for real estate leases.[58]

According to Fuller, "a 1925 salesman was a single purpose animal, trained for a short burst of speed. Office men got the prospects. The salesman was armed with a sales kit and a single selling story. He was selling one product, a vacant lot that was 'sure to double in value within 90 days.' He showed the prospect, wined and dined him, if necessary, bluffed, cajoled or talked the prospect out of 'earnest money,' and he was done. Others closed the deal."[59] The lots themselves might be isolated parcels in St. Pete or platted as a group, or they might be found inside a development. Numerous developments were unveiled in St. Pete during the boom and most had an impressive entranceway, though one hastens to add that infrastructure (electricity, streets, water, sewer lines, etc.) ran the gamut of being included, partially included, or the developer failed outright to include such.

Space limitations preclude a list of every subdivision hatched in St. Pete in the Twenties; however, among the signature developments there was Snell Isle (promulgated by C. Perry

Lavish hotels dotted the 1920s landscape of St. Petersburg. Developer "Handsome Jack" Taylor spared no expense on the Rolyat—his last name spelled backwards. Kiehnel & Elliot drew the plans. Today it helps form the Gulfport campus of Stetson University's School of Law (courtesy Florida Memory, State Archives of Florida).

nell, the city's biggest and richest developer); Pasadena Estates (developed by "Handsome Jack" Taylor), which contained a magnificent Spanish-styled hotel named the Rolyat (the name Taylor spelled backwards) and which later became part of Stetson University College of Law; Kenwood and Lakewood Estates, both developed by Charles R. Hall, who later gave the city Seminole Park; Jungle Prada, located on the city's western edge fronting Boca Ciega Bay, which was put forward by the aforementioned Walter P. Fuller (the Jungle Country Club Hotel today being part of Admiral Farragut Academy); while Shore Acres and part of St. Petersburg Beach became the pride and joy of developer N. J. Upham. The developers were quite different from one another in terms of background, education, and demeanor, but all had one common thread: they shared a profound faith in the future of St. Petersburg.

According to author Karl Grismer, "at least two-thirds of all the land on the lower peninsula, south of Pinellas Park, had been subdivided. It was later established that at least 150,000 building lots were placed on the market during the land boom—possibly 300,000 would have been more nearly accurate."[60] At the boom's peak in 1925, more than fifty subdivisions were operating in St. Pete. Most of the realty offices were located on Central Avenue. Grismer confirms that "in the fall of 1925 there were nearly 6,000 licensed real estate salesmen. Most of the salesmen wore knickerbockers, according to the fashion of the day."[61] One broker employed no one except retired ministers, for ex-ministers had little trouble in gaining the "confidence" of prospective buyers. Often assisting the legions of salesmen

St. Petersburg is studded with glorious homes that were built in the Roaring Twenties. Among them was this masterpiece conceived by architect Harry Cunningham for client Louis Raquet. It was christened "Granada Gables."

were "bird dogs" (many were women) who "talked-up" real estate to tourists and prospects wherever and whenever possible, whereupon the unsuspecting were collared and brought to the real estate magicians.[62]

In 1920, the population of St. Petersburg stood at 14,000 persons; by 1926, nearly 30,000 could be counted. The circulation of the *St. Petersburg Times* went from 3,137 customers in 1921 to nearly 11,000 in 1927. The paper would employ nearly two hundred workers in 1925. In the following year the operation would move into a new, eight-story office tower. Between 1920 and 1925, in order to keep up with the influx of people and development, the City of St. Petersburg spent nearly $12 million on new roads and bridges. Further, it opened a new million-dollar municipal pier in July 1926 that permitted cars to actually drive out upon it. In that same year the 260-acre Piper-Fuller Flying Field opened, the first in St. Pete, the third in the entire state. The city's skyline also began to change as new hotels and commercial buildings went up. Bank deposits soared, too, from $5.9 million in 1920 to an astounding $46 million by 1926. Building permits surged as well, from $2.8 million in 1920 to $24 million in 1925. Without question, the Twenties land boom had an enduring, transformational effect.[63]

Raymond Arsenault, the preeminent historian of St. Petersburg, reminds us that "more than any other single development, the opening of the Gandy Bridge was responsible for raising the boom to its dizzying apogee of 1925."[64] Prior to its construction, St. Petersburg and Pinellas County were separated from the mainland of Florida by Tampa Bay. The shortest route around the northern edge of the Bay, via Oldsmar, was forty-three miles. However, a bridge across the upper arm of Old Tampa Bay could reduce that jaunt to nineteen miles. And that was the motivation behind the Gandy Bridge project.

George Shepard "Dad" Gandy, a New Jersey native raised in Philadelphia, possessed an extensive transportation and construction background. A staunch believer in electrical traction, he built over a hundred miles of trolley lines in Pennsylvania and eventually became involved with the St. Pete trolley enterprise of publisher F. A. Davis, a fellow Philadelphian. Gandy conceived his bridge idea across Old Tampa Bay when he first visited St. Pete in 1902, though he felt that the potential traffic then between the two cities would be insufficient to cover costs and upkeep. But thirteen years later—having opened the La Plaza Theatre in St. Pete in 1912—Gandy initiated surveys of the bridge using the shortest possible route having the shallowest depth. Several enterprises were formed to oversee the entire project. In 1917, Gandy applied for a bridge permit from the Department of War in Washington, D. C. After no little opposition from rivals, the grant was made in February 1918. (Approval from the Florida legislature had been secured the year before.) But just as Gandy was about to launch construction, America found itself in the First World War. Construction materials and manpower became almost impossible to obtain as a result of the hostilities along with other obstacles.[65]

Fortunately, the setbacks proved temporary and in the fall of 1922—some twenty years after Gandy had conceived the plan and seven years after the surveys had been completed—financing and construction started. Finding all the necessary funds took a mere six months, thanks to an aggressive sale of preferred and common stock by a Gandy adjutant. No bonds were needed. It took 1,500 workers and some two years to complete the Gandy Bridge, which was hailed as the longest drawbridge in the world at the time—3¼ miles of causeways and a reinforced concrete bridge 2.5 miles long that was twenty-two feet wide. The structure was formally opened by Florida Governor Cary Hardee on 20 November 1924 by untying a rope of flowers in front of sixteen other state governors and a crowd of some 30,000 persons.[66]

No fewer than ten large hotels arose in St. Pete between 1923 and 1926. Among them were the seventeen-story Ponce de Leon; the 300-room Soreno (built by Soren Lund and the first to cost a million dollars to construct); the eleven-story Pheil Hotel (owner and ex-mayor Abram Pheil died before it was finished); the 118-room Suwanee; and the popular Mason Hotel which overlooked Williams Park (owner Franklin Mason ultimately built seventy-four other buildings). The previously-mentioned Rolyat at Pasadena Estates (designed by Pittsburgh architect Richard Kiehnel) sported superb Mediterranean Revival details as did the Jungle Country Club Hotel which Henry Taylor designed. The 312-room Don Ce-Sar, still in its flamingo pink dress and a gem on the St. Pete beachfront, opened in December, 1927, at a cost of $1.4 million. (Owner Thomas Rowe—born in Boston, orphaned at four, educated in England—named it after Don Cesar de Bazan, the principal male character in the musical opera *Mariana*.)

Perhaps the most lavish hostelry of all was the spectacular 375-room Vinoy Park, which was built by Pennsylvania oilman Aymer Vinoy Laughner on a twelve-acre site in the downtown waterfront park area. Conceived by architect Henry L. Taylor in Mediterranean Revival style and erected in ten months, the $3.5 million structure is today known as the Renaissance Vinoy Resort and Golf Club. In his authoritative history about St. Petersburg, Raymond Arsenault notes that "the Vinoy Park had everything: Moorish arches and tile-lined cupolas, elegant Georgian-style ballrooms with leaded glass windows and carved beam ceilings, scores of crystal chandeliers and ornamental urns, and 367 lavishly appointed rooms. A single room went for fifteen dollars a night during the mid–1920s, the highest rate in town, but a bargain considering that the hotel promised to surround its customers with the "quintessence of beauty" including "the blue sea and the sapphire sky and the same profusion of vivid flowers as greeted the earliest Spanish explorers on Florida shores."[67]

Whereas Laughner, along with his directors and architect, made all the key financial and design decisions about the facility, virtually all others regarding the Vinoy's furnishings, operations and personnel fell to the Managing Director, usually a coveted position in the hospitality world. Ultimately, the Vinoy board selected one of the best in the business: Karl P. Abbott, whose family owned and operated several resort hotels in the beautiful White Mountains of New Hampshire. After the pageant of autumn and before the snow began to fly, the Abbott family came south year-after-year to run Florida hotels in the winter tourist season, such as the posh Royal Palm in Fort Myers or the illustrious Gasparilla Inn in Boca Grande.

Karl Abbott eventually wrote a highly entertaining book about his life, devoting an entire chapter on how he was appointed to the Vinoy and what he achieved. "This was no project to play around with," Abbott relates, for "the hotel had to be completed, equipped and furnished and the grounds landscaped by the first day of the New Year, 1926."[68] Shortly after signing his employment contract with Laughner, Abbott headed north to New York City where he rented an entire floor of rooms at the Commodore Hotel. Since Laughner and his board had little knowledge of what it took to furnish a new hotel, much less how much funding would be needed, Abbott insisted they come to New York City. After the furniture in each of the rented rooms was removed, Abbott filled them with sales reps and their merchandise, and in this way the Laughner entourage were able to inspect merchandise first-hand and make the ever-important decisions about everything from linen supplies to carpeting, from silverware to flatware. In fact they met with all manner of representatives that sold drapery, elevators, printing equipment, and fire-fighting equipment; safe and vault people; refrigerator salesmen; office fixture folks; lamp and lampshade reps; plumbing fixture people; etc.

After the contracts for these essentials were let, Abbott then opened a New York office for the Vinoy so as to handle press relations, advertising, contacting some three hundred tourist bureaus, organizing a convention sales organization, getting out attractive color brochures, arranging for music and musicians to come to St. Pete, contracting for bulk food, hiring some three hundred employees, buying their uniforms, and arranging for their transportation to Florida, all this long before the age of computers.

I had promised the owners that we would open the Vinoy Park Hotel with a New Year's Eve party. That was a mistake! Three weeks before the hotel was to open the crew arrived to get the place ready. It wasn't ready to get ready! The dormitory to house and feed the help was not ready, much less furnished. The help camped out wherever they could, and we fed them in the main kitchen amid a clutter of uncrated equipment. The last twenty-four hours the dining room and housekeeping crews worked straight through, setting up the dining room and guest rooms. Thirty thousand dollars' worth of linen had to be laundered and put on the shelves. The hall carpets arrived in St. Petersburg by ship in such large rolls that we didn't have a door wide enough to get them into the building, so each carpet had to be unrolled outdoors and pulled up with block-and-tackle through the windows. Forty-eight hours before the hotel opened there was still no refrigeration. The Vinoy was due to open for dinner at exactly seven o'clock that New Year's eve. At five-thirty men were still laying the oriental rugs in the lobby, and electricians were feverishly trying out the lighting system in the huge ballroom while groups of housemen were giving the last cleaning up to the public space.

The owners wanted a show, and they were going to get it. Every light in every room on the front of the entire building was lighted. The great hotel that had been in darkness all these months sprang suddenly came to life. I looked out of my office window ... great crowds had gathered on the plaza in front of the hotel and down the waterfront looking up at the brilliant new Vinoy. It was now twenty-five minutes before the deadline! At five minutes to seven, four tall handsome doormen stepped out to the main entrance. They wore black boots with white kid tops, white trousers, long powdered-blue coats, and tall silk hats with a cockade at the side. At exactly seven o'clock they opened the doors and the great crowd entered the sparkling new, beautifully-appointed hotel and milled in the lobby and public rooms.

After allowing the crowd to oh-and-ah for five minutes, the clerk at the front desk pressed a buzzer. Out from the west wing marched the Superintendent of Service with the entire uniformed force—bellboys, pages, elevator operators, porters, and housemen, all in new powder-blue uniforms. Their shoes shone, their uniforms were pressed to a razor's edge. He brought them up to attention and then gave them the "Dismiss!" The bellboys took their stations, the elevator men manned the elevators, the clerks, cashiers and office force took over the desk. The two little pages—about four and a half feet tall, in blue trousers and vermillion jackets—started to page mythical people. The show received an ovation from the crowd.

Those who had dinner engagements proceeded to the dining room. At precisely seven-fifteen ... the entire dining room staff walked in: captains, wine stewards, waitresses, bus boys, and cutest of all, six pretty little brunettes with slanting eyes and plucked eyebrows, dressed in beautiful Chinese robes with their hair dressed high on top of their heads with huge black combs—they were to pass the relish trays, rolls, and later the petit fours. (I searched New York for those robes and combs!). At seven forty-five the entire crowd was dining at its leisure and the hotel was functioning as if it had been open for months. This is what I mean by opening a hotel with a crew that knows their business."[69]

Our vignette of St. Pete of the Twenties closes with a brief tribute to perhaps the greatest developer of that remarkable era: C. Perry Snell, Jr. (1869–1942). Snell left a remarkable legacy in St. Petersburg, one that is still greatly admired and cherished. Whereas many of his colleagues did not always conduct their affairs with the public in an honest, upright manner, Snell based his entire business reputation—despite being aggressive and sometimes ruthless—on professionalism, integrity and an eye for taste, even when the proverbial "chips were down."

A native of Kentucky who trained as a druggist, Snell began his real estate career in 1905 using a share of his wife's money. Four years later he began building homes in the northeastern section of St. Pete. In time, the transplant would develop an architectural passion for all things Italian, Spanish, and Moorish, which inspired him to help introduce Mediterranean Revival style to St. Pete. His work at Coffee Pot Boulevard, Beach Drive, and adjoining streets consisted of stucco and tile homes. His creative efforts in the Old Northeast sector resulted in one of the most stylish neighborhoods in all of Florida. Snell's career in real estate development continued to his death in 1942, "resulting in the improvement of more property in value than any other one man or group has ever developed on Pinellas Peninsula."[70]

Snell's investing strategy began on a modest scale. A suitable real estate parcel having potential was identified, he acquired it then it was later resold at profit. At times he purchased real estate with partners, his partnership with J. C. Hamlett lasting more than a decade whereupon Snell bought out his interest and dispensed with partners altogether. The purchase of small parcels gave way to larger and costlier properties, sometimes risky ones. When necessary, he obtained mortgage monies. Lot buying and "flipping" eventually led to home building and subdivisions. With each success, Snell's pool of capital increased. In time the ex-druggist would develop all the property east of Fourth Street, from Fifth Avenue north to the north limit of Snell Isle. He and his associates also developed much of the land around Mirror and Crescent lakes, plus he undertook two developments on the keys, one of them at Bennett Beach near Pass-a-Grille.

One of Snell's most impressive achievements was the Snell Arcade Building at Fourth and Central, a $750,000 commercial structure regarded as one of the most beautiful in the South. Its "arcade" at street level consisted of retail shops. Snell eventually lost the building, completed in 1928 and designed by the famed architect Richard Kiehnel, during the Great Depression. (The structure still stands today, many floors containing condominiums). It should also be noted that it was Snell who gave the city a major portion of its waterfront— from Thirteenth Avenue north to Coffee Pot. Snell was also the city's foremost world traveler and a patron of the arts.

Thanks to the scholarship of Judy Lowe Wells, an excellent account of Snell's life now exists.[71] Chapter Eleven of her book focuses on Snell's greatest visual and housing extravaganza—Snell Isle. Bounded by Coffee Pot Bayou, Tampa Bay and Smack's Bayou (later called Placido Bayou), "The development of this property was definitely Snell's largest project. With an eye on achievement, he set about in 1924 to dredge and fill the shoreline when only

Elegant subdivisions also dotted the St. Pete landscape during the Twenties. Perhaps the ultimate was Snell Isle, developed by the legendary Perry Snell. The desirable enclave is studded with stunning homes, many of which now sell in the millions.

thirty-nine of the 275 acres were reportedly above water at high tide. During the develop-ment phase of Snell Isle, the weekly payroll for the workers was said to have been $25,000."[72]

From the get-go, Snell believed that the Snell Isle would require "a high moral obliga-tion" because of its stunning location and his deep appreciation for all things beautiful. A reinforced concrete seawall would surround the area, and sufficient land would be trucked in to elevate the setting substantially above sea level for good drainage. Utilities would be pre-installed, including underground electric and telephone lines, along with sidewalks, storm and sanitary sewers, streets and street lighting. The streets themselves would be broad and literally wind through the development. Park and plaza land would be embellished with statuary from Europe. A hotel was planned for but never built, though a golf course and clubhouse were—the latter having minarets, heavily bracketed cornices, keyhole arches, and onion domes. (The Andalusian–like edifice is now part of the Renaissance Vinoy Golf Club.)

Lots in Snell Isle were offered for sale in October 1925, starting at $7,500. Within a few days of the opening bell some $7 million in sales were recorded. Deed restrictions were in evidence: no outbuildings, no visible clotheslines, boat docks had to be pre-approved; only white or Caucasian persons could purchase, no signs could be displayed, nor could any owner retain livestock. Snell's sales manager for the project eventually became Walter P. Fuller, whom he housed in an elegantly furnished sales office on Central Avenue and Fourth Street. Immediately after the successful sales launch, Snell left for Europe and spent about a million dollars on more artwork and antiquities. Sadly, he returned to find a town that had "gone bust." Though development of Snell Isle temporarily halted and some purchasers defaulted on their lot purchases, Snell eventually resumed his efforts and honored every commitment—unlike other boom-era developers who eventually stopped altogether or out-right bailed.

Not only did Snell himself build spec homes in Snell Isle, including one for himself, but other developers bought lots and erected products as well. Among the latter was Samuel V. Schooley, who purchased lots near Coffee Pot Bayou whereupon he commissioned noted architects, like the aforementioned Richard Kiehnel, to design prestigious residences, some of which today sell in the millions of dollars. As one of Schooley's period promotional pieces stated, "This home is ideally located for viewing the rising sun and especially the full moon in all of its gorgeous splendor, rising over the limpid waters of Coffee Pot Bayou and Tampa Bay, o'er which the gentle zephyrs blow. Embodied in the Schooley Homes are liberal features incorporating every desirable and artistic phase of the Mediterranean environment plus the departures of improvement that please individual American tastes and conveniences. They are homes that encourage real fascination for abiding in comfort and permanency."[73]

Although family, friends, and business associates sometimes had varying opinions of Perry Snell the man—from a brilliant man to a gambler, from a tough bargainer to someone having a disagreeable personality—the fact remains that he was an icon in the boom years and one of St. Pete's greatest boosters. His achievements, like the era in which he found success, are forever etched into Florida history.

## Davis Islands and Davis Shores

South of Tampa's inviting Hyde Park neighborhood and across a short bridge lay the famed Davis Islands. The renowned setting boasts Tampa General Hospital, landscaped parkways and streets, businesses, hotels, apartments, and homes, with many structures exhibiting pseudo–Spanish, Mediterranean and Italian architecture. During the 1920s the

Davis Islands would emerge as one of the most distinctive developments in all of Florida that was inaugurated by one human being: David Paul Davis.

As the principal center of population and commerce on Florida's west coast, Tampa suffered less than most municipalities after the great land boom petered out in 1926. But even with its strong industrial backbone, which most boom-era settings sorely lacked, it was really not until 1928 that Tampa's painful real estate deflation began to recover. One of the very first tests of the turnaround was a public auction of seven buildings on February 1 at the Davis Islands Country Club. Among the properties to be auctioned were the Bay Isle Building (a two-story office structure), the Biscayne Hotel, the Augustine Apartment house (fifty-two furnished apartments), and the three-story Davis Islands Garage that held 183 cars. Had he lived, D. P. Davis—as he wished to be addressed in the media—would likely have been soured by the proceedings, but the successor firm of his island Utopia, Stone and Webster of Boston, who ended up completing the project through a subsidiary, needed to create cash flow and retire certain liabilities from the endeavor.[74]

Tampa began the Roaring Twenties on a sour note as well. The unusual prosperity that the city enjoyed as a result of the war years had basically passed. According to author Karl Grismer, "The first blow suffered by the city was the closing down of the Tampa Dock Company and the Oscar Daniels Company which had employed more than 5,000 men during 1918. To add to the city's troubles the cigar industry was prostrated by a general strike."[75] Cigar workers wanted shorter hours and more pay, while cigar manufacturers supported an "open shop" (membership in the union being optional). Negotiations eventually collapsed. The union struck, all 159 cigar factories closed, and 7,613 men were thrown out of work for the rest of 1920. The financial gloom continued as the nation passed through a sharp recession as a result of America adjusting to a peacetime economy. Then, a destructive hurricane came ashore.[76]

Setbacks aside, Tampa—as well as other Florida locales—also witnessed then stirrings of another kind: tourists and newcomers flocking to the state in greater numbers. "Some of the adventurers came in palatial yachts, ships and private railroad coaches. Others less affluent came by Pullman and day coach. And many, many more others came in automobiles they had never used before for long journeys. Now, with the war over, the proud owners had the chance to ramble southward. To make sure they would have a place to sleep and something to eat, they piled their cars with tents, and bedding, and great boxes of canned food. They soon became known as Tin Can Tourists."[77]

To accommodate these winter visitors makeshift tourist camps sprang up almost overnight, though many Florida towns made the point of extending no hospitality whatsoever. Tampa did. In fact at DeSoto Park the motor tourists banded together in the 1921–1922 winter season and organized the "Tin Can Tourists of the World." In retrospect these tourists and their conventional counterparts, including those that came by rail and water, dumped millions of dollars into the Florida economy in the Twenties, not only on food and lodgings but for building lots and homes. According to author Grismer, they were the land boom's progenitors.

Grismer goes on to say that "the greatest activity in high-class residential properties [in Tampa] occurred on Interbay Peninsula, due in large measure to the development work done years before in the Bayshore and Palma Ceia sections."[78] Development of Interbay was given a tremendous boost during the winter of 1922–1923 when it became certain that the long-talked about Gandy Bridge to St. Petersburg would become a reality, it finally opening on 20 November 1924. Other notable Interbay subdivisions included New Suburb Beautiful, Belmar, Virginia Park, Sunset Park, and Two Pines. As the boom soared in 1923–1924, choice properties that once sold for $50 an acre zoomed to nearly $10,000.

Other developments flourishing in the metro Tampa area included Forest Hills, Parkland Estates, Beach Park, and Temple Terrace, the latter having been developed in northeastern Hillsborough County by the Burks Hamner-Collins Gillett syndicate. (It was planted with Temple oranges developed by M. E. Gillett, father of Collins.) A subsidiary, Temple Terrace Estates, Inc., proceeded to develop a golf course, country club, streets, and Mediterranean-style homes along with a hotel and an apartment building. Temple Terraces, Inc. developed 5,000 acres of orange groves, then the largest in the world. In 1924, part of Temple Terraces changed gears from being strictly an orange grove development to an upscale residential development called Temple Crest.[79] But for many, the most spectacular development of all in greater Tampa was not the foregoing but the fabled Davis Islands.

What had initially caught the interest of D. P. Davis were two islands and mudflats in Hillsborough Bay. Big Grassy Island (104.5 acres) and Little Grassy Island (16.3 acres) were once part of the Fort Brooke military reservation created in 1824. Through subsequent years the ownership of each had changed. Little Grassy was often submerged in strong high tides, while Big Grassy usually remained dry. (Both islands were underwater in the aforementioned hurricane of 1921.) But it was not D. P. Davis who first thought about developing the islands. That vision belonged to the aforementioned Tampa developer Burks Hamner, who also helped develop Forest Hills, Parkland Estates and Golfland. In brief, Hamner visualized man-made islands sitting atop the smaller natural ones, a dream that Davis would eventually exploit.

Rodney Kite-Powell, curator of the Tampa Bay History Center and America's foremost authority on Davis, notes in several works that the developer had been born in 1885 at the resort town of Green Cove Springs, on the St. Johns River. His father, George Davis, served aboard steamboats. Eventually the Davis family moved to Tampa, where the father became a marine engineer with the "Favorite Line" of steamboats that plied Tampa Bay and nearby waters. According to Kite-Powell, "D.P." grew up selling newspapers, clerking for a law firm, and later serving as a steamboat mate with his father. In 1904 he began working for Knight and Wall, a Tampa hardware and sporting goods store. Three years later Davis opened a real estate partnership known as Davis and Arnold, but for reasons not known he became a book-keeper the following year.[80]

Forever restless, D. P. Davis eventually moved to New York City and left there for Colon, Panama, to sell real estate, He returned to New York City in 1910. Before long, though, the wanderlust struck again, and next we find the future developer in Buenos Aires, possibly running a cattle business. In late 1914 or early 1915 he relocated to Jacksonville where he married Marjorie Merritt. A short stint as a shoe salesman followed. He then joined a movie film exchange company where, in time, he became an officer of the firm. But in 1919, Davis tossed in the towel and moved his family to the Magic City of Miami where he might again cast his lot in the world of real estate.[81]

Shakespeare made Brutus once speak, "There is a tide in the affairs of men which, taken at the flood, leads on to fortune." That line from *Julius Caesar* best describes what next happened to David Paul Davis. "Noticing that a developer had tried to sell some lots but had been turned down because the subdivision was two and one-half miles from Miami City Hall—a distance too far the real estate men decreed—Davis offered to advertise the lots at his own expense if he could raise the price from $165 a piece to $275 and keep the profits. The developer agreed to the proposition with Davis spending one thousand dollars on advertising in the daily newspapers and selling all lots within a short time."[82]

The foregoing experience in lot buying and reselling allowed Davis the opportunity to accumulate some capital. From here the short, blue-eyed Davis now moved into the field of development and subdivisions. Organizing United Realty, he christened his first development project Commercial Biltmore, which was located in the Miami suburb of Buena Vista. From the get-go, Davis pursued two strategies: completing all promised infrastructure to purchasers and aggressively advertising the setting. In the non-business section of Commercial Biltmore he would erect bungalows having Colonial and Federal design influences. The project—finished in late 1921—proved a big success and allowed for another in Buena Vista: Shadowland, strictly a residential neighborhood. Fancy stone columns marked its entrance, and inside the development there were wide streets, sidewalks and tropical landscaping. The average cost of a building lot was about $2,500.

Once again Davis hit the jackpot, which further enhanced his financial condition and permitted the unveiling of yet another development: Shadowland Extension. An aggressive newspaper advertising campaign for the development began in January 1922. In return, the *Miami Herald* also ran favorable "stories" about the development and its creator, a technique often used by the newspaper trade for regular advertisers. Other Davis communities in Miami included Bellaire and Alta Vista. "All were successful ... and Davis realized an estimated five million dollars or more from his Miami ventures.[83]

The year 1922 also proved to be a sad time for Davis, for his wife Marjorie died shortly after giving birth to their second child—David Paul Davis, Jr. Fortunately, family members came to Miami to assist the distressed husband, thereby allowing him time to complete his realty endeavors. In January 1924, Davis and his two sons exited the Miami scene, about four years after the family first arrived. (He allowed his development firm, D. P. Davis, Inc., to remain open.) One of the reasons why he left was that persistent dream he had of developing several grassy islands in Tampa's Hillsborough Bay.

According to Kite-Powell, before Davis actually left Miami he became involved with another Florida development—Carleton Terrace in Cocoa, the latter an attractive hamlet consisting then of some 1,500 persons. In December 1923, the Cocoa newspaper announced that Miami developer Davis had purchased a large waterfront tract to accommodate upscale housing. Milton Davis, brother of D.P., who had come to his brother's aid when his wife passed away in Miami, would be a partner in the undertaking. The tract itself was acquired by D.P.'s Miami real estate firm, United Realty. In April 1924, a development plat was filed in Brevard County. A local real estate firm, Trafford Realty, was named another partner—the firm's owner having first interested Davis in developing the picturesque setting. Milton Davis ultimately oversaw the project.

According to the late James Covington of the University of Tampa, "The thoughts of D. P. Davis now turned to those mosquito-infested islands in Hillsborough Bay where he had hunted rabbits as a boy. It was Burks L. Hamner, developer of Temple Terrace and organizer of B. L. Hamner Realty Company, who brought the attention of Davis to the Tampa Bay area where many opportunities were still available. With his Miami sales training, Davis would transform these islands into profitable real estate ventures."[84]

The first hurdle Davis faced was actually acquiring the islands and the adjoining mudflats. Whereas he readily obtained the publicly-owned portion of Big Grassy Island from its rightful owners for $150,000, title to Little Grassy Island (along with the non-public portions of Big Grassy and all adjacent submerged lands of both islands) rested with the City of Tampa. To guide the sticky acquisition, Davis wisely engaged Giddings Mabry as counsel, a former attorney for the City of Tampa and Hillsborough County.

But city officials, unsure of how much Davis would end up dredging and filling, did not immediately give their assent to the project. Undeterred, Davis then initiated a public relations campaign. Among those eventually supporting the Davis proposal were the Tampa Board of Realtors, the Tampa Board of Trade, several major businesses, and Peter O. Knight—Tampa's most powerful business and civic leader who ran Tampa Electric. However, certain home owners living on Bayshore Boulevard opposed the purchase because their view of Hillsborough Bay would be impacted by the development and the City of Tampa, they felt, did not have the legal right to sell the submerged bottomlands. By March 1924, the opposition was put to rest and the City accepted Davis's offer for $200,000. The contract itself called for the posting of a performance bond by Davis, thus assuring the City that the dredging and completion of the development would cost not less than five million dollars; that a concrete bridge would be built to link the mainland with the development; and, that a park on the island would be created. The stipulations were to be met within four years. In April, Tampa voters approved the sale: 1,128 votes for, 59 against.[85]

So as to absolutely confirm the City of Tampa had the legal right to sell the aforementioned real estate, a legal opinion was sought from the courts. The testimony of Davis at the subsequent hearings, along with various exhibits, proved convincing especially when the developer promised to spend at least $500,000 on the project as early as June 1924. The case was ultimately heard by the Florida Supreme Court in special session which, in the end, ruled for the City and paved the way for transferring title to Davis. (The Army Corps of Engineers would give approval for the island bridge in August 1924.) Unfazed by the legal goings-on, Davis went about organizing D. P. Davis Properties, Inc. with a capitalization of $3.5 million and additionally made plans for a posh sales office at 502 North Franklin Street.[86]

There now began the Herculean task of creating the 834-acre island Utopia. Davis wasted little time in negotiating contracts and lining up contractors. In August, 1924, he signed a $2 million contract with Northern Dredge and Dock Company of Minneapolis for dredging no less than nine million yards of cubic fill. Locally, the Tampa Sand and Shell Company received a $5,000 contract for building a temporary bridge (with a twenty-foot wide roadway and a five-foot wide sidewalk) leading from De Leon Street on the mainland to the first island. Among other tasks, Davis also hired a Chicago sales manager for the project and an advertising expert from Connecticut. On 24 September 1924, Davis formally announced that his development would hereafter be called Davis Islands. A fifty-five-acre park thereon would be christened Marjorie Park, in memory of his wife who had died in 1922.[87]

Even though the project was still in its infant stages, Davis authorized the sale of building lots so as to create cash flow. The first sales session took place at the Hillsboro Hotel on Saturday, October 4. Three hundred lots in the yet-to-be-built Hyde Park Section would be available for purchase on a first come, first served basis. (Each buyer could only purchase two lots maximum.) Heavy newspaper advertising preceded the event, which was so effective that lines of prospects began forming at the hotel some forty hours before the sale. In fact, thousands would eventually appear, and supposedly the first person in line chained himself to the hotel's front door! In three frenetic hours that Saturday all lots were sold, despite all three hundred still being under water! Sales amounted to $1,683,000 (today's money: some $29.5 million). Many purchasers wanted nothing more than to buy a lot then "flip" it for profit. "Penn Dawson, of Dawson-Thornton Dry Goods, purchased his limit of two lots and, before he had left the hotel, sold them to E. W. Cloughton of Atlanta for a profit of one thousand dollars."[88] Another sale went off on October 13, this time in the new sales office of Davis Islands. One thousand lots in the yet-to-be-built Bay Circle Section went on the market. Again, lines of purchasers appeared, and by nightfall only forty-one lots were left unsold. Sales revenues that day amounted to $1,028,200.

This is an early view of Tampa's Davis Islands in Hillsborough Bay. Bulkheads surround much of the setting; behind them, sand was pumped in. A wooden bridge to the mainland is visible in the upper left (courtesy Florida Memory, State Archives of Florida).

With the treasury refreshed, the dredge and filling work continued at breakneck speed as well as other construction details. In all, some eighty-nine thousand cubic feet of sand would be pumped up from Hillsborough Bay. Building materials were stockpiled in the Hyde Park neighborhood of Tampa until the temporary bridge to the development was opened. Davis now proceeded to sign a million dollar contract for an upscale apartment hotel with Wynne-Claughton Realty of Atlanta. "On December 4th, Davis awarded a contract to G. H. Cooper to build six homes of Spanish and Italian design at a cost of $10,000 apiece. An advertisement appeared in the Tampa papers telling about a business section being planned on Davis Islands with a sketch showing an old Spanish restaurant, a florist, and a candy store."[89]

Davis Boulevard, the main thoroughfare leading to the development, was nearly complete in October, but the temporary bridge from De Leon Street remained unfinished; thus construction materials could not be efficiently conveyed. Approval was now sought, and obtained, for drinking water from the City of Tampa. Finally, the temporary bridge from the mainland opened in November 1924, allowing cars, trucks and construction materials to directly access the development. (Arthur Milam, the secretary-treasurer of D. P. Davis Properties, a wealthy Jacksonville attorney and a well-known figure in the Florida legislature, drove the first car over the structure.) Elsewhere, "the dredge *Burlington* was busy pumping sand through seventeen hundred feet of twenty-inch pipe to a level of seven feet above low tide and held in position by concrete bulkheads placed by the A. M. Grain Company."[90] Newspaper articles mentioned that Davis would spend some $30 million on Davis Islands, that his development could eventually accommodate 15,000 residents. Further, the extravaganza would contain eleven miles of waterfront having seawalls and twenty-seven miles of streets and boulevards along with several miles of canals.

Davis's frenzied sales campaign never seemed to halt. In fact he had to open a branch sales office on Tampa's East Main Street to accommodate the abundance of prospects. Women received a complimentary corsage, an orchestra provided background music, and prospects were conveyed by busses to the development site. Temporary dining rooms were even opened on the island to serve meals. Davis opened other sales offices in St. Petersburg and Clearwater. A fleet of commodious touring busses were also acquired, which dashed about the state collecting sales prospects. Davis also aroused interest in his project by arranging speedboat races, hiring stunt airplane flyers and engaging sports personalities. (He paid $10,000 to the Olympic swimmer Helen Wainright to swim around the project.) Some 260 lots now went up for sale in the Yacht Club Section, a promotion that yielded another $1,250,000 in revenues. (Overall, Davis envisioned eight sections or neighborhoods, though not all were built.) After disposing of most of the residential building lots, the developer aggressively encouraged the construction of commercial buildings. Among those built was the Davis Islands Coliseum, organized by investors who owned such a building in nearby St. Petersburg. T. H. Eslick, who had designed ballrooms in distant Australia and India, subsequently drew plans for a 40,000 square foot facility in Moorish Revival style that would hold five thousand persons. When the City of Tampa needed a new site for a municipal hospital, Davis offered for sale a fifty-acre site near Marjorie Park, albeit the parcel was then still under water.

A number of commercial structures existed at the development by March 1925. The $50,000 Davis Islands Administration Building had been completed along with the Tennis

Club Building. Construction was also well underway on numerous homes, apartment buildings and hotels, many of which still stand today. Landscaping and beautification of the
development fell to Frank Button, whose outstanding work could be seen in Coral Gables
and Miami Beach. Thousands of palm trees were brought in along with tropical plantings
and flowers, many coming from the Davis-owned nursery. Soil was trucked in from the
mainland, which helped control any blowing, shifting sand.

     With one of the most spectacular Florida developments on its way to completion, it
seems almost impossible that David Paul Davis would launch—at the same time—a project
of even greater magnitude, despite his stating publicly that he was annually earning in
excess of $800,000.[91] But in 1925, the land boom's zenith year, that was exactly what the
restless entrepreneur would do. In fact, news of Davis Shores in St. Augustine broke that
fall. The October 15 edition of the *St. Augustine Evening Record* issued a forty page supplement that day—likely paid for by the Davis publicity machine—to describe the mammoth
undertaking. In brief, Davis would create a ready-made community on Anastasia Island by
bulkheading and filling in five partially submerged and marshy islands between the Matanzas
River and the Atlantic Ocean, a project that would require no fewer than fifteen miles of
seawalls.

     Davis delighted in saying that he would spend some $60 million on Davis Shores, twice
the amount he projected to fully spend on the Davis Islands. A $1.5 million hotel was envi-
sioned along with a $250,000 country club, yacht club, Roman pool, casino, two 18-hole
golf courses, fifty miles of streets, one hundred miles of sidewalks, and lush landscaping.
The architect selected to create his second island masterpiece was Carlos Schoeppl, whose
partnership—Hedrick and Schoeppl—had a national reputation.

     The initial idea for Davis Shores actually belonged to the aforementioned Arthur Milam
of Jacksonville, an officer of D. P. Davis Properties in Tampa, who, in 1925, was Speaker of
the Florida House of Representatives. Along with his brother Robert Milam, a future president of the Florida Bar Association, and other Jacksonville investors, this inner group
brought considerable political, legal, and financial clout to the table. Also in that group of
players was Clifford Foster, adjutant general of the Florida National Guard, who acquired
for the syndicate some 1,500 acres during the summer of 1925. That August, Davis even
gave the City of St. Augustine $6,000 to widen the new bridge approach onto Anastasia
Island from the historic city, though the famed Bridge of Lions—"The Most Beautiful
Bridge in Dixie"—would not open until February 1927.[92]

     The old city hall in St. Augustine became the temporary sales office for Davis Shores.
A public reception for the developer and his colleagues went off on November 12, at which
time plans for the project were formally detailed. Two days later all available building
lots at Davis Shores were completely sold out within a few hours. Sales revenues amounted
to $16,268,000 (today's money: some $213 million), another example of how hungry the
public was for Florida real estate investments. However, one must remember that most lot
sales throughout Florida were closed on the installment plan—so much down and so much
a month. Thus, gross revenues that day did not reach the company's coffers all at once. As
an aside, the building lots themselves contained restrictions, including this one: "No part
of said land or any interest therein, shall be given, loaned, rented, leased, encumbered or
conveyed to any person of Negro blood."[93] A proper sales office for Davis Shores was even-

Aggressive newspaper advertising greatly contributed to the success of Davis Islands in Tampa, a strategy that developer D. P. Davis had previously used in his Miami endeavors.

**The purpose of this advertisement was to illustrate the proximity of St. Augustine proper to the Davis Shores development being built on Anastasia Island. Likely its clever developer, D. P. Davis, suggested the copy.**

tually established at the Blenmore Hotel, after Davis had the structure remodeled. (Today it is the home of the American Legion.)

In order to create Davis Shores it was necessary to undertake an enormous dredge and fill operation. A record thirteen million cubic feet of fill would be needed for the endeavor, the dredging itself beginning that October. "Two-ton concrete slabs were cast on site and hydraulically jetted into place to form the seawall that encircled about three-fourths of Davis Shores. These tongue-and-groove slabs were then topped with a twenty-inch wide reinforced cap and secured with concrete tie-backs."[94]

One of the first buildings to be erected at the new development was another sales office, on Arredondo Avenue. By April 1926, the local newspaper in St. Augustine reported that four apartment buildings were nearing completion and that the Schindler Realty Company contracted with Davis to build six Mediterranean Revival homes, the only "original" houses ever completed at the development.

Despite the hoopla at Davis Shores, with each passing day in spring 1926 it was becoming increasingly evident that the great Florida land boom of the Twenties was ending. As the July issue of *The Nation* magazine summarized, "The world's greatest poker game, played with building lots instead of chips, is over."[95] With installment payments on lots becoming

Virtually every upscale development in Florida during the Twenties had a touring bus or a fleet of such. Davis Shores was no exception. While prospects were shuttled about the proposed community, salesmen delivered honeyed pitches (courtesy Florida Memory, State Archives of Florida).

delinquent, along with mortgage payments being skipped on homes and buildings, cash flow problems forced the cessation of many statewide development projects. More than one developer, financier, and investor began fretting, sweating, perhaps trembling at the possible consequences.

Possibly one of the foregoing was David Paul Davis, who now "booked passage to France on the White Star liner, *Majestic*, supposedly to investigate a project on the French Riviera. On the night of October 12, 1926, the 41-year old Davis either jumped or fell overboard from the porthole in his stateroom and disappeared into the Atlantic. The ship turned around to look for him, but his body was never recovered. The circumstances surrounding his death remain a mystery."[96]

Whereas the death of D. P. Davis would likely have placed his two developments into jeopardy, that was not entirely the case. In fact, a "white knight"—at least at Davis Islands—was already on the scene before Davis had sailed: the Boston engineering firm of Stone and Webster, managers of several utilities including Tampa Electric Company where Peter Knight, a Davis Islands investor, was president. A summer 1925 article in the *Tampa Tribune* suggested that Davis was going to sell out to the firm. Davis refuted the statement but admitted that Stone and Webster might lend financial support. After reviewing the Davis Islands books and inspecting the property, Stone and Webster concluded that the development—though short of cash and incomplete—was very much solvent. In early August 1926, Peter Knight announced from a Manhattan hotel that the Boston entity had formed a new subsidiary—Island Investment Company—which would issue $2.5 million in stock

**Elegant and substantial amenities were projected for Davis Shores, such as this stunning golf and country club. But the grandiose sketch remained just that and nothing more.**

so as to acquire control of D. P. Properties. (D. P. himself was given a 49 percent stock interest in the new firm.) Big changes now started to occur at Davis Islands. Stone and Webster moved its downtown office to the location, the entire real estate operation was revamped and certain infrastructure was at last completed including the golf course and the Roman Pool.[97]

The picture at Davis Shores was not as bright. Although Davis pledged some of his new stock in the Stone and Webster subsidiary as collateral for a much-needed loan at St. Augustine, the "fix" proved temporary. A few months later Davis was dead, and the reversals began in earnest: the Yacht Club was left partially completed, the stupendous Marion Hotel—centerpiece of the development—was never built, only a smattering of homes and buildings stood, the waterfront bathing casino fell by the wayside, and most of the much-needed seawalls remained uncompleted. According to a *New York Times* article on 6 March 1927, irate lot owners—led by Fanny Hartman of Chestertown, Maryland—petitioned the Federal court for a receivership to protect their interests. Approval was granted, and realtor Joseph Dunn of Jacksonville was named receiver. Despite the legal interventions, Davis Shores began to wither, the spoils eventually playing into the hands of other developers and builders. All the while the kaleidoscopic story of David Paul Davis began fading into Florida history.

# 7

# Down Comes the Curtain

Friends, you are now in Cocoanut Manor, one of the finest cities in Florida. Of course we still need a few finishing touches. But who doesn't? This is the heart of the residential district. Eight hundred beautiful residences will be built right here. You can have any kind of a home you want to. You can even get stucco—Oh, how you can get stucco!

—Groucho Marx, *The Cocoanuts*

Our concluding chapter explores several topics that contributed to the demise of Twenties land boom, together with an astute summary of the phenomenon by a renowned expert. Among the topics discussed are the schemes of shady real estate operators, the response to the fraudulent activities by Governor John Martin, the effects of two deadly hurricanes, and a devastating banking crisis. No single factor was more sinister than the other, though many devotees of the Twenties land boom story still insist that only one event triggered the collapse: the disappearance of real estate purchasers and investors. In one sense that is true, but hopefully what follows will enlarge our appreciation of the other contributing factors.

The fantastic sums of money being made in Florida during the Roaring Twenties naturally attracted an undesirable element—crooks and scoundrels who were trying to obtain something for nothing or close to it. Among those who found the "effortless riches" irresistible was the infamous Charles Ponzi of Boston, originator of a fraudulent investment scheme that promised to pay fabulous returns to investors, not necessarily from profits earned by the entity but from monies paid in by the latest suckers.

While waiting to serve a prison sentence in Massachusetts for investment fraud, Ponzi had the temerity to unveil a scam in Florida in September 1925, called Charpon Land Syndicate—"Charpon" being an amalgam of Charles Ponzi's name. The Italian immigrant, who never became an American citizen, envisioned selling no fewer than ten million (yes, million!) minuscule building lots "near Jacksonville." However, the lots themselves were in reality situated some sixty-five miles west of the "Gateway City," in a desolate section of Columbia County, approximately nine miles south of Lake City, amidst heavy scrub oak, palmetto and swamp water.[1]

According to Professor Mitchell Zuckoff of Boston University, Ponzi's able biographer, the dapper and charming criminal, who lived in the lap of luxury, borrowed seed money for his Florida "flyer" from a few remaining friends.[2] In addition to selling the lots through the

155

United States mail, he also offered ownership interests in Charpon. Of particular note were his "unit certificates of indebtedness," which cost $310 apiece and paid the remarkable dividend of 200 percent in sixty days! Profits from certificate sales helped Ponzi (the syndicate's only trustee) to acquire the "best land obtainable for the least amount of money" in Columbia County.[4] In a public statement, Ponzi disclosed that his subdivision, including land, subdividing costs, plotting, staking, advertising, office rental, and salaries and other incidental overhead costs, cost him $40 an acre, "as she lays."[5]

The first tract to go on the market was named for Ponzi's wife, Rose Maria. Each acre was divided into no fewer than twenty-three building lots, a feat that prompted Harvard economist John Kenneth Galbraith to cheekily remark years later that "Ponzi believed in good, compact neighborhoods."[6] Lots were offered to the public for $10 apiece or $230 an acre. According to the Charpon prospectus, if there was sufficient cash on hand at dividend time, then each unit certificate holder was to receive thirty dollars for each $10 certificate he or she owned; or, in lieu of the cash dividend, the holder could instead have three $10 lots. If the syndicate had no available cash at dividend time, then each owner of record would receive three $10 lots for every $10 certificate they owned. In this way, notes another economist, "Ponzi disposed of any possible dividend problem."[7]

The only physical sign of activity at Rose Maria were some survey stakes, "so purchasers who might visit the tracts might find their lots."[8] (The two other tracts, Oreste and Imelde, were named for Ponzi's parents.) Although Ponzi did not guarantee any improvements at Charpon, his prospectus further assured buyers that each lot would face a street measuring forty feet wide.

Before long purchaser complaints about Charpon began to mount, and were subsequently investigated by the National Better Business Bureau, the Florida Chamber of Commerce, the Florida Association of Real Estate Boards, and the Florida Real Estate Commission. Several states' attorneys and federal postal officials also got onboard. On 8 February 1926, Ponzi was indicted for violating Florida's Declaration of Trust laws as well as marketing Charpon without a permit and failing to pay the proper license fees. (Both Ponzi and Charpon were headquartered in the Springfield section of Jacksonville.) Interestingly, the indictment came just three days after a combined drive against real estate "sharks" had been announced by the National Better Business Bureau and the Florida State Chamber of Commerce. Later, on April 2, Ponzi was found guilty for violating Florida statutes pertaining to land trusts, indiscretions that carried a sentence of two years in the state prison and a fine of $1,500.

As Professor Zuckoff relates, "Ponzi beat the charges of land fraud, but was sentenced to one year in jail for violating Florida's securities laws."[9] The notorious crook, however, remained free while pending an appeal during which time he changed his name and physical appearance and faked a suicide. He then hopped aboard a freighter from Tampa, Florida, bound for Texas where—after a nationwide manhunt—he was ultimately apprehended, arrested, and extradited to New England.

Despite making personal appeals to U.S. President Calvin Coolidge and the Italian dictator Benito Mussolini, Ponzi entered the Massachusetts State Prison in February 1927, where he spent his days sewing underwear. Paroled in 1934, he was immediately deported to his native Italy. The infamous schemer died in 1949 at age sixty-six, in the charity ward of a Rio de Janeiro hospital.[10] The Florida investors were hopelessly defrauded.

Another fraud involving marketing—one of many that surfaced during the Twenties land boom—involved Manhattan Estates, the name no doubt catching the eye of many New Yorkers. Located in northern Florida and heavily marketed (like Charpon) through the United States mail, its prospectus noted that the subdivision was located "not more than three-fourths of a mile from the prosperous and fast-growing city of Nettie."[11]

But after scrutinizing a state map, shrewd investors discovered that no such town or city existed in Florida, though such savvy investors were the exception and not the rule. Those that actually viewed the subdivision realized that the setting was nothing more than an abandoned, burned-over turpentine camp. Who Nettie was named for and why has not been learned. What has been learned was that the forty or so acres comprising the promotion were entirely waterlogged.

Melbourne Gardens, advertised as a "suburb" in southern Brevard County, also attracted a share of unsuspecting purchasers. In brief, the development proved to be a most unsuitable tract of land located some fifteen miles from the city limits of Melbourne. In order to reach it, one had to travel over a dirt road that became a trail through prairie muck lands. Occasionally a tree came into view. The circuitous route only worsened until automobiles became hopelessly mired in mud, about three miles from the site. Then, one had to tramp through low-water swamp. Building lots in Melbourne Gardens were priced around $1,000, the size of each approximately 150 feet by 150 feet. Few purchasers actually inspected their investments, despite the setting being heavily advertised as "very suitable for homes and gardens." Similar stories abounded for Melbourne Heights and Melbourne Manor.[12]

One of the more interesting real estate frauds involved Fulford By-the-Sea, north of Miami. A special bulletin issued by the National Better Business Bureau in May 1926 stated that Fulford's developer, Merle C. Tebbetts, had been arrested for using the U.S. mails to defraud lot purchasers. Further, the Florida Cities Finance Company, which Tebbetts and others operated for the benefit of lot purchasers, was "in the hands of a receiver, and that its sales of lots in the last five years aggregated $10,692,180, of which it had received $2,307,830.95 in cash and had $4,855,038.55 due on lots payable in 1926, 1927, and 1928."[13] The report also revealed that 5,085 lots had been sold to some 3,600 individuals, the average per lot price being $2,102.69. Because so many sales had been conducted through the mail, a team of postal solicitors and investigators descended on the location to investigate purchaser complaints.

According to the *New York Times* of 4 August 1926, the Postmaster General of the United States was informed that the Fulford Company had stated in Miami-area newspapers, during July 1925, that it had spent over a million dollars on "sidewalks, roads, beautifying homes and building business blocks." However, postal investigators confirmed that "absolutely no steps had been taken to put into effect certain improvements promised purchasers of lots." In reality, purchase monies had been siphoned off by Tebbetts and insiders. The same newspaper reported on August 20 that forty-two persons, along with several firms connected with Fulford, had been formally indicted, including the Stanley Realty and Development Company which at the time was promoting Arcadia Gardens in Arcadia.

**Sales prospects in Miami wishing to see the Fulford development in North Miami had only to board the developer's vessel for the quick trip up to the Uleta River. Busses stood at the ready, which brought the excited crowds to the development proper.**

In addition to bringing charges of mail fraud against Tebbetts, the government investigation revealed that the Fulford Company had unwisely built a speedway for racing cars at a cost of $663,379, "an unsightly affair which depreciated the value of the high-priced lots adjacent to it."[14] (The wooden Miami Speedway, built with help from Carl Fisher of Miami Beach, was completely destroyed by the 1926 hurricane.) In 1927, Fulford By-the-Sea (which was not at all located by the sea!) was sold by its receiver to a group of Chicago financiers. Four years later it was voted to change the setting's name to North Miami Beach. Perhaps the best remaining icon of the development is a splendid mosaic-domed entrance fountain at NE 172nd Street and NE 23rd Avenue.

Fraudulent marketing schemes naturally disturbed purchasers, the public at large, along with government agencies and officials. Among those that vociferously criticized such practices during the Twenties land boom was *Advertising and Selling Magazine*, which summarized the goings-on in its issue for 4 November 1925.

> The fact remains that the advertising technique of some Florida promoters constitutes nothing short of scandal. This indictment does not include all Florida real estate promotion. There are some notable exceptions which are all together reputable and as sound as might reasonably be expected in these times of instability and soaring prices; but these exceptions are often greatly overshadowed by the rank and file of ballyhoo shouters.
>
> To say that the truth is being violated is to put the situation in its mildest and most polite

terms. Beautifully illustrated and suavely worded advertisements beguile the reader with exotic pictures of life in America's sub-tropics. All he need do is to send in his check to "get in on" a marvelous development. Close, analytical perusal may disclose the fact that the "developments" so charmingly described to the eye and the mind have as yet failed to develop and are merely proposals; that their sites are at present inhabited by alligators and are shielded from the burning rays of the southern sun by three or four feet of malaria-infested water. Motion picture scenery, trick photography, impressionistic art, distorted and un-scaled maps—every twist and turn of the fake advertiser from the Year One—appears in the Florida advertising of these unscrupulous promoters. Their publication advertising is bad enough, but their direct mail literature is several times worse.

How any person above the category of a moron could accept at face value some of these statements, passes our comprehension, but apparently the checks, properly made out and duly signed, keep pouring in just as they have done for every campaign of a similar nature to which the public reacted in the same way. And there will be the same grand howl when the crash comes, just as there has always been.

Examples of fraudulent real estate practices during the Twenties could never be fully eradicated. If anything they precipitated a cataract of negative press. The stories not only served to cast doubts in the minds of potential purchasers and investors, but they antagonized out-of-state government officials as well as bankers, who became alarmed over the huge outflows of monies going into speculative Florida investments. The charges reached a stentorian level just as the land boom reached its zenith year—1925.

Ohio passed "blue sky" laws that forbade certain firms to sell Florida real estate in Ohio. The purpose of the move, reported the *Cleveland Plain Dealer* newspaper, was to protect the investor who had no means of investigating the reliability of such real estate ventures. Walter J. Greenbaum, a Chicago investment banker, also voiced his opposition to the Florida movement. So many investors in Massachusetts savings institutions withdrew their funds for land speculation that the Massachusetts Savings Bank League began cautioning depositors. J. H. Tregoe, Executive Manager of the National Association of Credit Men, also undertook to sound a warning. The New York Times observed that withdrawals from northern, mid-western, and western banks had been enormous, while Oscar Smith, Commissioner of Immigration in Minnesota, predicted the Florida Boom will burst with a bang.[15]

Florida Governor John Martin responded to the criticisms and critics by holding a luncheon news conference on 9 October 1925 at the Waldorf-Astoria Hotel in New York City. It was entitled "The Truth about Florida." Martin insisted that his state was being made the victim of considerable misrepresentation. Accompanying him were thirty prominent figures, among them Barron Collier, United States Senator T. Coleman du Pont, H. H. Raymond of the Clyde Steamship Company, publisher John Perry, and S. Davies Warfield, president of the Seaboard Air Line Railway.

The delegation circulated to press attendees negative advertisements and articles denouncing Florida by out-of-state individuals and entities, declaring that most of the accusations were completely false and unjustifiable. "Mr. Collier asked for cooperation in sifting 'the goats from the sheep' among advertisers," while George Sebring, founder of Sebring, Florida, criticized the practices of "curbstone real estate dealers."[16] How beneficial the conference proved is uncertain, but it confirmed that Florida was not going to sit on its hands. Although the Florida Legislature approved, in the following month, "An Act Regulating Real Estate Brokers and Salesmen" (Chapter 11336), the fraudulent schemes and negative press did not cease.

A definite lull in Florida real estate sales began in early 1926. Fewer people came to the state and, consequently, fewer real estate sales occurred. Real estate advertising also became less aggressive and, in many cases, was reduced in frequency. But by no means was the land boom completely over. The *New York Times* ran an article on February 13 entitled "Lull in Florida Disturbs Buyers: Small Investors Fear Failure to Resell Before the Next Payment is Due." It noted that the mid–February real estate boom that was heralded by Florida realtors during the previous three months had failed to materialize. "Hundreds of investors who bought land expecting ready turnovers with handsome profits are now unable to dispose of their holdings even at purchase price. The more optimistic see nothing alarming in the situation. Real estate values, they say, are merely stabilizing. Real estate men say a digestive period has set in."

Overall, lot sales and resales definitely slowed during the remainder of 1926. Further, that construction work on many subdivisions ceased and more than one developer folded as a result of little or no buyer activity. Aggravating the situation was the fact that many lot owners began defaulting on their installment purchases. Construction and mortgage loans were also becoming difficult to obtain as bankers and mortgage loan firms began to tighten loaning criteria. There was also growing competition from another investment opportunity, perhaps one far more lucrative than real estate, that many Americans were deeply fascinated by and involved in: the stock market.

Two setbacks from the hand of nature also wreaked havoc with the land boom. The disastrous 1926 hurricane, equivalent to a Category 4 storm of today, made landfall between Coral Gables and South Miami in the wee hours of September 18. Not only did it destroy greater Miami, but it ravaged Hollywood-by-the-Sea and Fort Lauderdale. It then crossed the peninsula, south of Lake Okeechobee, and hit Fort Myers and Sanibel Island, whereupon it went up into the Gulf of Mexico and battered the Florida Panhandle and Alabama. Some 6,300 people were injured, 400 persons perished, and some 18,000 individuals were made homeless.

In Miami, where winds of 140 miles per hour were recorded, most residents did not evacuate as warnings were not issued until a few hours before the blow. Further, many of the newer residents knew nothing about hurricane preparedness. A fifteen-foot tidal surge rolled in causing unprecedented damage to old and new homes, businesses, commercial buildings, roads, bridges, causeways, marinas, and boats, as well as destroying miles of tropical landscaping. Many Miami residents went out and about during the storm's midpoint lull—for about thirty-five minutes—and were killed when the rear eye wall arrived. The rising waters of Lake Okeechobee broke the earthen dike at Moore Haven, flooding the town and drowning many of its residents.[17]

The University of Miami in Coral Gables, which opened its doors for the first time a few days before the storm, subsequently named its athletic teams the Hurricanes. The Red Cross rushed to South Florida as did medical personnel from everywhere. But certain parties did not want the extent of damage played up in the press, thinking it would discourage out-of-state tourists and home seekers from coming to the Magic City, folks that the realty magicians and developers desperately needed. In the 18 October 1926 issue of the *Wall Street Journal*, an official of the Seaboard Air Line Railway, which served Miami, expressed concern in an article that the solicitation of Red Cross funds for hurricane relief would "do more damage permanently to Florida than would be offset by the funds received." Nevertheless,

# the Truth about
# FLORIDA
## *is good enough!*

DISCOUNT the stories about Florida all you will, the Truth remains—here is the new "Land of Good Fortune" because the world has awakened to Florida's four great realities: 1. The year 'round pleasantness of her Climate, and the easiness of her Life. 2. The matchless fertility of her soils, where every month is a growing season and each acre can yield, not one, but several profits. 3. The supreme beauty and charm of her natural playground areas of beaches, lakes and woodlands, which with magnificent hotels are making Florida the world's vacation Mecca. 4. Her easy tax condition—Florida's constitution prohibits state income or inheritance taxes, encouraging productive investment of capital.

Your faith in Florida has impressive endorsement —America's greatest building and industrial corporations have contracts running into HUNDREDS OF MILLIONS for new edifices and equipment in Florida. These far-sighted corporations know what they are doing. The big financial institutions and insurance companies have loaned still other SCORES OF MILLIONS for Florida's development. They too have faith that Florida's prosperity is *permanent*.

Have a share in Florida—in her matchless Destiny.

### Warning to Investors

INVESTIGATE BEFORE YOU INVEST. Come and see for yourself. In any event, deal only with responsible business concerns. Local volunteer business bodies such as Chambers of Commerce, Real Estate Boards, Banks and Better Business Bureaus are cooperating with the Florida Chamber of Commerce in vigorously contesting the activities of unscrupulous, fly-by-night operators who think to reap enormous profits from credulous and uninformed investors. Investigate before you invest.

*Make all railroad, steamship and hotel reservations earlier this year*

### Herman A. Dann, President
## Florida Chamber of Commerce
421 Consolidated Building, Jacksonville, Florida

-----------TEAR OFF HERE------------

Florida Chamber of Commerce
    421 Consolidated Building, Jacksonville, Florida
I am interested in Florida and will appreciate your sending without obligation on my part information about

Name..........................................................

Street.........................................................

City............................................................

---

As the land boom years advanced, fraudulent sales schemes in Florida multiplied. To clear the air, ads such as this were run by city, county and state agencies.

**Unimaginable destruction occurred in Dade County during the 1926 hurricane. This scene was snapped at Miami Beach. Many homes and commercial buildings that were destroyed had just been built in the land boom—obviously not to today's hurricane codes.**

many residents left Miami and neighboring communities for good, clearing their bank accounts in the process.

Another destructive blow occurred two years later. The 1928 hurricane pummeled the coast from Pompano Beach to Jupiter. Arriving on September 17 with winds of 145 miles per hour and a storm surge ten feet high, the storm destroyed some 1,700 homes in West Palm Beach alone, many having been hastily built with cheap materials during the earlier years of the land boom.

Severest hit was the southern edge of Lake Okeechobee, where flood waters spilled over the lake's earthen dike for hundreds of square miles, in some places as high as twenty-feet above ground. Homes and buildings were literally lifted off their foundations or wrecked by the rising waters in Canal Point, Belle Glade, Pahokee, and South Bay. In all some 2,500 people perished, about 75 percent of the fatalities being migrant farm workers. The gathering-up of drowned bodies went on for weeks, with many of them being buried in mass graves in Port Myakka. In all, the 1928 hurricane would cause some $25 million of damage. Eliot Kleinberg's book *Black Cloud* (see Bibliography) expertly recounts the disastrous story of America's second deadliest hurricane.

As stated in this work's Introduction, a vital ingredient of any successful land boom is having access to capital, usually lots of it. It is the indispensable lubricant of a free market economy. Capital enabled the acquisition of land, land boom promotion, development costs, the construction of products, monies for payrolls and bills, mortgages for purchasers, rewards for developers, and sundry other items.

Florida banks played a key role during the palmy days of the Twenties land boom. Capital was, for the most part, readily available. It proved inevitable that banks and bankers would form close relationships with developers and promoters, and often bankers themselves would reap attractive rewards. While unscrupulous actors initiated fraudulent marketing and promotion schemes in real estate, certain banks and bankers were orchestrating their own criminal endeavors, and the losers—as in real estate—often became the "Common Man" as banks floundered or failed.

Whereas space limitations here prevent a detailed account of this dark chapter, the reader has only to consult the definitive tome on the subject: *Panic in Paradise,* by Tallahassee author and attorney Raymond Vickers. The book convincingly describes what went on during the Twenties land boom from a banking perspective, and includes a list of the bad actors, their motives, and what they achieved and lost. "I haven't found a single bank failure that didn't involve a conscious conspiracy to defraud," claims Vickers. By obtaining access to records that in some cases have been sealed for almost seventy years, the author provides a shocking story of professional corruption and conspiracy. On 23 May 1989, the *Wall Street Journal* published an article by Vickers entitled, "Sleazy Banking in the '20s and Today."

For decades, the opinion prevailed that it was the Florida land boom that brought down the state's banking system. But through meticulous research, Vickers presents a different opinion. "The 1926 banking crash devastated Florida's economy and drove its recession into a depression. Bank assets in Florida fell more than $300 million in 1926. Between 1926 and 1929, they declined 60 percent, from $943 million to $375 million. The sad story told by these [banking] records is that insiders looted the banks they pledged to protect. They tried to get rich by wildly speculating with depositors' money, and when their schemes failed so did their banks."[18]

Ever since the Twenties land boom ended in Florida there has been no shortage of individuals who have attempted to explain how it first took flight, prospered and eventually collapsed. Among those parties are historians, academics, authors, economists, financial specialists, and free-lance writers. Even the dissertations of graduate students help enrich our understanding of the topic. But if one person truly comprehended the migration and building episode, moreover actually witnessed and participated in the spectacle itself, it was the nationally-known financial counselor and investment advisor, Roger Ward Babson (1875–1967).

A native of Massachusetts who maintained a winter home in Lake Wales, Florida, Babson made possible Babson College in Wellesley, Massachusetts, and Webber College in Babson Park, Florida, a city he founded. Entrepreneur, educator, philanthropist, author of some fifty books, Babson is perhaps best remembered as having organized an information clearinghouse about financial investments, and publishing the famed *Babson Reports* which investors everywhere relied upon for decades.

A graduate of the Massachusetts Institute of Technology, Babson received no fewer than six honorary doctoral degrees during his lifetime, including one from the University of Florida in 1927 where at he gave the commencement address. His articles about the Florida land boom appeared in myriad publications, such as the *Saturday Evening Post*, *Forbes Magazine*, the *New York Times* and the *American Review of Reviews*. In his autobiography, *Actions and Reactions*, the financial pundit devotes two timely chapters about his Florida experiences, one of which forms a penetrating analysis of the land boom.

Babson claimed that every generation in Florida—ever since the 1880s—had experienced some sort of a land boom. "There has never been more than one Florida boom within one generation. It has been impossible to catch the same people twice, but it has always been possible to catch each generation."[19]

As to how the boom manifested, Babson felt the speculative fever began with northern and mid-western folk who eventually tired of cold winters and looked for some kind of relief. "As a generation becomes older, it feels the cold more, and also is able to take winter vacations which it could not take when younger." Finally these people to go to Florida for the winter, and while there they are attracted by what appears to be a very low price for land. Babson observed that while the price per acre was low compared with prices in the North

and mid–West, the productivity of the Florida land is proportionately less. This latter fact "is not recognized, and these people purchase a little property. Other people come down who also purchase property. The result of all this buying is that prices go up and some of the early purchasers sell and take a profit. Instead of carrying the profit back North with them, they reinvest it in other Florida land. This makes the price of land go even higher. Soon, everyone is making a profit on land as well as enjoying a healthful and pleasant winter."[20]

The financial wizard also felt that the stories of quick profit-taking in Florida real estate were enthusiastically communicated to family and friends "up North" which, in turn, brought even more people down to Florida to investigate and verify the stories. The preponderance of nationwide newspaper and magazine articles about the "effortless riches" also contributed to the mania. "Yet, strange to say, at no time have the Florida people themselves been responsible for starting one of these booms. In every instance, in every generation, the Florida boom has unconsciously been started by Northern visitors and systematically been cultivated by Northern real estate vultures. The native Florida people of each generation have not got excited until the boom was about ready to culminate. Then these unfortunate Florida natives,

Roger Ward Babson, the renowned American financial expert, participated in the Twenties land boom firsthand and wrote extensively about it. His sage commentary on why and how the phenomenon occurred makes for cogent reading.

instead of being content to take their profit and salt it down in good securities, have put it back into more land at fictitiously high prices. In many cases old Florida families, who had been out of debt all their lives, mortgaged their properties at the height of the boom excitement and lost everything."[21]

Although Babson did not particularly care for the Magic City of Miami—he thought it a northern metropolis with palm trees—he was nevertheless privy to its orgy of real estate doings. "In this city, corner business lots, which sold for $2,500 in 1920, sold freely for $50,000 in the spring of 1926. These purchases were not made by promoters and speculators, but by some of the shrewdest bankers and biggest business men of the North. Often a business lot starting at $20,000 would be resold four times in a month, at a profit each time of perhaps $5,000."[22] He further notes that a hundred dollars a front-foot was a standard price for lots in the wilderness, while land prices were retailing for up to five hundred dollars a front-foot for east coast ocean lots. "The whole thing was ridiculous, and yet all the people who bought at these outrageous prices expected to sell at a profit."[23] The laying out and building of subdivisions, Babson says, naturally caused a boom in the construction industry which resulted in great temporary benefit to merchants, artisans, and common labor. In addition to the construction boom, he also witnessed promotions within the state of everything from banana plantations to oil explorations. "Pandemonium reigned," he said, and to prove it Babson insists that "there were more Rolls-Royces and Lincolns in the State of Florida in 1926 than in any other state in the country."[24]

The Twenties land boom, Babson claims, might not have been so bad at the end if buyers and sellers had kept everything more or less on a cash basis. But as the boom advanced, most people became so hungry for profits that they began borrowing in order to buy more land than they otherwise would. The fact, too, that real estate was usually sold on the installment plan had accelerated transactions which, in and of itself, carried with it a corresponding increase in prices. "Most people did not realize until the spring of 1927 that the boom had ended; yet, land boom statistics reached their zenith in September, 1926. When the tide turned, the boom quickly collapsed."[25]

Following the collapse, the Mediterranean fruit fly appeared which prompted the Federal government to place an embargo on all exported fruit from the state. "Then came the general stock market collapse in 1929," says the revered pundit, "which was a blow to Florida as well as the rest of the country."[26] If that were not enough, a huge storm swept the state in 1930 which blew off a large percentage of the citrus fruit, wrecked buildings, and felled trees. Bank failures came in 1931, when about three-fourths of the banks in Florida closed.[27]

Babson concludes his analysis by discussing one of the less-known dimensions of the 1920s boom: the municipal bond mania, which Florida communities promulgated in order to pay for the seemingly endless list of infrastructure improvements like municipal buildings, roads, causeways, bridges, etc. Babson knew first-hand that many "were issued with legal opinions from the best New York municipal bond attorneys, they yielded 6 percent interest and they were exempt from federal income taxes. Yet, when the boom broke, these 'municipals' gradually began to greatly default. These defaults continued to increase until seven-eighths of the cities of Florida refused to pay either principal or interest."[28] Whereas most of the "municipals" had sold freely in 1926 at par, practically all of them crumbled in price. "Five years before these defaults," Babson says, "no banker or bond expert in the United

States would have believed that such municipal bond repudiation would have been possible."[29] Even Babson himself fell victim to the onslaught. "I bought largely without visiting these Florida cities and seeing for what purposes the money was being spent. If I had done this, I would have seen that most of this money was being spent, at the solicitation of irresponsible real estate promoters and contractors, for the building of asphalt roads through undeveloped property which would not be occupied for fifty years."[30]

And on that note, our journey into one of the greatest building and migration episodes in American history comes to a close. Although Florida will continue to experience land booms in future years, that which occurred in the Roaring Twenties will forever remain a remarkable and colorful chapter in the state's storied past.

# Chapter Notes

## Introduction

1. Boorstin, *The Americans*, 278.
2. *New York Times*, 13 September 1925.
3. Mormino, *Land of Sunshine*, 45.
4. Shelby, "Florida Frenzy," 179.
5. Hancock, "New Towns in Florida," 69.
6. Shelby, "Florida Frenzy," 177.
7. Buchanan, "Miami's Bootleg Boom," 13.
8. Webb, "Ten Years of Florida Journalism," 23; Wynne, *Paradise for Sale*, 59.
9. Galbraith, *The Great Crash*, 11.
10. Ibid., 8–9.
11. Villard, "Florida Aftermath," 635
12. Ibid., 636.

## Chapter 1

1. Van Dyke, *Millionaires of a Day*, 8.
2. Dumke, *The Boom of the Eighties*, 275.
3. Ibid.
4. Van Dyke, *Millionaires of a Day*, 38.
5. Ibid., 40.
6. Ibid., 41.
7. Ibid.
8. Ibid., 41–42.
9. Dumke, *The Boom of the Eighties*, 4.
10. Ibid.
11. Ibid.
12. Ibid.
13. Allen, *Only Yesterday*, 235; Sisto, "Miami's Land Gambling Fever of 1925," 60; Weigall, *Boom in Paradise*, 50.
14. Dumke, *The Boom of the Eighties*, 275.
15. Turner, *A Journey into Florida Railroad History*, 52–53.
16. Ibid., 105–107.
17. George, "Passage to the New Eden," 445–448.
18. Turner, *A Short History of Florida Railroads*, 75.
19. Bush, "Playground of the USA," 159–160; George, "Passage to the New Eden," 451.
20. George, "Passage to the New Eden," 440–441.

21. Ibid., 441; Powell, "Simply Staggering," 19; *Federal Writers Project*, 61.
22. Boyer, *The Oxford Companion*, 844–845.
23. Turner, *A Journey into Florida Railroad History*, 160–162.
24. Weigall, *Boom in Paradise*, 37.
25. George, "Passage to the New Eden," 451.
26. Powell, "Simply Staggering," 19.
27. *Division of Elections*, S-13.
28. Baruch, *American Industry in the War*, 86.
29. Gordon, *An Empire of Wealth*, 289.
30. Hicks, *Rehearsal for Disaster*, 12.
31. Hanna and Hanna, *Florida's Golden Sands*, 334.
32. Ibid.
33. McDonell, "Rise of the Businessman's Politician," 44.
34. Ibid., 45.
35. *Florida's Resources and Inducements*, 22.

## Chapter 2

1. Roberts, *Sun Hunting*, 137.
2. *Federal Writers Project*, 208.
3. George, "Brokers, Binders, and Builders," 29.
4. Ibid., 30.
5. Vanderblue, "The Florida Land Boom," Part 2, 255.
6. Vanderblue, "The Florida Land Boom," Part 1, 120.
7. George, "Brokers, Binders, and Builders," 34.
8. Ibid., 45.
9. Roberts, *Sun Hunting*, 144.
10. George, "Brokers, Binders, and Builders," 35.
11. Ballinger, *Miami Millions*, 35–36.
12. Roberts, *Sun Hunting*, 145.
13. *Federal Writers Project,*, 210.
14. Stewart, "The Madness That Swept Miami," 62.
15. Redford, *Billion Dollar Sandbar*, 112.
16. Ballinger, *Miami Millions*, 109.
17. Ibid., 110–11.
18. Parks and Klepser, *Miami, Then and Now*, 111.
19. Roseberry, *Glenn Curtis*, 425; Bramson, *The Curtiss-Bright Cities*, 14.

20. Roseberry, *Glenn Curtiss*, 429.
21. Bramson, *The Curtiss-Bright Cities*, 14.
22. Ibid., 81.
23. Ibid., 82.
24. Ibid.
25. *Opa-locka Times*, 23 February 1927.
26. Fitzgerald-Bush, *A Dream of Araby*, 4; Lynn, "Dream and Substance," 166.
27. Lynn, "Dream and Substance," 178–183.
28. Turner, *A Milestone Celebration*, 127–130.
29. Varona, "Bernhardt E. Muller Collection," 4.

## Chapter 3

1. Galbraith, *The Great Crash*, 9.
2. Stockbridge and Perry, *Florida in the Making*, x.
3. Fox, *The Truth About Florida*, 171.
4. Allen, *Only Yesterday*, 236.
5. Fox, *The Truth About Florida*, 165.
6. *Federal Writers Project*, 48.
7. Ibid.
8. Babson, "Florida's Future," 447.
9. Allen, *Only Yesterday*, 234.
10. Grismer, *The Story of Fort Myers*, 222.
11. Ibid., 222–23.
12. Vanderblue, "The Florida Land Boom," 118.
13. Weigall, *Boom in Paradise*, 107.
14. Matthews, *Venice*, 277; Turner, *Venice in the 1920s*, 114.
15. Turner, *Venice in the 1920s*, 96.
16. Webb, "Ten Years of Florida Journalism," 9.
17. Ibid., 48–49.
18. Ibid., 49.
19. *New York Times*, 13 June 1926. A noteworthy graduate dissertation about Roberts and his creative output on 1920s Florida has been prepared by James Ricci. See Bibliography.
20. Ibid.
21. Parks, *George Merrick's Coral Gables*, 44–45.
22. Weigall, *Boom in Paradise*, 131–32.
23. Turner, *Venice in the 1920s*, 115.
24. Weigall, *Boom in Paradise*, 133.
25. Turner, *Venice in the 1920s*, 115; *Cocoa Tribune*, 8 March 1923.
26. LaHurd, *Sarasota*, 56.
27. Ballinger, *Miami Millions*, 49.

## Chapter 4

1. Beach, *The Miracle of Coral Gables*, 11.
2. Freeland, "George Edgar Merrick," 4.
3. Parks, *George Merrick's Coral Gables*, 14.
4. *New York Times*, 15 March 1925.
5. Cleary, "Denman Fink," 4–15.
6. Patricios, "Phineas Paist," 5–27.
7. Standiford, *Coral Gables*, 110–119.
8. LaRoue and Uguccioni, *The Biltmore Hotel*, 24–64.
9. Standiford, *Coral Gables*, 131.
10. Bramson, *Coral Gables*, 77–88.
11. Freeland, "George Edgar Merrick," 7.
12. Parks, *George Merrick's Coral Gables*, 34.
13. Peterson, "History of Miami Shores," 1–3; Bramson, *Boulevard of Dreams*, 36–37.
14. *Miami Shores Thematic Group*, Section 8, pg. 3; *New York Times*, 31 March 1937.
15. Peterson, "History of Miami Shores," 2–4; *Miami Shores Thematic Group*, Section 8, 1–2; Bramson, *Boulevard of Dreams*, 36–37.
16. Peterson, "History of Miami Shores," 2–5.
17. Ibid.; *New York Times*, 31 March 1937; *Miami Shores Thematic Group*, Section 8, pg. 8. Peterson, "History of Miami Shores," 3–4.
18. *New York Times*, 31 March 1937.
19. Peterson, "History of Miami Shores," 5–9.
20. *Miami Shores Thematic Group*, Section 8, pg. 6; *New York Times*, 17 January 1926.
21. *Miami Shores Thematic Group*, Section 8, pg.6.
22. Peterson, "History of Miami Shores," 11.
23. *New York Times*, 1 February 1927.
24. *New York Times*, 31 March 1937.
25. Roberts, *Hollywood*, 7.
26. Ballinger, *Miami Millions*, 41.
27. "Hollywood History," City of Hollywood Florida, 2.
28. Mickelson, *A Guide to Historic Hollywood*, 20.
29. "Hollywood History," City of Hollywood Florida, 2.
30. Mickelson, *A Guide to Historic Hollywood*, 8–27.
31. *Federal Writers Project*, 320.
32. Ibid, 320–321.
33. Ibid., 319.
34. "Hollywood History," City of Hollywood Florida, 2.
35. Mickelson, *Joseph W. Young, Jr.*, 133–134.
36. Mickelson, *A Guide to Historic Hollywood*, 84.
37. Mickelson, *Joseph W. Young, Jr.,* 171–174.
38. Roberts, *Sun Hunting*, 13–14.
39. Amory, *The Last Resorts*, 352.
40. Showalter, *The Many Mizners*, 43–53.
41. Ibid., 48.
42. *Historic American Buildings Survey*, 3.
43. Ibid.
44. Curl, *Mizner's Florida*, 41–48.
45. Ibid., Chapter 4.
46. Curl, *Florida Architecture of Addison Mizner*, xxxix.
47. Curl, *Mizner's Florida*, Chapter 4.
48. *Historic American Buildings Survey*, 5.
49. Curl, *Mizner's Florida*, 138; Curl and Johnson, *Boca Raton, A Pictorial History*, 44–53.
50. Curl, *Mizner's Florida*, 139–145; Gillis, *Boomtime Boca*, Chapter 2.
51. Vickers, *Panic in Paradise*. See Bibliography.
52. Vickers, "Addison Mizner," 381–407.
53. Ibid.; *New York Times*, 25, 29 November 1925.
54. Vickers, "Addison Mizner," 381–407.
55. Seebohm, *Boca Rococo*, Chapters 18, 19.
56. Ibid., 237.
57. Ibid.

58. *New York Times*, 1 March 1933
59. Gillis, *Boomtime Boca*, 92–97.
60. *Federal Writers Project,* 496.
61. Ibid., 499.
62. Ibid., 500.
63. *Sebring, Florida, The City of Health and Happiness*, 54.
64. Altvater, "The Boom: 1924–1925–1926," 1.
65. Ibid.
66. Ibid., 2.
67. Ibid., 2–17.
68. Ibid., 5
69. Ibid., 2–17.
70. Olausen, *Sebring, City on the Circle*. For additional information and superb images see Susan and Randall MacDonald's *Sebring* in Bibliography.
71. Olausen, *Sebring, City on the Circle*, 38–100.
72. Turner, *A Journey into Florida Railroad History*, 200–201; Turner, *A Short History of Florida Railroads*, 124–125.
73. Altvater, "The Bust: 1928–1931," 1–13.

## Chapter 5

1. Abbey, *Florida Land of Change*, 178.
2. *Railway Age*, "Florida Roads Have Experienced," 979.
3. Ibid.
4. Ibid.
5. Turner, *A Journey into Florida Railroad History*, 188.
6. Shelby, "Florida Frenzy," 178.
7. *Railway Age*, "Florida Roads Have Experienced," 979.
8. Ibid., 979–80.
9. Ibid., 981.
10. *Railway Age,* "Florida Roads Spent Millions," 1037–38.
11. *Railway Age*, "Florida Roads Have Experienced," 978.
12. Ibid.
13. Turner, *A Journey into Florida Railroad History*, 191; Bramson, *Speedway to Sunshine*, 99–108. Statistical material for this segment extracted from the annual reports of the Florida East Coast Railway, 1920–31.
14. Turner, *A Journey into Florida Railroad History*, 191.
15. Ibid., 192.
16. Ibid., 192–93; Campbell, *Across Fortune's Tracks*, 210–11.
17. Turner, *A Journey into Florida Railroad History*, 194.
18. Ibid., 194.
19. Ibid., 194–199.
20. Hoffman, *Building a Great Railroad*, 210–11.
21. Turner, *Railroads of Southwest Florida*, 55–88; Turner, *A Short History of Florida Railroads*, 77–90.
22. Turner, *Railroads of Southwest Florida*, 55–58.
23. Turner, *A Journey into Florida Railroad History*, 199–200. Other factual material for this segment

was extracted from the corporate annual reports of the Seaboard Air Line Railway, 1918–1932.
24. Shrady, *Orange Blossom Special*, 14.
25. Turner, "The Seaboard's Fort Myers-Naples Extension," 14–29.
26. Turner, *A Milestone Celebration*, 17–178.
27. Ibid.; Turner, *A Journey into Florida Railroad History*, 205–06; Turner, *Florida Railroads in the 1920s*, 81–88.
28. Turner, *A Journey into Florida Railroad History*, 89.
29. Morrison, *The Oxford History*, 224.
30. Ibid., 225.
31. Ibid.
32. Ibid., 227.
33. *Federal Writers Project*, 74.
34. Miller, "Greater Jacksonville's Response," 31, 51.
35. *Federal Writers Project*, 61.
36. Fox, *The Truth About Florida*, 140–142.
37. Roberts, *Florida*, 19.
38. *New York Times*, 17 April 1926.
39. McDonell, "Rise of the Businessman's Politician," 45.
40. Stockbridge and Perry, *Florida in the Making*, 145.
41. Stager and Carver, *Looking Beyond the Highway*, 3.
42. Ibid., 3, 4.
43. Ibid., 5.
44. Davis, "The Tamiami Trail," 2.
45. Wright, "Building a Million Dollar Private Road," 11–12.

## Chapter 6

1. Turner, *Venice in the 1920s*, 9–13; Matthews, *Venice*, 194–196.
2. Matthews, *Venice*, 205–217; Turner, *Venice in the 1920s*, 13–18. For further information on the renowned surgeon see Louella Albee's, *Doctor and I* and Fred H. Albee's, *A Surgeon's Fight to Rebuild Men*.
3. Glass, "John Nolen and the Planning of New Towns," 21–45; Hancock, "John Nolen: New Towns in Florida," 69–87; Turner, *Venice in the 1920s*, 13–18; Rice, *Venice-Nokomis, 30 Miles of Shore Front, The White City on the Gulf*, 1–6.
4. Turner, *Venice in the 1920s*, 18–19.
5. Hillman, *The Labor Banking Movement*, 148–149.
6. Ibid., 210–211.
7. Brotherhood of Locomotive Engineers, "Report of the Committee of Eight," 304.
8. *Jacksonville Times-Union*, 20 September 1925; Matthews, *Venice*, 229.
9. *Locomotive Engineers Journal*, "Venice Begins to Grow," 413.
10. Turner, *Venice in the 1920s*, 26–38. French's uncle was artisan Daniel Chester French, sculptor of the Lincoln Memorial.
11. *Locomotive Engineers Journal*, "Venice Begins to Grow," 410.

12. Ibid., 413; Turner, *Venice in the 1920s*, 34–35.

13. Turner, *Venice in the 1920s*, 44–53.

14. Ibid., 54–55

15. Ibid., 57–68.

16. Matthews, *Venice*, 265, 277.

17. Ibid., 69–82.

18. Ibid., 79–80; Turner, *Florida Railroads in the 1920s*, 53–76; Turner, *A Journey into Florida Railroad History*, 243.

19. Matthews, *Venice*, 266.

20. Turner, *Venice in the 1920s*, 83–94.

21. Ibid.

22. Ibid., 199–122; Matthews, *Venice*, 314–315; Hillman, *The Labor Banking Movement*, 248–251.

23. Hillman, *The Labor Banking Movement*, 249–250.

24. Hancock, "New Towns in Florida," 72.

25. Stockbridge, *Florida in the Making*, 266.

26. *The Disston Lands of Florida*, 3.

27. LaHurd, *Gulf Coast Chronicles*, 13.

28. Ibid., 14; *Sarasota and Sarasota County Florida, 1925–1926*, 3.

29. Weeks, *Ringling*, 39.

30. Grismer, *The Story of Sarasota*, 199–200.

31. Puig, *Spend a Summer This Winter*, 1–6; Weeks, *Ringling*, 74–80.

32. Puig, *Spend a Summer This Winter*, 6–8.

33. Morrison, *The Works of Dwight James Baum*, 11–14.

34. Grismer, *The Story of Sarasota*, 205–206.

35. McDonough, "Selling Sarasota," 12.

36. Craig, *The Architecture of Francis Palmer Smith*, 120–127.

37. Nolen, "Report on Planning Proposals and Zoning," 3–23.

38. McCarty, *Ca'd'Zan*, 3.

39. *New York Times*, 2 December 1938; Weeks, *Ringling*, 84; 91–92; 255.

40. McCarty, *Ca'd'Zan*, 21–63; Morrison, *The Work of Dwight James Baum*, 11–13.

41. Weeks, *Ringling*, 73–75; Puig, *Spend a Summer*, 1–7.

42. Weeks, *Ringling*, 75; 90–91; Puig, *Spend a Summer*, 11.

43. Grismer, *The Story of Sarasota*, 211–213 Weeks, *Ringling*, 95–96.

44. Weeks, *Ringling*, 97.

45. Ibid., 98; Puig, *Spend a Summer*, 11–13; McDonough, "Selling Sarasota," 29–30; LaHurd, *Gulf Coast Chronicles*, 61–62.

46. Weeks, Ringling, Chapter 9.

47. Grismer, *The Story of St. Petersburg*, 132.

48. Ibid., 132–133.

49. Fuller, *This Was Florida's Boom*, 63.

50. Abbott, *Open for the Season*, 200.

51. Arsenault, *St. Petersburg*, 189; Fuller, *This Was Florida's Boom*, 8–9.

52. Sitler, "Selling St. Petersburg," 25.

53. Arsenault, *St. Petersburg*, 186.

54. Fuller, *This Was Florida's Boom*, 51; Grismer, *The Story of St. Petersburg*, 134; Arsenault, *St. Petersburg*, 188.

55. Grismer, *The Story of St. Petersburg*, 134–135.

56. Fuller, *This Was Florida's Boom*, 7.

57. Ibid.

58. Ibid., 25.

59. Ibid., 24–25.

60. Grismer, *The Story of St. Petersburg*, 151–152.

61. Ibid, 152.

62. Ibid., 152–153.

63. Arsenault, *St. Petersburg*, 195; Grismer, *The Story of St. Petersburg*, 148.

64. Arsenault, *St. Petersburg*, 197.

65. Ibid., 196–97; Grismer, *The Story of St. Petersburg*, 139–143.

66. Ibid.

67. Arsenault, *St. Petersburg*, 202.

68. Abbott, *Open for the Season*. See Bibliography.

69. Ibid., 201–218.

70. Grismer, *The Story of St. Petersburg*, 302.

71. Wells, *C. Perry Snell: His Place in St. Petersburg, Florida History*. See Bibliography.

72. Ibid., 99.

73. Sully, *Casa Florida*, 93.

74. *New York Times*, 22 January 1928.

75. Grismer, *Tampa*, 247.

76. Ibid., 248.

77. Ibid., 249.

78. Ibid., 251.

79. For additional information consult *Temple Terrace* by Lana Burroughs. See Bibliography.

80. Kite-Powell, *History of Davis Islands*, 26.

81. Ibid., 28.

82. Covington, "The Story of the Davis Islands," 30.

83. Ibid., 32–33; Kite-Powell, *History of Davis Islands*, 33–38; Kite-Powell, "In Search of David Paul Davis," 24–33.

84. Covington, "The Story of the Davis Islands," 34.

85. Kite-Powell, *History of Davis Islands*, 45–50.

86. Ibid.

87. Covington, "The Story of the Davis Islands," 35.

88. Ibid.; Kite-Powell, *History of Davis Islands*, 61.

89. Covington, "The Story of the Davis Islands," 35.

90. Ibid., 36.

91. *New York Times*, 13 May 1925.

92. Bowen, *Bridge to a Dream*, 13–19.

93. Ibid., 15.

94. Ibid., 17.

95. Ibid., 19.

96. Ibid.

97. Kite-Powell, *History of Davis Islands*, 89; 100–108.

## Chapter 7

1. Vanderblue, "The Florida Land Boom," Part 2, 260.

2. Zuckoff, *Ponzi's Schemes*, 305.

3. Vanderblue, "The Florida Land Boom," Part 2, 260.

4. Galbraith, *The Great Crash*, 9–10.

5. Vanderblue, "The Florida Land Boom," Part 2, 260.

6. Galbraith, *The Great Crash*, 10.

7. Vanderblue, "The Florida Land Boom," Part 2, 260.

8. Ibid., 261.

9. Zuckoff, *Ponzi's Schemes*, 306.

10. Ibid., 306–307.

11. Vanderblue, "The Florida Land Boom," 261.

12. Ibid.

13. Ibid., 262.

14. Ibid.

15. Sessa, "Anti-Florida Propaganda," 43–44.

16. *New York Times*, 10 October 1925.

17. For more information on the 1926 hurricane see http://www.pbs.org/wgbh/amex/miami/peopleevents/pande07.html.

18. Vickers, *Panic in Paradise*, 5.

19. Babson, *Actions and Reactions*, 237.

20. Ibid., 238.

21. Ibid.

22. Ibid., 239.

23. Ibid.

24. Ibid.

25. Ibid.

26. Ibid., 240.

27. Ibid.

28. Ibid., 243.

29. Ibid.

30. Ibid.

# Bibliography

Abbey, Kathryn Trimmer. *Florida Land of Change.* Chapel Hill: University of North Carolina Press, 1941.

Abbott, Karl P. *Open for the Season.* New York: Doubleday, 1950.

Agassiz, Garnault. *Florida in Tomorrow's Sun.* New York: L. H. Bigelow, 1925.

Albee, Fred H. *A Surgeon's Fight to Rebuild Men.* New York: E. P. Dutton, 1943.

Albee, Louella B. *Doctor and I.* Detroit: S. J. Bloch, 1951.

Allen, Frederick Lewis. *Only Yesterday.* New York: Harper & Row, 1931.

Altvater, Allen C. "The Boom: 1924–1925–1926." *The Way It Was in Early Sebring History.* Sebring: Sebring Historical Society, 1982.

_____. "The Bust: 1928–1931." *The Way It Was in Early Sebring History.* Sebring: Sebring Historical Society, 1982.

Amory, Cleveland. *The Last Resorts.* New York: Harper & Brothers, 1948.

Arsenault, Raymond. *St. Petersburg and the Florida Dream, 1888–1950.* Gainesville: University Press of Florida, 1996.

Babson, Roger W. *Actions and Reactions: An Autobiography of Roger W. Babson,* 2d rev. ed. New York: Harper & Brothers, 1950.

_____. "Florida's Future," *Review of Reviews,* November 1925, 477–480.

Ballinger, Kenneth. *Miami Millions: The Dance of the Dollars in the Great Florida Land Boom of 1925.* Miami: The Franklin Press, 1936.

Barbour, Ralph Henry. *Let's Go to Florida! Information for Those Who Haven't Been, But Are Going, Those Who Have Been and Are Going Back, and Those Who Don't Expect to Go but Will.* New York: Dodd, Mead, 1926.

Baruch, Bernard M. *American Industry in the War.* New York: Prentice-Hall, 1941.

Beach, Rex. *The Miracle of Coral Gables.* New York: Currier and Hartford, 1926.

Blassingame, Wyatt. "When Florida Went Wild." *Reader's Digest,* January 1961.

Boorstin, Daniel J. *The Americans: The Democratic Experience.* New York: Random House, 1973.

Bowen, Ruth Rogero. *Bridge to a Dream, Building of the Bridge of Lions and Davis Shores, 1925–27.* St. Augustine: The St. Augustine Historical Society, 2010.

Boyd, Orton W. "Accounting Problems of the Florida Real Estate Boom." *The Accounting Review,* 1, no. 3 (September 1926), pp. 64–73.

Boyer, Paul S. *The Oxford Companion to United States History.* New York: Oxford University Press, 2001.

Bramson, Seth H. *Boulevard of Dreams: A Pictorial History of El Portal, Biscayne Park, Miami Shores and North Miami.* Charleston: The History Press, 2007.

_____. *Coral Gables.* Charleston: Arcadia, 2006.

_____. *The Curtiss-Bright Cities: Hialeah, Miami Springs & Opa Locka.* Charleston: The History Press, 2008.

_____. *From Farms and Fields to the Future, The Incredible History of North Miami Beach.* Charleston: The History Press, 2009.

_____. *Miami, The Magic City.* Charleston: Arcadia, 2007.

_____. *Miami Beach.* Charleston: Arcadia, 2005.

_____. *Speedway to Sunshine: The Story of the Florida East Coast Railway.* Erin, Ontario: Boston Mills Press, 1984.

Bricker, Lauren Weiss. *The Mediterranean House in America.* New York: Abrams, 2008.

Brotherhood of Locomotive Engineers. "Report of the Committee of Eight." August, 1929, 302–309.

Buchanan, Patricia. "Miami's Bootleg Boom." *Tequesta,* 30 (1970), pp. 13–31.

Burroughs, Lana, Tim Lancaster and Grant Rimbey. *Temple Terrace.* Charleston: Arcadia, 2010.

Bush, Gregory W. "Playground of the USA: Miami and the Promotion of Spectacle." *The Pacific Historical Review,* 68, no. 2 (May 1999), 153–172.

Campbell, Walter E. *Across Fortune's Tracks: A Biography of William Rand Kenan, Jr.* Chapel Hill: University of North Carolina Press, 1996.

Clark, Peggy Beucher. *Howey-in-the-Hills.* Charleston: Arcadia, 2011.

Cleary, Malinda Lester. "Denman Fink, Dream Coordinator to George Merrick and the Development of Coral Gables, Florida." Master's thesis; University of Miami, 1996.

Covington, Dr. James W. "The Story of Davis Islands, 1924–1926." *Sunland Tribune,* IV (November 1978), pp. 28–50.

Craig, Robert M. *The Architecture of Francis Palmer Smith, Atlanta's Scholar-Architect*. Athens: University of Georgia Press, 2012.

Curl, Donald W. "Boca Raton and the Florida Land Boom of the 1920s." *Tequesta*, XLVI (1986), pp. 20–34.

_____. *Florida Architecture of Addison Mizner*. New York: Dover, 1992. Unabridged republication of the work originally published by William Hellburn, Inc., New York, in 1928, with a new introduction by Donald W. Curl.

_____. *Mizner's Florida, American Resort Architecture*. New York: Architectural History Foundation and the Massachusetts Institute of Technology, 1987.

Curl, Donald W., and John P. Johnson. *Boca Raton, A Pictorial History*. Virginia Beach: Donning Company, 1990.

Davis, Doris. "The Tamiami Trail: Muck, Mosquitoes and Motorists." http://www.nps.gov/bicy/history culture/upload/History-of-Tamiami-Trail.pdf.

DeBerard, Philip E., Jr. "Promoting Florida: Some Aspects of the Use of Advertising and Publicity in the Development of the Sunshine State." Master's thesis: University of Florida, 1951.

*The Disston Lands of Florida*. Philadelphia: Florida Land & Improvement Company, 1885.

Division of Elections, Proclamations and Executive Orders, 1845–1995, Series S-13. Tallahassee: State of Florida, 1995.

Dovell, J. E. *Florida: Historic, Dramatic, Contemporary. Volume II*. New York: Lewis Historical, 1952.

Dumke, Glenn S. *Boom of the Eighties in Southern California*. Los Angeles: Anderson, Ritchie & Simon, 1944.

Eades, John F. "City Planning in West Palm Beach during the 1920s." *The Florida Historical Quarterly*, 75, no. 3 (Winter, 1997), pp. 276–288.

Federal Writers Project. *Florida: A Guide to the Southernmost State*. American Guide Series. New York: Oxford University Press, 1939.

FitzGerald-Bush, Frank S. *A Dream of Araby, Glenn H. Curtiss and the Founding of Opa-locka*. Opa-locka: South Florida Archaeological Museum, 1976.

*Florida's Resources and Inducements, Eighteenth Biennial Report, 1923–24*. Tallahassee: Department of Agriculture, 1924.

Fox, Charles Donald. *The Truth About Florida*. New York: Charles Renard Corporation, 1925.

Frazer, William, and John J. Guthrie, Jr. *The Florida Land Boom: Speculation, Money, and the Banks*. Westport, CT: Quorum, 1995.

Freeland, Helen C. "George Edgar Merrick." *Tequesta*, I no. 2, (August 1942), pp. 1–7.

Fuller, Walter P. *This Was Florida's Boom*. St. Petersburg: St. Petersburg Times Publishing Company, 1954.

Galbraith, John Kenneth. *The Great Crash 1929*. Boston: Houghton Mifflin, 1954.

George, Paul S. "Brokers, Binders, and Builders: Greater Miami's Boom of the mid-1920s." *The Florida Historical Quarterly* 65, no. 1 (July 1986), pp. 27–51.

_____. "Passage to the New Eden: Tourism in Miami from Flagler through Everest G. Sewell." *The Florida Historical Quarterly*, LX, no. 4 (April 1981), pp. 440–463.

_____. "Traffic Control in Early Miami." *Tequesta*, XXXVII (1977), pp. 3–16.

Gillis, Susan. *Fort Lauderdale, The Venice of America*. Charleston: Arcadia, 2004.

Gillis, Susan, and Boca Raton Historical Society. *Boomtime Boca: Boca Raton in the 1920s*. Charleston: Arcadia, 2007.

Glass, James Arthur. "John Nolen and the Planning of New Towns." Master's thesis; Cornell University, August 1984.

Gordon, John Steele. *An Empire of Wealth*. New York: Harper Perennial, 2004.

Grismer, Karl H. *History of St. Petersburg, Historical and Biographical*. St. Petersburg: Tourist News, 1924.

_____. *The Story of Fort Myers*. St. Petersburg: The St. Petersburg Printing Company, 1949.

_____. *The Story of Sarasota*. Tampa: Florida Grower Press, 1946.

_____. *Tampa, A History of the City of Tampa and the Tampa Bay Region of Florida*. St. Petersburg: St. Petersburg Printing Company, 1950.

Hancock, John. "New Towns in Florida (1922–1929)." *The New City*, University of Miami School of Architecture, Fall 1991.

Hanna, A. J., and Kathryn Abbey Hanna. *Florida's Golden Sands*. New York: Bobbs-Merrill, 1950.

Hicks, John D. *Rehearsal for Disaster*. Gainesville: University of Florida Press, 1961.

Hillman, Sidney, *The Labor Banking Movement in the United States*. Princeton: Princeton University Press, 1929.

Historic American Buildings Survey, Department of the Interior. "Everglades Club." Washington, D.C.: Department of the Interior (HABS No. FLA-226), 1980. http://lcweb2.loc.gov/pnp/habshaer/fl/fl01 00/fl0177/data/fl0177data.pdf.

Hoffman, Glenn. *Building a Great Railroad: A History of the Atlantic Coast Line Railroad Company*. Richmond: CSX Corporation, 1998.

Hollywood Historical Society. *Hollywood, Then and Now*. Charleston: Arcadia, 2009

*Hollywood History*, City of Hollywood Florida—Records and Archives Division, 1–6. Richard Roberts, Director of Records and Archives. http://www.hollywoodfl.org/records_archives/ARC.asp?DeptN=ARC&Pagehistory.

Hughes, Melvin Edward, Jr. "William J. Holley and His Florida Dreams, *The Florida Historical Quarterly*, 66, no. 3 (January 1988), pp. 243–264.

*Jacksonville Times-Union*. "Brotherhood of Locomotive Engineers Buy Large Tract." 20 September 1925, 2.

Jeffers, Dennis Willard. "An Analysis of Florida Land Boom Content in Two Miami Daily Newspapers from 1924 through 1926." Master's thesis, University of Florida, 1968.

Kessler, Karl W. *Florida from the Inside*. Toledo: George B. Ricaby, 1925.

Kite-Powell, Rodney. "David Paul Davis' Unfulfilled Dream: Davis Islands from October, 1926 until the

Crash of 1929." *Sunland Tribune* 25 (December 1999).

_____. *History of Davis Islands, David P. Davis and the Story of a Landmark Tampa Neighborhood.* Charleston: The History Press, 2013.

_____. "In Search of David Paul Davis." Master's thesis, University of South Florida, 2003.

Kleinberg, Eliot. *Black Cloud: The Great Florida Hurricane of 1928.* New York: Carroll & Graf, 2003.

LaHurd, Jeff. *Come on Down! Pitching Paradise Through the Roaring 20s.* Sarasota: Sarasota Alliance for Historic Preservation, 1995.

_____. *Gulf Coast Chronicles: Remembering Sarasota's Past.* Charleston: The History Press, 2005.

_____. *Quintessential Sarasota: Stories and Pictures from the 1920s to the 1950s.* Charleston: The History Press, 2004.

_____. *Sarasota: Roaring Through the 20s.* Sarasota: Peppertree Press, 2007.

LaRoue, Jr., Samuel D., and Ellen J. Uguccioni. *The Biltmore Hotel, an Engaging Legacy.* Miami: Arva Parks & Company and Centennial Press, 2002.

*Locomotive Engineers Journal.* "Venice Begins to Grow." June, 1926, 411–415.

Lynn, Catherine. "Dream and Substance: Araby and the Planning of Opa-Locka." *The Journal of Decorative and Propaganda Arts*, 23. Florida Theme Issue (1998), pp. 162–189. The Wolfsonian-Florida International University, 1978.

MacDonald, Susan Priest, Randall M. MacDonald, and the Sebring Historical Society. *Sebring.* Charleston: Arcadia, 2008.

Mackle, Elliot. "Two Way Stretch: Some Dichotomies in the Advertising of Florida as the Boom Collapsed." *Tequesta* XXXIII (1973), pp. 17–29.

Matthews, Janet Snyder. *Venice, Journey from Horse and Chaise.* Sarasota: Pine Level Press, 1989.

McCarty, Ronald R. *Ca'd'Zan: Ringling's Venetian Palace.* London: Scala Publishers Limited, 2010.

McDonell, Victoria H. "Rise of the 'Businessman's Politician': The 1924 Florida Gubernatorial Race." *The Florida Historical Quarterly*, LII, no. 1 (July 1973), 39–50.

McDonough, Michael. "Selling Sarasota: Architecture and Propaganda in a 1920s Boom Town." *The Journal of Decorative and Propaganda Arts*, 23. Florida Theme Issue. The Wolfsonian-Florida International University, 1998.

McIver, Stuart B. *Dreamers, Schemers and Scalawags, Volume 1.* Sarasota: Pineapple Press, 1994.

Merz, Charles. *The Great American Bandwagon.* Garden City: Garden City, 1928.

*Miami Shores Thematic Group*, National Register of Historic Places Inventory, Nomination Form. Tallahassee: Division of Historical Resources, Bureau of Historic Preservation, September, 1988. pdfhost.focus.nps.gov/docs/NRHP/Text/64000116.pdf

Mickelson, Joan. *A Guide to Historic Hollywood.* Charleston: The History Press, 2005.

_____. *Joseph W. Young, Jr., and the City Beautiful: A Biography of the Founder of Hollywood, Florida.* Jefferson, NC: McFarland, 2012.

Millas, Aristides J. and Ellen J. Uguccioni. *Coral Gables, Miami Riviera, An Architectural Guide.* Miami: Dade Heritage Trust, 2003.

Miller, Philip Warren. "Greater Jacksonville's Response to the Florida Land Boom of the 1920s." Master's thesis: University of Florida, 1989.

Mitchell, Charles R. and Kirk W. House. *Glenn H. Curtiss, Aviation Pioneer.* Charleston: Arcadia, 2001.

Morison, Samuel Eliot. *The Oxford History of the American People, Volume Three.* New York: Oxford University Press, 1972.

Mormino, Gary R. *Land of Sunshine, State of Dreams.* Gainesville: University Press of Florida, 2005.

Morrison, William, ed. *The Work of Dwight James Baum.* New York: Acanthus Press, 2008.

*The Nation's Business.* "Simply Staggering." May 1925.

*New York Times*: "Miracle Men on Florida's Gold Coast" 8 March 1925; "Florida Migration Has a Series of Precedents" 13 September 1925; "Gov. Martin Sees Plot to Hit Florida" 10 October 1925; "Florida Has Vision of a New Economic Life" 15 November 1925; "Miami 'Happy Town' Opens" 17 January 1926; "Journalistic Kaleidoscope of the Florida Boom" 13 June 1926; "Miami Shores Named in Bankruptcy Suit" 1 February 1927; "Liabilities 8 Million, Assets Put at $400: H. M. Anderson was Head of Ambitious Florida Scheme in Boom of 1925" 31 March 1937; "John Ringling Dies of Pneumonia" 2 December 1938.

Niemeyer, Glenn A. "Oldsmar for Health, Wealth, Happiness." *The Florida Historical Quarterly*, 46, no. 1 (July 1967), pp. 18–28.

Nolen, John. *Report on Planning Proposals and Zoning for the City of Sarasota, Florida.* Cambridge: John Nolen & Associates, 1924.

Nylander, Justin A. *Casas to Castles: Florida's Historic Mediterranean Revival Architecture.* Atglen, PA: Schiffer, 2010.

Olausen, Stephen A. *Sebring, City on the Circle.* St. Augustine: Southern Heritage Press, 1993.

Orr, Christina. *Addison Mizner, Architect of Dreams and Realities.* Palm Beach: Norton Gallery of Art, 1977.

Ossman, Lauren, and Heather Ewing. *Carrere & Hastings, The Masterworks.* New York: Rizzoli International, 2011.

Parks, Arva Moore. *George Merrick's Coral Gables: "Where Your 'Castles in Spain' Are Made Real!"* Miami: Centennial Press, 2006.

_____. *Miami, The Magic City.* Miami: Centennial Press, 1991.

Parks, Arva Moore, and Carolyn Klepser. *Miami, Then and Now.* San Diego: Thunder Bay Press, 2002.

Patricios, Nicholas. "Phineas Paist and the Architecture of Coral Gables, Florida." *Tequesta* LXIV (2004), pp. 5–27.

Peterson, Thelma. "History of Miami Shores." Typescript. Miami Shores and Fountania Pageant Ephemera, 1926–1980. HistoryMiami Archives & Research Center.

Pinney, Charles Bartlett. "The Effects of the Real Estate Boom on Florida State Banks." Master's thesis; University of Florida, 1934.

Powell, Willis B. "Simply Staggering!" *The Nation's Business,* May, 1925.

Puig, Francis J. *Spend a Summer This Winter in Sarasota, Four Key Figures in Sarasota's Development.* Sarasota: Archeological Consultants, 2002.

*Railway Age Magazine,* "Florida Roads Have Experienced a Phenomenal Development," (Part I) 19 November 1927; "Florida Roads Spent Millions in Construction During Boom," (Part II) 26 November 1927, pp.1037–42.

Reardon, R. L. *The Florida Hurricane & Disaster.* Miami: Miami Publishing Company, 1926. Reprinted 1986 by Arva Parks & Company of Coral Gables, Florida.

Redford, Polly. *Billion-Dollar Sandbar: A Biography of Miami Beach.* New York: E. P. Dutton, 1970.

Ricci, James M. "Reporting the Florida Land Boom of the 1920s: Kenneth L. Roberts in Florida." Master's thesis, University of South Florida, 1980.

Rice, Roger C. *Venice-Nokomis, 30 Miles of Shore Front: The White City on the Gulf.* Sales brochure. Sarasota: The Roger C. Rice Company, n.d.

Roberts, C. Richard. *Hollywood.* Charleston: Arcadia, 2003.

Roberts, Kenneth L. *Florida.* New York: Harper and Brothers, 1926.

_____. *Florida Loafing: An Investigation into the Peculiar State of Affairs Which Leads Residents of 47 States to Encourage Spanish Architecture in the 48th.* Indianapolis: Bobbs-Merrill, 1925.

_____. *Saturday Evening Post:* "Florida Diversions," 20 February 1926, 24–25, 141–142, 145; "Florida Fever," 5 December 1925, 6–7, 207, 209–210; "Florida Fireworks," 23 January 1926, 12–13; "Florida Loafing," 17 May 1924, 20–21, 125, 129, 133; 1"Florida Prophets," 3 February 1926, 20–21, 99, 101–02, 106; "Good Warm Stuff," 9 January 1926, 12–13, 78, 80, 82, 84; "In the Wake of the Hurricanes," 27 November 1926, 6, 7, 54, 56, 59–60, 62; "The Sun Hunters," 15 April 1922, 6–7, 56, 60; "The Time-Killers," 1 April 1922, 6–7, 56, 60; "Tropical Growth," 29 April 1922, 8–9, 77–78, 80, 83, 85; "Tropical Parasites," 2 January 1926, 12–13, 78, 80, 83.

_____. *Sun Hunting: Adventures and Observations Among the Native and Migratory Tribes of Florida, including the Stoical Time-Killers of Palm Beach, the Gentle and Gregarious Tin-Canners of the Remote Interior, and the Vivacious and Semi-Violent Peoples of Miami and Its Purlieus.* Indianapolis: Bobbs-Merrill, 1922.

Roseberry, C. R. *Glenn Curtiss: Pioneer of Flight.* Garden City, NY: Doubleday, 1972.

Sakolski, Aaron M. *The Great American Land Bubble, The Amazing Story of Land-Grabbing, Speculations and Booms from Colonial Days to the Present Time.* New York: Harper & Brothers, 1932.

*Sarasota and Sarasota County Florida, 1925–1926.* Sarasota: Sarasota County Chamber of Commerce, 1925.

*Sarasota Herald.* "Adair Marvels at Growth of Sarasota During Past Year Says Future Very Promising," 3 January 1926.

*Sebring, Florida: The City of Health and Happiness.* Sebring: Sebring Board of Trade, 1920.

Seebohm, Caroline. *Boca Rococo, How Addison Mizner Invented Florida's Gold Coast.* New York: Clarkson Potter, 2001.

Sessa, Frank B. "Anti-Florida Propaganda and Counter Measures during the 1920s." *Tequesta* 21 (1961), pp. 45–51.

_____. "Miami in 1926," *Tequesta* XVI (1956), pp. 15–36.

_____. "Miami on the Eve of the Boom: 1923." *Tequesta* 1, no. 11 (1951), pp. 3–25.

_____. "Real Estate Expansion and Boom in Miami and Its Environs during the 1920's." Doctoral dissertation: University of Pittsburgh, 1950.

Shelby, Gertrude Mathews. *Harper's Monthly Magazine,* "Florida Frenzy," January 1926, pp.177–186; *Outlook:* "The Crisis of Florida Fever," 5 May 1925, 24–27.

Showalter, J. Camille, ed. *The Many Mizners, California Clan Extraordinary.* Oakland: The Oakland Museum, 1978.

Shrady, Theodore, and Arthur M. Waldrop. *Orange Blossom Special, Florida's Distinguished Winter Train.* Valrico, FL: The Atlantic Coast Line and Seaboard Air Line Railroads Historical Society, 2000.

Sisto, Benedicte. "Miami's Land Gambling Fever of 1925." *Tequesta,* LIX (1999), 52–73.

Sitler, Nevin D. "Selling St. Petersburg: John Lodwick and the Promotion of a Florida Paradise." Master's thesis: University of South Florida, 2006.

_____. *Warm Wishes from Sunny St. Pete.* Charleston: The History Press, 2014.

Stager, Claudette, and Martha Carver. *Looking Beyond the Highway.* Knoxville: University of Tennessee Press, 2006.

Standiford, Les. *Coral Gables, The City Beautiful Story.* Coral Gables: The Coral Gables Chamber of Commerce and Atlanta Riverbend, Ltd., 1998.

Stanton, James Russell. "A Study of Public Relations in the Miami Land Boom of the 1920s." Master's thesis, University of Florida, 1974.

Starr, Kevin. *Inventing the Dream, California Through the Progressive Era.* New York: Oxford University Press, 1985.

"Statement by City Planning Commission." http://www.sarasotagov.com/NDS/LongRange/NolenPlan/NolenPlan.htm.

Stewart, Doug. "The Madness That Swept Miami." *Smithsonian Magazine,* 31, no. 10 (January 2001), pp. 60–67.

Stockbridge, Frank Parker and John Holliday Perry. *Florida in the Making.* New York: DeBower, 1926.

Sully, Susan. *Casa Florida.* New York: Rizzoli International, 2005.

Tarbell, Ida M. *McCall's Magazine:* "Florida—and Then What?" Part 1, Vol. 53 (May 1926); Part 2, Vol. 54 (June 1926); Part 3, Vol. 55 (July 1926).

Taylor, A. D. "The Planning of Sebring, a Lake-Front Town in Florida." *The American City* 24 (January 1921), p. 65

TenEick, Virginia Elliot. *History of Hollywood 1920 to 1950.* Hollywood: City of Hollywood, Florida, 1966.

Turner, Gregg M. *Florida Railroads in the 1920s.* Charleston: Arcadia, 2005.

_____. *Fort Myers, Florida, The City of Palms.* Charleston: Arcadia, 2001.

_____. *Fort Myers, Florida, in Vintage Postcards.* Charleston: Arcadia, 2005.

_____. *A Journey into Florida Railroad History.* Gainesville: University Press of Florida, 2008.

_____. *A Milestone Celebration: The Seaboard Railway to Naples and Miami.* Bloomington: Author House, 2004.

_____. *Railroads of Southwest Florida.* Charleston: Arcadia, 1999.

_____. *A Short History of Florida Railroads.* Charleston: Arcadia, 2003.

_____. *Venice in the 1920s.* Charleston: Arcadia, 2000.

Turner, Gregg M., and Seth H. Bramson. *The Plant System of Railroads, Steamships & Hotels: The South's First Great Industrial Enterprise.* Laury's Station, PA: Garrigues House, 2004.

Vanderblue, Homer B. *The Journal of Land & Public Utility Economics*: "The Florida Land Boom," Part 1: Vol. 3, No. 2 (May 1927), pp. 113–131; Part 2: Vol. 3, No. 3 (August 1927), pp. 252–269.

Van Dyke, Theodore Strong. *Millionaires of a Day: An Inside History of the Great Southern California Boom.* New York: Fords, Howard & Hulbert, 1890.

Varona, Esperanza B. "Bernhardt E. Muller Collection, 1925–1960," University of Miami Special Collections, 1–5. http://proust.library.miami.edu/findingaid/?p=collections/findingaid&id=887&q.

Vickers, Raymond B. "Addison Mizner: Promoter in Paradise." *The Florida Historical Quarterly.* Vol. 75 (Spring 1997), pp. 381–407.

_____. *Panic in Paradise, Florida's Banking Crash of 1926.* Tuscaloosa: University of Alabama Press, 1994.

Villard, Henry. "Florida Aftermath." *The Nation*, 6 June 1928.

Webb, Martha Gwendolyn. "Ten Years of Florida Journalism from 1920 to 1930 with Special Emphasis on the Land Boom Period." Master's thesis; University of Florida, 1957.

Weeks, David C. *Ringling: The Florida Years (1911–1936).* Gainesville: University Press of Florida, 1993.

Weigall, T. H. *Boom in Paradise.* New York: Alfred H. King, 1932.

Wells, Judy Lowe. *C. Perry Snell: His Place in St. Petersburg, Florida History.* Orlando: Orange Blossom Press, 2006.

Werndli, Phillip Alton. "J. C. Penney and the Development of Penney Farms, Florida (1924–1934)." Master's thesis, University of Florida, 1974.

Wright, Hamilton M. "Building a Million Dollar Private Road Through the Florida Everglades." *The Highway Magazine*, XIX, no. 11 (December, 1923).

Wynne, Nick, and Richard Moorhead. *Paradise for Sale, Florida's Booms and Busts.* Charleston: The History Press, 2010.

Young, June Hurley. *The Don Ce-Sar Story.* St. Petersburg: Partnership Press, 2007.

Zuckoff, Mitchell. *Ponzi's Schemes.* New York: Random House, 2005.

# Index